6322

SCIENCE
AT
WAR

SCIENCE
at
WAR

By George W. Gray

When besieged by ambitious tyrants I find a means of offense and defense in order to preserve the chief gift of nature, which is liberty.

—Leonardo da Vinci, NOTE ON WAR

HARPER & BROTHERS PUBLISHERS

NEW YORK   LONDON

This book is complete and unabridged
in contents, and is manufactured in strict
conformity with Government regulations
for saving paper.

To my Mother
Virginia Williams Gray

PREFACE

THE term science is used in this book in a comprehensive sense. It includes the search for knowledge, the search for ways of putting knowledge to use, and the system of techniques and skills attained through these efforts. I am aware that a distinction is usually made between the "pure" science of the natural philosopher who is only following his desire to explore and discover, and the "applied science" of the inventor and engineer whose efforts are directed toward industrial ends. For purposes of classifying personnel and activities, and of distinguishing between the functions of discovery and those of application, the distinction is logical and useful. But when we view human progress as a whole, and contemplate science as an aspect of man's thought and of man's society, the line between the pure and the applied becomes artificial. Pasteur pointed out many years ago: "There exists no category of the sciences to which the name 'applied science' could rightly be given. We have science and the application of science, which are united together as the tree and the fruit."

So the reader is to understand by science the work of all who are engaged in exploring nature or in harnessing its forces. This includes such persons as the astronomer studying the secrets of stars with a photo-electric tube, and the metallurgist whose studies of metals made the photo-electric tube a possibility; it includes the acoustical engineer picking up attenuated sound waves, and the medical man recording brain waves. Stars, metals, sound waves, and brain waves are only four of thousands of phenomena that scientists are prospecting in the national war effort, but they are representative of the wide range of interests and endeavors. Research has been expanded to a volume and accelerated to a pace beyond anything known in time of peace.

Some of the new developments are so important to the war effort, and their secrecy on that account is so closely guarded, that not even a hint of their nature has been released for publication. But it is possible, without violating any of the necessary safeguards, to review the interrelationship of science and war and recognize the kinds of contributions that have been made. All the sciences have been drawn upon. It would be difficult to name a field of natural knowledge that is regarded as irrelevant to the war effort, but the sciences which have been most active are physics, mathematics, chemistry, biology, and psychology, and the present report will focus on certain of their contributions.

All fields of battle—in the air, on the land, on the sea and under the sea—bear witness that science has mightily influenced the methods and instruments of war. It is not so obvious that war has influenced science. How the massive impact of a world-encircling struggle will mold the shape of civilization even the wisest can only surmise. Of this we may be sure: the new and swifter and cheaper ways of producing munitions, and the increased control over the forces of nature which has been gained through war research, will carry over and will affect the postwar world. These vastly enhanced resources of knowledge, methods, skills, and equipment can serve the citizen as they have served the warrior. If a humane world society is to be the fruit of our victory, organized science will be as necessary to the waging of peace as it has been to the waging of war.

CONTENTS

SCIENCE
AT
WAR

PROLOGUE

Science and the Warrior

Science does not make war more terrible, it merely
makes it seem more terrible, which is a very desirable
result.

—George R. Harrison, ATOMS IN ACTION

ONE of the names in Renaissance science is that of Niccolo
Tartaglia, born in Brescia near the Italian Alps. He was still a child
in 1512 when a French army under Gaston de Foix overran Lom-
bardy, and in the ensuing sack of his city the boy was horribly
mutilated. He was one of numerous non-combatant victims, for
civilians did not have to await the invention of dive bombing to
learn what war could do to them, their homes and possessions. It
is said that Brescia, one of the fairest and wealthiest of Lombard
cities, never completely recovered from that Sixteenth-century
blitzkrieg.

Fortunately the boy Niccolo did recover, though only after a
long illness undergone in dire poverty. By some miracle of self-
education he became proficient in mathematics, and rose to a pro-
fessorship in Verona. Here he became acquainted with the master
of ordnance at the castle. Tartaglia has described his friend as "a
man of experience, very skillful in his art," but apparently the
artilleryman felt that there was room for improving his art, for

one day he asked the professor if mathematics could tell how to aim a gun so as to give it its greatest range.

Tartaglia had no practical knowledge of artillery, never having fired a single round with bombard or other gun, but the artillery-man's question provided the professor with an interesting mathematical problem, so he set to work with his equations. Eventually he was able to report that at an elevation of $45°$ a gun possesses its greatest range.

It is second nature with a man of science to make known the results of his study, and Tartaglia immediately thought of writing a treatise on the art of artillery, "to bring it," as he said, "to a degree of perfection capable of directing fire in all circumstances, assisted only by a few particular experiments."

But as he meditated the undertaking, his mind conjured up a picture of war. Perhaps he remembered the tragedy of his childhood; the cannon balls crashing into the roofs of Brescia, the destruction, the wounds, the deaths. He turned from his project in horror. It seemed to him "a thing blameworthy, shameful and barbarous, worthy of severe punishment before God and man, to wish to bring to perfection an art damageable to one's neighbor and destructive of the human race, and especially Christian men, in the wars they wage on one another."

Not only did he turn his attention to other studies, but, as he later revealed, "I even tore up and burnt everything which I had calculated and written on the subject, ashamed and full of remorse for the time I had spent on it, and well decided never to communicate in writing that which against my will had remained in my memory, either to please a friend or in teaching of these matters which are a grave sin and shipwreck of the soul."

But circumstances alter decisions. In 1537 the Saracens were on the move with a formidable invasion force directed at the Italian peninsula, and Tartaglia had a change of heart. "In sight of the ferocious wolf preparing to set on our flock, and of our pastors united for the common defense, it does not seem to me any longer proper to hold these things hid and I have decided to publish them, partly in writing, partly by word of mouth, for the benefit of Christians so that all should be in better state either to attack the common enemy or to defend themselves against him."

He was sorry he had abandoned his earlier studies of ballistics, for "I am certain that had I persevered I would have found things of the greatest value, as I hope yet to find." So he hurried into print a treatise on the theory and practice of gunnery, dedicating it to the Duke of Urbino in "the hope that your Lordship will not disdain to receive this work of mine so as better to instruct the artillery-men of your most illustrious government in the theory of their art, and to render them more apt in its practice."

THE DILEMMA OF CONSCIENCE

Tartaglia's vacillation is understandable. It represents not only the dilemma of the scientist but that of every civilized person who has any conscience at all about this business of war. Why should the choicest products of man's mind—the beautiful and precise tech-niques of mathematics; the laws of immutable nature whose dis-covery through the ages is a supreme accomplishment of the human spirit; the time-saving, labor-economizing, wealth-producing ma-chines and processes which technology has wrung from the findings of science: gifts which could work endlessly for the healing of the nations and the freeing of their peoples from want and fear—why should these priceless gains be turned to purposes of destruction, deception, enslavement and death? Why?

One answer is that the persons who explore nature and add new knowledge to the treasure house of science do not have control over the use that is made of their discoveries; at least not in ordinary times. In science there is no secrecy; as new findings are made they are promptly published and become the common property of all; therefore any person who is so disposed can take a beneficent result and pervert it to any malign end that suits his desires. The wide-spread use of the radio by the European dictators is an example of this perversion of a gift of science. The radio even more than the airplane has made the modern totalitarian state possible, for without the ability to speak instantly to large masses it would be difficult to manipulate the thinking and feeling of a whole people.

There is another answer to our why. It comes when war ceases to be an abstraction and becomes a reality to be dealt with in the person of an aggressor. Who can deny the morality of self-defense? The idea of killing is repugnant, but the idea of being killed is also repugnant. On what ground could any useful talent be excused or exempted from rendering full service against the ruthless force that threatens the looting and enslavement of all the nation's resources, human as well as material?

Appeasement, as appeased aggressors repeatedly have demonstrated, is a road to suicide. There is no negotiating with the lust for power. We can only fight.

THE CHOICE OF WEAPONS

If we are to fight, what are we to fight with? Surely not with outmoded tools of war simply because there is a tradition which accepts them as chivalrous. If war is accepted, it is no more immoral to fight with aerial bombs than to fight with rifles and 16-inch guns, with makeshift sticks and stones, or with naked muscles in the brutality of hand-to-hand struggle.

It has been said that the new weapons provided by modern technology have transformed war from a retail to a wholesale operation. Technology, in breaking down nature's barriers of space and time and providing means to promote communication and bring the nations into one neighborhood, also made it possible for war to reach farther, strike more suddenly, and destroy lives and property over a wider area than was possible in the days when cavalry represented the utmost of lightning attack. Airplanes, tanks and radio have projected war over whole continents and across seas, penetrated to capital cities, industrial centers, workers' settlements, churches, schools, hospitals and other civilian communities, and drawn non-combatants into the conflict. "The citizen," says Nicholas J. Spykman in *America's Strategy in World Politics*, "no longer lives in comparative safety behind a front held by military forces. The war is no longer far away; it is fought out all around him, over his garden, his back yard, and the ruins of his home, and it kills without impartiality both civilian and soldier."

Isn't there an iron justice in this transfer of the battlefront to the citizen's back yard? If it makes war seem more terrible to the civilian, remember that war has always been terrible to the soldier on the firing line. If war is the expression of national policy, it is scrupulously right that the people who are responsible for the national policy, whose votes ordain it and sustain it, who expect to benefit from its success should share the terrors, feel the privations, suffer the wounds and taste the death that have been the lot of the soldier from the earliest days of organized armies.

To condemn science because it provides more effective weapons is to misunderstand not only the nature of war and of science but the nature of morality. The choice of weapons is merely incidental to the moral issue. The moral issue in the Ethiopian War, for example, was not the fact that 45,000,000 civilized Italians suddenly turned machine guns, aerial bombs and gas attacks on 10,000,000 poorly equipped, half-naked, almost defenseless Ethiopians. The moral obloquy would be just as great if the Italians had limited their weapons to whatever degree of mechanization the Ethiopians possessed. If the Italians had charged with cavalry sabers, bows and arrows upon the neighbors whose land they coveted it would still be aggression; and a peculiarly unjustifiable type of aggression, since both the Italian government and the Ethiopian government were sister members of the League of Nations and therein had already at hand a means of settling, or at least of mutually considering, their differences. By the time she was ready to pounce on Albania—celebrating Good Friday of 1939 by this act of rapacity upon a nearer neighbor whose land also looked good—Italy had withdrawn from the hypocrisy of league membership. "A people exuberant with life which is suffocated within the narrow space of territory where it is imprisoned" cannot escape being urged on by an "expansionist impetus," apologized one of the Roman fortnightly journals. To stab in the back a fallen France and to provoke war with neutral Greece were in character with this Fascist principle, and with Italian acceptance of it.

Of course Italy is not alone, nor is the record of the democratic nations free of predatory incidents, but Italy presents a peculiarly apt and current example of our thesis. The fact that is hideous in human behavior, the accusation of history that has never been answered beyond a shoulder-shrugging "Am I my brother's keeper?" is the cold and calculating use of war as "a continuation of political intercourse." The use of force to gain possession of another people's land, to enslave the population, to impose the trade, politics or religion of the conqueror upon the conquered— these of course are familiar practices from the days when the

Assyrians "came down like a wolf on the fold" to the "new order" of our modern Assyrians. Predatory war is revolting for what it does to the body; it is even more horrible for what it does to the human spirit: the fanatical prejudices that it creates or stirs into hatreds, the false faces that it puts upon the real motives, its cultivation of emotionalism and denial of reason—above all, its lack of integrity which poisons human relations at the source. The Fascist's "exuberance of life" is just a name for these emotional drugs, which feed war as alcohol feeds delirium.

The method of science is the antithesis of prejudice, pretense, evasion and antisocial self-seeking. It asks no special favors, no exemption from examination or criticism, no reverence for its dignity or tradition, no acquiescence in what it says because it says it. Science asks only that the facts of any situation be sought honestly, and that in so far as the facts are ascertainable they be used to guide human action. In the postwar world of reconstruction and reconciliation we have more to expect from these strict standards of integrity than from any other system of thinking and acting.

Also, we have more to expect from science *in the successful prosecution of the war* than we can hope to obtain through any other existing system of thinking and acting. The modern soldier, sailor and airman are in effect practicing scientists, using the term in its broadest sense. The highly mechanized equipment of modern warfare requires a degree of technical training and a proficiency in making use of machines, instruments, optical and electrical apparatus and other engineering devices far beyond anything required of the rank and file in previous wars. And because warfare is thus mechanized it requires the active assistance of research workers, a laboratory front to back up the military front, to discover, develop and apply the best brains, methods and mechanisms for outthinking and outfighting the enemy.

These relations of science to war grow out of the nature of science. The scientist's participation can be understood only if we have a clear perception of what science is.

THE STRUGGLE WITH THE WORLD OF NATURE

Science is man's struggle with nature. It is first of all a battle against ignorance—for more knowledge. And second, it is a battle against impotence—for more control over the natural forces. Nature is the environment that surrounds us: the universe of stars and planets and radiation; our revolving globe of rock, metal, water, gases and soil; and its thin film of life green with chlorophyll, red with hemoglobin, so sensitive, so vulnerable in its delicate balance of forces, and yet so resilient, adaptable, enduring. Man is of this world, made of its very dust, and yet he is somehow a creature apart, outside the world; able to study it, to pry into it, to learn a bit of its secret mechanism—to practice his science.

The practice of science yields two supreme results: ever-increasing knowledge of the environment and ever-increasing control of it. Sometimes the pursuit of knowledge has been the chief aim of research. Other times control has been the driving motive. But eventually all knowledge finds use, even such seemingly remote findings as those gleaned from the stars. It was in a star—remember? —that helium was first seen. Today, extracted from rich deposits in the Texas clays, this noninflammable lightweight gas is serving the United Nations in dirigible balloons, divers' decompression chambers, and other military and medical uses; and for all its benefits our thanks must go first to the astronomer who discovered it 93,000,000 miles out in space.

Through the practice of science man has climbed from the cave man's cave to the aeronaut's ship in the sky. Between those two extremes of human habitation lies a vast sequence of discoveries, inventions, trials and errors, false trails and sure achievements, representing the labor of many generations of thinkers, experimenters, doers. On the way up man tampered with fire, and at length harnessed its heat in engines. He snatched at the lightning, and eventually found a way of generating it in machines and conducting it along wires to do useful work and finally a way of flinging it through limitless space to carry his messages. From study of his environment man found that he could improve animal and vegetable stocks, fertilize exhausted soils, banish famine, control destructive floods and lead their waters off into useful work, cure devastating diseases, increase the health rate and lower the death rate.

Along this trail too he discovered, quite early, that the knowledge which could be used in so many ways to improve the conditions of life could be applied quite as successfully in the opposite direction.

If there was a grudge against another human creature or group—rivalry, hatred, anger, covetousness—something could be done in self-interest. The forces that helped and promoted life could be turned against the other fellow, to hinder his life and if possible destroy it.

So science could be used to wage war. And inasmuch as science was simply man's knowledge, and since man wanted to wage war, why not?

THE STRUGGLE WITH THE WORLD OF MAN

All this is obvious, of course, but it is fundamental. Science is a purely human preoccupation, subject to the limitations as well as to the capacities of the human brain. Indeed, science is only man —man adventuring, man exploring and discovering, man putting his new-found knowledge to use. And if he decides to put it to such uses as torpedoing ships and bombing cities, apparently there is no one to say him nay but another man.

So we have man struggling against man. War becomes an extension of man's battle with nature. In nature he fought against summer heat and winter cold, fire, lightning, the wind, the sea, the wild beasts. Now he is confronted by a new kind of force, belligerent man. The new force is more formidable than the forces of nature, because it is more cunning, more ingenious, able to shift its tactics, to develop and adapt new means of destruction. It can use its science; and the only way to counter it successfully is to use superior science.

In war the enemy becomes part of the environment, and his efforts to isolate his opponent, starve him out, blast his defenses, burn his possessions, poison his air or riddle his body can only be regarded as part of the phenomena of nature, like overflowing rivers, failing crops and multiplying bacteria. As science has been successful in controlling floods, famines and pestilences, so now it is called on to control and overcome submarines, planes, tanks, and other extensions of enemy nerves and enemy muscles.

This is the rationale of science in war. This is how its discipline, the function of which is to understand and control nature, becomes man's most powerful resource for controlling human aggression. Under a war program the efforts of science are narrowed into channels that bear directly on the war effort; though even then it is not wise to neglect fundamental research, for theoretical knowledge has a surprising way of becoming practical and applicable. Part of the office of science is to think ahead, analyze the probabilities, and prepare for contingencies not yet on the horizon but which nevertheless are latent influences whose neglect now may work to the advantage of the enemy later. This anticipating and preparing for the future is one of the vital roles of research in a nation at war.

CHAPTER 1

The Physicists' War

If the War of 1914–'18 was a chemists' war, the present affliction, with its extensive mechanization, radio propaganda and aeronautical developments, is a physicists' war. Aerial bombardment alone might almost be called a nightmare of complex physical problems the solution of which would need the efforts of more than the whole of the country's physicists.

—NATURE, August 30, 1941

BY SATURDAY, November 18, 1939, the second world war was in its twelfth week. Poland had been crushed during September. Thereafter the pace slowed. There were sporadic raids on German and British bases, some sinkings of naval and merchant fleets, a few aerial dogfights—but, on the whole, October and early November were a period of waiting and watching on both sides. British airplanes bombarded German cities with leaflet "Notes to the German people." German troops guarding their western front posted signs which proposed "Don't shoot and we won't shoot." Poilus inhabited the vast, labyrinthine, underground fastnesses of their Maginot Line with prideful confidence in its impregnable forts, sleek guns, airconditioned quarters and other modern conveniences.

Meanwhile the conqueror of Poland was making a peace drive, inaugurated by his Reichstag speech of October 6th in which he said, "Let those who consider war to be the better solution reject my outstretched hand." But it was a hand already busy with systematic plans for the next aggression. In the light of subsequent events we know that those weeks of stalling were a period of preparation, the lull before the fiery storm soon to break over the Low Countries, Norway and France; a softening-up phase which some American critics, smug in their fancied isolation, derided as "the phony war."

THE EPIDEMIC OF SHIP SINKINGS

It was no make-believe war to the passengers and crew of the Dutch merchant ship, the *Simon Bolivar*, which was navigating waters off the east coast of England that Saturday, November 18. By a quirk of fate this neutral ship bearing the name of a New World patriot became an instrument for demonstrating the effectiveness of one of Hitler's secret engines of destruction. As the unsuspecting vessel pushed her way through the impartial sea there was a tremendous explosion which seemed to come from beneath her hull, the steel bottom was crushed upward, and the *Bolivar* sank with the loss of many lives.

Other sinkings which followed the same general pattern occurred on Sunday in the same or neighboring waters. On Monday four more merchant vessels went down, bringing the week-end's toll to 10 ships and 200 lives. On Tuesday a Japanese liner, the *Terukuni Maru*, met a similar rendezvous with death near the mouth of the Thames; and before that day ended the British destroyer *Gypsy* also had been blown in two, leaving 21 of her crew maimed besides the 40 who went down with the ship.

The fact that these explosions occurred in near-by coastal waters which were closely patrolled, where mine sweepers operated at frequent intervals and where submarine detection was at a maximum, added an element of mystery to the epidemic of disasters.

British lookouts had reported a curious aerial visitation the night before the *Terukuni Maru* and *Gypsy* sinkings. In the semi-darkness German airplanes were seen hovering over the water within sight of the English shores, and one flew low over the Thames Estuary. Fighter planes of the Royal Air Force rose to meet the enemy, but the Germans turned and disappeared into the southeast.

Wednesday night the visitors were back. Their aircraft, marked with the black Prussian cross, circled over the broad mouth of the Thames, and this time alert watchers saw "dark objects" dropping from the planes. The objects floated down leisurely, supported by parachutes, and on reaching the water were lost to view. As before, the Germans scurried homeward when pursued, but next morning an odd cylindrical shape was sighted resting on a sandbank opposite the Essex seashore town of Shoeburyness.

THE SECRET WEAPON

Here was one of those "dark objects" waiting in the light of day to be seen, examined and exposed. The patrol took a few pot shots at it, but fortunately their marksmanship was poor; the mine was not hit and did not explode. Thus the experts of the British Admiralty's mine experimental department had preserved for them by lucky accident a sample of the secret weapon which was causing such destruction in supposedly protected waters.

It was a metal cylinder 8 feet long and 2 feet in diameter, shaped somewhat like a torpedo. But there was no steering gear or propelling mechanism such as torpedoes customarily carry, nor was there any chain, cable, or other mooring gear such as is attached to the usual buoy type of mine. Suspecting that it might be a magnetic device, the experts divested their pockets of keys, tools, and other things of steel or iron before approaching the contraption. Then they made careful measurements of its exterior, noting joints, seams and other features, and from these data prepared special tools of non-magnetic material to use in dismembering the mine.

The story of how Lieutenant-Commander John G. D. Ouvry volunteered to open this infernal machine and explore its unknown mechanism has been told in interesting detail by Professor A. M. Low in his *Mine and Countermine*. It took courage of a high order to go alone to that isolated sandbank and lay a prying hand on the deadly invention, knowing, as Ouvry must have known, of the German predilection for planting booby traps.

"He had no idea," relates Professor Low, "whether the mine did not contain some special device for exploding it should any attempt be made at dissembly, but having told his staff exactly what he proposed to do and what parts he would tackle first, he set out across the flats on his perilous mission. It was necessary that he should first explain what he intended to do, in order that, if he were blown up, others should have some knowledge of what not to do on any subsequent occasion."

Ouvry's first step, continues Professor Low, "was to remove a small fitting which he assumed to be a detonator. By the evening he and his assistant had removed the outer case of the mine, with various other fittings, one of which they were startled to discover was a second detonator. By that time they were satisfied that the mine had been made innocuous; it was thereupon put upon a lorry and sent to Portsmouth for further examination."

The casing was a light metal, resembling duralumin. The charge, about 650 pounds of high explosive, was carried in the forward part. Just back of it was a compartment containing the firing mechanism, whose control was a magnetic needle. Finally, there was evidence that the construction originally included a rear compartment in which was carried a parachute. The total weight was around 1,200 pounds. As the mine dropped from the mine-sowing airplane the sides of its rear compartment opened, the parachute unfolded and the load was eased down to the sea. On reaching the water it sank to the bottom, while an automatic device freed the parachute and another controlled by water pressure set the firing mechanism. As soon as it was thus rendered "alive" the mine became sensitive to any iron presence within the range of its magnetic influence.

This range appears to have been about 30 feet. Any large object of iron or an iron alloy, such as the steel hull of a ship, would affect the magnetic needle when it came within 30 feet of the mine; the swing of the needle would close an electric circuit to the detonator, and this in turn would set off the charge.

A huge concentration of steel, such as a superbattleship, might deflect the needle at a greater distance, but for the usual warship or merchant vessel 30 feet represent the effective zone of activation. It was for this reason that the Germans selected the Thames Estuary, the mouth of the Humber and other shore waters of 40-foot depth or less for sowing their new-style seeds of destruction Most steel ships ride at least 10 feet under water; therefore, in passing over a mine resting on a 40-foot sea bottom, their hulls would come within range of the mine's influence.

Torpedoes and ordinary naval mines which detonate on contact usually strike a ship on the side, and there are many instances in which a vessel so wounded has limped into port. But not so the victims of the magnetic mine; it does not count many wounded.

Striking from below, it hits a vessel in the most vulnerable part, and its blow usually is fatal. Ships' bottoms are broken in two by the massive impact of updriven water, and sink quickly with little opportunity for salvage or life saving. Not only was this type of weapon peculiarly destructive but it was peculiarly insidious, lying in wait on the sea bottom out of reach of the mine sweepers.

FIGHTING MAGNETISM WITH MAGNETISM

Once shorn of the secret of its mode of operation, the new weapon was soon rendered futile. The very principle of physics that activated the firing mechanism could be used to neutralize the mine, as British scientists soon demonstrated.

For the force which makes a magnetic mine respond to a passing steel ship is terrestrial magnetism. And this derives from the well-known fact that the Earth is a magnet. As our planet whirls along its path around the Sun, invisible lines of force spray out from the north magnetic pole and bend around the Earth to join the south magnetic pole. This vast globe-enveloping pattern constitutes the Earth's magnetic field. Just what the lines of force are is a detail the authorities can't explain, but they know that by virtue of this field all steel objects on or near the surface of the Earth are feebly magnetized. Thus the steel hull of a ship moving over the sea is a magnet, with one of its ends serving as the north-seeking pole, the other as the south-seeking pole—which end is which depending on the ship's position with reference to the direction of the Earth's magnetic field. Also, the steel needle poised in the mine down on the sea bed is a magnet. It is known that when one magnet is brought near another, like poles repel, opposite poles attract; hence the needle in the mine swings either toward the ship or away from it. In whichever direction it moves the device is so arranged that it forms a contact, and closes an electric circuit which sets off the explosive.

But this can happen only if the thing that approaches the needle is a magnet, and the ship is a magnet only by reason of the Earth's magnetic field. All right, said the British scientists, let's take our ships out of the magnet class. They found they could do this by winding a coil of wire around the hull and sending through the coil a suitable current of electricity. If the current was rightly proportioned to the strength of magnetism induced in the ship by the Earth, a magnetic field of opposite polarity which exactly equaled the magnetic field imposed by the Earth was set up, and this artificial field canceled the effect of the natural field. Thereby the steel ship was denuded of its magnetism. Thereafter it had no more influence on a mine's needle than any wooden ship.

The coil of wire which is strung around ships to protect them against this clever perversion of magnetism is known as a de-gaussing girdle. It is so called because the unit of magnetic flow is a gauss. The name is derived from that of the eminent German physicist, Carl Frederick Gauss (1777-1855), who formulated the laws of terrestrial magnetism about a hundred years ago. He is second only to the pioneering British experimenter William Gilbert (1544-1603) in this branch of physics. It is a tribute to the international character of science that both British and German researchers (as well as those of other nationalities) have contributed to our knowledge of magnetism. And the same pool of knowledge which provided the German genius for war with a secret weapon of offense was promptly turned by the beleaguered British to purposes of defense. By December, 1939, virtually all steel ships navigating waters susceptible of infestation with magnetic mines were protected with de-gaussing girdles. When the 85,000-ton *Queen Elizabeth* made her maiden voyage to New York in March, 1940, she wore her protective girdle and passed unscathed through the uncertain waters.

It seems strange that the British had made no preparations to counter the magnetic mine in advance of the German attack; for the principle of the device was well known, and in fact had been tried in a small way in World War I.

It also seems strange that the Germans unleashed this weapon so early in the war and apparently without making it part of their grand strategy. If the magnetic mine had been held in reserve for the projected invasion of Britain, for example, and had suddenly been used in concert with extensive air and naval raids, it is possible that the new device might have had a longer period of effective use. The strain and excitement of fighting off squadrons of bombing planes and invasion forces might have complicated and unduly delayed the task of developing a counterweapon. As it was, when

Reichsmarshal Göring launched his all-out attack in August, 1940, the defenders had long ago disposed of the menace of the magnetic mine and were able to concentrate their forces on the German bombers.

THE BATTLE OF BRITAIN

No matter how fierce the fighting, how acute the perils or how crucial the issues of subsequent conflicts may be, this battle which was fought in the skies over England will rank in history as one of the decisive battles of civilization. If it had been lost, the war would have been lost in 1940.

The Battle of Britain occupied twelve weeks of almost continual aerial warfare, waged at heights of three to six miles; a battle without precedent, weird, magnificent, awesome, aimed at the destruction of a nation. It began on August 8th with an attack on two coastal convoys, and for the first ten days the Germans' objective was the destruction of British shipping and port facilities. They succeeded in sinking five ships, damaged five others, and strafed several channel ports; but they paid the heavy toll of 695 aircraft lost in the effort, and on August 18th abandoned the attacks. That was phase 1 of the battle.

After a pause of five days, apparently to give their Luftwaffe a rest, the Germans resumed the attack in a new phase. This time the fury of the bombers was directed at the airfields, particularly at the R.A.F.'s inland fighter fields. The obvious effort was to destroy the British facilities for taking off and landing, and thus to ground the Royal Air Force. Some damage was inflicted, some serious destruction of aerodrome facilities, but at the end of twelve days of these tactics most of the fields were still functioning. Meanwhile 610 German planes had been shot down, including 39 lost on reconnaissance flights during the five-day lull—and again Göring shifted his attack.

Phase 3 of the battle began on September 7th with raids on the industrial cities of England, particularly London. The fighting mounted to a swift and terrible tempo as the Germans increased the size of their squadrons and the frequency of their raids, only to be met by the vigilant R.A.F. and the shattering fire of their Hurricanes and Spitfires. Some enemy bombers got through to

London; fires were started, docks destroyed, homes demolished. Buckingham Palace and other notable buildings were struck, civilians were killed and wounded, but the majority of the raiders never reached their objectives; many were turned back, many were shot down. Thus on September 7th the Germans lost 103 aircraft and 297 airmen killed or missing; on the 9th their losses were 52 planes and 208 airmen; on the 11th, 89 planes and 183 men; on the 15th, "the great day" when 500 planes of the Luftwaffe were hurled at the British capital in wave after wave, the losses mounted to 185 planes and 516 pilots; on the 18th, 48 planes and 183 men; on the 27th, 133 planes and 150 men. The next day, September 28th, it is said that 800 German planes crossed the channel, but not one of them was able to reach London. For a fortnight the number of wrecked German aircraft cluttering the English countryside was so great that two battalions of British infantry were required to guard them. Someone wrote that the rural districts of Kent were "ankle deep" in Messerschmitts and Heinkels. By October 5th the efforts to strafe London and other industrial cities had lost the Germans 883 planes, and Göring was willing to call a halt on daylight raiding. Thereafter the bombers increasingly restricted their visits to the night hours; and finally, as October ended, it became apparent that the Battle of Britain was over.

During the eighty-seven days the German raiders had shot down 600 British planes, they had destroyed thousands of buildings and other valuable property, they had inflicted on London and other cities wounds and scars that can never be compensated, they had killed 14,281 persons and wounded 20,325 others (nearly all civilians). But against these achievements they had to weigh many failures: they had not broken British resistance, they had not wiped out British shipping, they had not seriously interrupted British war production. Above all, they had not grounded the Royal Air Force, though the Luftwaffe had lost 2,375 of its own aircraft over England in the battle. How many Germans fell at sea or failed to reach their home ports can only be conjectured.

The human factor was indispensable to the prodigies of effort which won this victory. Without the quality of personnel that manned the aircraft and ground stations, no other resources could have made up for its lack. But in an air battle in which the foe is numerically superior, indomitable courage and naked skill are not enough. The R.A.F. had two advantages of technological equipment that contributed decisively to its success.

The first was superior aircraft. The British Spitfires could fly faster than the German Messerschmitts, and though the British Hurricanes were not so speedy they were more maneuverable. Both were better armored and better armed than the German fighters. The Messerschmitt carried five guns: a cannon firing through the propeller hub, two machine guns in the top fuselage and two in the wings. But the Hurricane and the Spitfire each carried eight machine guns mounted in the wings in a line, four on each side. When all eight guns were firing their combined output was 160 shots per second, and that massive concentration of fast-moving slugs slashed Nazi planes to ribbons, slicing off wings, cutting fuselage, crippling propellers, ripping fuel tanks, puncturing engines, and even when they did not send a ship down in flames accounted for the sudden death of many a skilled enemy airman.

The fact that the British had better planes must be credited not alone to their engineering skill. British tardiness in recognizing the menace of the totalitarians proved in this connection to be an actual benefit. For it was in 1936 that Göring standardized the German aircraft types. Mass production was necessary to provide the air power that Hitler craved. His Junkers, Heinkels, Dorniers and Messerschmitts excelled the British planes of 1936, indeed were the best designs then in sight, so he fixed on them for mass production. German factories, tools and production schedules were geared to turn out the adopted types by the thousands and the ten thousands. But it was not until the shock of Munich that John Bull awoke to his danger. Then began the feverish rush to rearm. Although the first Hurricanes had already been produced, British aircraft designs were not yet standardized. Their jigs and tools were still to be set, and in consequence the planes which came out of the British factories in 1939 and 1940 were able to embody improvements unknown to the standardizers of 1936-'37.

Not only did the Royal Air Force have superior planes but it possessed a second advantage in a secret weapon of defense—secret until the summer of 1941, when the Air Ministry announced its use; a device called by the British authorities the radiolocator.

THE GOLDEN COCKEREL

Lord Beaverbrook, in a radio address broadcast in June, 1941, described the new device as "our golden cockerel," referring to Rimsky-Korsakov's pantomime-opera "Le Coq d'Or." This is a dramatization of Pushkin's story of a king whose land was sorely beset by an aggressive enemy, who was sleepless because his small army was unable to know from which direction invasion was coming, when an astrologer appeared bearing a mysterious object.

"I have brought thee a magic bird, O Sire, a Golden Cockerel which is ready to serve as thy watchman by night and by day," said the man of science to the anxious king. "Set it upon the highest spire, and it will keep a faithful watch upon the farthest borders of thy realm. When no danger threatens it will remain quiet. But at the first approach of enemies, even afar off, my Golden Cockerel will spy out their presence, he will lift his comb, flap his wings, turn his beak in the direction of the raiders, and crow 'Cock-a-doodle-do! Beware!' "

The British Minister of State did not explain how the radio-locator simulates the comb-raising, wing-flapping, danger-facing and crowing routine of the golden cockerel. The truth is, precious little has been revealed of the design and operation of this ingenious instrument. Its principle, however, is well known, and has been made use of in other ways for years. Its utility lies in the fact that whenever a radio beam strikes a surface which conducts electricity, the beam is reflected off the surface like light. This was observed a number of years ago, long before the war. It was observed by scientists studying the Kennelly-Heaviside layer, a zone of electrified particles in the upper atmosphere. The layer surrounds the earth as a tenuous roof of electricity, and it is because of this roof of the world 70 to 150 miles above us that a radio signal is able to go around the earth. The radio waves striking the layer are reflected down to the ground, which in turn reflects them back to the layer, and so by a series of zigzags a broadcast travels from New York to Melbourne.

Radio researchers are accustomed to probing the Kennelly-Heaviside layer with short-wave radio beams, and were able by these means to measure its height and stratification. In the early years of these studies the investigators would sometimes get a sudden quick reflection which was too short to have come from the Kennelly-Heaviside layer. Later they discovered that a passing airplane had chanced to intercept the beam, and its metal surface had reflected the waves back to the ground.

Here was something that might be very useful. The plane which had reflected the beam downward was passing overhead. But suppose the plane was approaching from a distance; and suppose the beam had been flashed in its direction, and had collided with the oncoming plane? The radio waves would be reflected back. Thus they could be used to detect the presence of an airplane before it was visible, or even before the sound of its motors was picked up by the microphones. By installing the transmitter in an elevated place, such as the top of a building or tower, and sweeping its beam through space the sky might be combed for invisible aircraft. As radio travels with the speed of light, and can go around the earth eight times in a second, any news that it could give of even the most distant aircraft would be received almost instantaneously.

From such observations emerged the aircraft warning system. Many refinements have been made, both in the transmitting part of the instrument and in its receiving end, and its precision is amazing. "It finds the enemy in the darkness," said Beaverbrook, "seeks them out through the clouds," and "it is in radio," he assured the British people, "that we will find a way to spread the covering wings of science over the multitudes who inhabit our vast cities."

The plane-detecting device received its definitive test in the Battle of Britain. "Though millions of pounds have been spent on radiolocators," said Air Marshal Sir Philip Joubert, "it is safe to say that the entire cost has already been saved. This instrument was of such incalculable help that independent observers have stated categorically that the Battle of Britain was won by the fighters of the Royal Air Force *and* the radiolocators."

Hundreds of locator stations were set up in various parts of the British Isles and because of them the Royal Air Force "was enabled to do away with the maintenance of standing patrols, relying on the vast detection system to give ample warning of the approach of bombers and the exact direction they were following."

No description of the apparatus, and very little of its history, has been released; but enough is divulged to show that this invention was no sudden makeshift hurriedly improvised in the fear of threatened invasion. On the contrary, it is a prewar development. Not only in Britain but in the United States as well scientists had early recognized the military possibilities of radio reflections. In each country, independently, devices had secretly been developed. The Americans called their instrument the radar, coining the word from the initials of "radio detecting and ranging." But because the British radiolocator was the first to see actual battle service it was the first to get into the news. "It was born," said Air Marshal Joubert, "in a rather ancient lorry on a fine March morning in 1935 on a road near Daventry."

The father of the British radiolocator is Robert Alexander Watson Watt, a research physicist who in 1935 was superintendent of the radio department of the British National Physical Laboratory. Just what happened in the ancient lorry on the English country road in that year has never been published; but it is on record that a few months later Dr. Watson Watt was transferred to the Bawdsey Research Station where radio investigations for the Royal Air Force are carried on. Then, in 1938, the Air Ministry and Ministry of Aircraft Production made him director of communications. Other scientists and engineers collaborated in the long sequence of experiments and tests, for like most scientific developments the new weapon is the product of much teamwork; and it is because of these men of the laboratories, because of their scientific imagination, their technological skill, their attention to small details of natural phenomena—in a word, because of their *science*—that Britain had its golden cockerel ready and set to crow the approach of the enemy.

SCIENCE IN THE WAR

"It is the scientist who heals our wounds," declared Beaverbrook, in his tribute to the creators of the radiolocator. "It is the scientist who will protect us. It is the scientist who will save our homes and guard our hearthstones." Although this admittedly is oratory, it is more than rhetoric. Never have nations appreciated the talents of their scientists, and recognized the practical value of the contributions of science, as now.

This is true not only of Great Britain but of all the countries currently engaged in the business of war. Russia's rugged and unbreakable resistance, which surprised even her friends and gave the lie to the gloomy predictions of her critics, was not unrelated to a comprehensive U.S.S.R. program of years of scientific research aimed at improving and strengthening the equipment of the Red Army.

The Kaiser's war venture of 1914 was founded on German possession of vast technological resources which were counted on to win before the Allies could sufficiently equip themselves to meet the challenge. And even more was Hitler's gigantic gamble based on his belief in the invincibility of superior science. He depended on science for synthetic nitrates with which to make explosives, for new alloys and other synthetic materials with which to make German planes, for synthetic fuel with which to fly them, and for the hundreds of other substitutes for or improvements upon natural products which entered into the bloody business of extending his dictatorship.

The use of science by an aggressor to impose his will by force necessarily calls for the use of science by the defender who would resist and insure his freedom. The only way to overcome the magnetic mine was to assign to the problem men who were thoroughly at home with the science of magnetism. The only way to outclass the Luftwaffe's equipment was to assign to the task of designing airplanes men who were abreast of the latest advances in aeronautical science. The Germans used radio beams to guide their planes to a distant target in the dark; the British countered by using radio beams to feel out their enemy afar off. Today, as through the centuries, new science is used to oppose old science, and in turn it is countered by still fresher applications of the laws of nature.

With the prospect of war in 1939, the British government wisely decided to classify its men of science in categories that would permit the nation to make the most effective use of their abilities. Several months before the invasion of Poland the Royal Society, at the request of the government, compiled a register of scientific personnel which became of the greatest value when the storm burst. Britain had learned a bitter lesson during the first world war. Then thousands of technically trained specialists were allowed to volunteer for the military service, or were drafted into it, simply because they were of military age. Later the government had to call many of these young men back from the army, navy, or air force and reassign them to laboratories, production plants, and other technological posts where their special knowledge and skill were urgently needed. In some instances the enemy's bullets claimed these exceptional brains before they could be recalled for more urgent service at home. A tragic example of this was the loss of Henry G. J. Moseley at Gallipoli in 1915. Moseley was a younger Rutherford, for at the age of 26 at Cambridge he had discovered and formulated one of the most important laws of atomic physics; but his career ended at the age of 28 with a piece of Turkish lead singing through his brain. Britain resolved in 1939 that Moseleys could do more for their country in the laboratory than in the trenches.

And so it turned out, as winter melted into the spring of 1940, and spring distilled from the dark eastern skies that mortal rain of fire and metal which fell upon Rotterdam, Louvain and other trusting cities, and with unbelievable ferocity and speed reduced them to death or slavery. It was war then—no longer bundles of leaflets to Germans, no longer the truce of "Don't shoot and we won't shoot." Three hundred and thirty thousand soldiers huddled on a narrow beachhead, without allies, without arms except for a last-stand rear guard; the green channel waters in front, behind the roar and whistle of the German artillery, the rumble of the oncoming tanks with their stuttering machine guns, and from above the eternal threat of the dive bombers! It was then that the R.A.F. was called on to perform its first prodigy of defense, to provide a protective canopy for the thousands of ships, boats, and other rescuing craft. And that performance in the air plus the performance down on the surface of the sea was the miracle of Dunkirk.

It was then that the Hurricanes and Spitfires first showed their mettle in dueling the Luftwaffe. And it was then that Britain began to reap the harvest of that prudence which had reserved her scientists for technical services. They were needed in the munitions factories and in the research that lay back of and accelerated the factories; for at Dunkirk Britain had saved only her soldiers. All their equipment, guns, tanks, ammunition and other supplies had been lost in Flanders. Now the soldiers must be rearmed with everything that technology could provide. There was no time for muddling or perfectionism. Speed, invention, improvisation, pushing the available resources to the last limit of tolerance—these were the watchwords in that somber emergency when Britain stood alone and the conqueror of a continent gathered his forces for her destruction. Nobody talked now about science taking a ten-year holiday. The time-saving, labor-economizing, future-piercing stratagems and tactics of the laboratory were available, and trained men capable of using them were on duty, and both men and methods were supremely needed. "It is the scientist who will save our homes and guard our hearthstones."

PHYSICS IN THE WAR

The scientist who has played the most conspicuous part in these efforts is the physicist. It was among physicists that the shortage of technical men first made itself felt in Great Britain. And as the United States began to shift its resources for military preparedness, it was the physicists who were increasingly called upon by the army and navy for consultation, advice, research, and collaboration on technological problems. When the President set up the National Defense Research Committee in the summer of 1940 to mobilize America's scientific brains, he selected as its chairman a man whose training and experience had been in the branch of applied physics which we call electrical engineering. The following summer the President expanded the committee into the Office of Scientific Research and Development, endowing it with resources and powers beyond that of any previous coalition between science and government in this country, and he kept the engineer in the technological high command.

By that time the government had mobilized many thousands of scientists in the war effort, and hundreds of laboratories in universities, research institutes and industrial plants had been geared into the systematic search for new and better ways of fighting the dictators. One finds among the scientists engaged in the war effort scores of different specialties represented, but in America as in Britain it is the physicists who have been called upon more than any other group.

"It's a physicists' war," said President James B. Conant of Harvard when he returned from a visit to the British laboratories in the spring of 1940, echoing a phrase which was current among scientists whom he met on that trip.

But why is it a physicists' war?

Because the new tools of offense and defense are primarily physical, rather than chemical or biological contributions. Note the wide use of aeronautics, motorized equipment, radio and other forms of electrical communication, mechanical control of gunfire, and such innovations as the magnetic mine, the radiolocator and the bombsight. Even the Germans' famed psychological warfare is largely dependent for its effectiveness on a physical tool, the radio. In 1914-'18, when aeronautics and radio were feeble infants, it was the chemists who held the center of the stage, with their startling contributions of nitrogen fixation, improved explosives and incendiaries, and gas warfare.

Today's struggle is a physicists' war only in the sense that powerful and spectacular weapons have been introduced through applications of physics—certainly not in the sense that they alone are indispensable to our arsenal. It would be difficult to find one of the new physical weapons that is not dependent on the collaboration of specialists in other fields. The airplane, to take but one example, is pre-eminently a child of physics. Its lineage can be traced through studies of mechanics, ballistics, gravitation, gaseous pressure, air flow, strength of materials, and a whole catalogue of other physical specialties, back to Newton and Galileo. More than any other group the physicists, including the engineers, are responsible for refinements which make the modern airplane one of man's greatest intellectual achievements. For it is a supreme triumph of the creative spirit, even though at present, as Joad has said, "it has fallen into the hands of the apes." But while physicists design and develop it, others also have contributed to the creation of the airplane. How far would it have advanced if chemists had not discovered ways to extract and alloy aluminum? Or if biologists had not studied the physiology of aviation and devised means which make the airman independent of the unaccustomed conditions of the stratosphere? Without many contributions such as these the 1943 airplane would not exist.

The physicists cannot win their war without the collaboration of mathematicians, chemists, biologists, psychologists and many others, for there is no field of science which the enemy may not invade and appropriate to his purpose. The sudden launching of a massive gas attack by the Axis might change the war overnight into a chemists' war. Other developments might shift the emphasis to a biologists' war. Every conceivable outcome must be anticipated. There is no department of natural knowledge which the democratic nations can afford to ignore or neglect as they throw their forces into the titanic struggle.

CHAPTER II

The Historical Relationship of War and Science

Not but what abstract war is horrid
I sign to thet with all my heart,—
But civlyzation does git foorid
Sometimes upon a powder cart.

—James Russell Lowell, THE BIGELOW PAPERS

THE classic example of science engaged in war is the defense of Syracuse against the Romans in 215 B.C. Apparently the only detail the defenders neglected was psychology. They had the most competent physicist of antiquity, and he responded loyally to his country's need and served as a combined national research director and chief of ordnance. Plutarch relates that Archimedes not only repelled the invaders, sinking their ships, wrecking their siege machine and decimating their ranks, but so terrified the Roman soldiery with his mechanical weapons that "if they did but see a little rope or a piece of wood from the city's walls, instantly crying out that there it was again—Archimedes was about to let fly some engine at them!—they turned their backs and fled."

MATHEMATICS INTO WEAPONS

Archimedes (287-212 B.C.) was a mathematician by profession, and indulged in physics only as a hobby and to demonstrate his problems in geometry. Once, in a letter to King Hiero, monarch of Syracuse, he made the assertion that any weight, no matter how heavy, could be moved if sufficient force were applied, and added that if a fulcrum could be found he would move the Earth. Hiero wanted to be shown this wonder. Could the mathematician actually demonstrate the movement of a great weight by a little machine? In the king's arsenal was a large ship of burden, a vessel which could be drawn out of the dock only with the labor of many men, and Archimedes selected it for his demonstration. "Loading her with many passengers and a full freight, sitting himself the while off, with no great endeavor, but only holding the head of the pulley in his hand and drawing the cord by degrees, he drew the ship in a straight line, as smoothly and evenly as if she had been in the sea." The king was so convinced of the might of mechanics that he prevailed on Archimedes "to make him engines accommodated to all the purposes, offensive and defensive, of a siege."

This was the origin of the formidable weapons installed at Syracuse, magnificent and opulent Greek city on the eastern coast of Sicily. King Hiero never had occasion to use them, for his long reign was an interval of peace, but shortly after his death these measures of preparedness were vindicated. For in the year 215, as part of Rome's bitter feud with Carthage, the Roman general Marcellus led a large naval and military force against Syracuse and demanded its submission.

Archimedes was now 72 years old, and however his achievements in science may have impressed the populace in times past, their confidence sank at the approach of the world-shaking Roman legions. The attackers threw themselves against the city's walls in two places, and at once "fear and consternation stupefied the Syracusans, believing that nothing was able to resist that violence and those forces."

But the venerable Archimedes was not shaken. Presently he began to ply his scientific weapons. From mechanical slings he hurled "immense masses of stone," missiles that "came down with incredible noise and violence, against which no man could stand— for they knocked those upon whom they fell, in heaps, breaking all their ranks and files."

Meanwhile, the Roman navy of sixty galleys, each with five rows of oars, assaulted the walls on the city's waterfront. The naval equipment included a huge bridge of planks laid upon eight ships chained together to support a giant catapult.

But the sea attack fared no better than the land attack. "Huge poles thrust out from the city's walls over the ships sank some of them by the great weights which they let down from on high. Other ships they lifted up into the air by an iron hand like a crane's beak, and, when they had drawn them up by the prow, and set them on end upon the poop, they plunged the ships to the bottom of the sea. Or else the ships, drawn by engines within, and whirled about, were dashed against steep rocks that stood jutting out under the city's walls, with great destruction of the troops that were aboard them. A ship was frequently lifted up to a great height in the air—a dreadful thing to behold!—and was rolled to and fro, and kept swinging, until the mariners were all thrown out, when at length it was dashed against the rocks, or let fall."

As for the Romans' proudest weapon, that giant catapult which they had brought upon the bridge of ships, the story goes that while it was yet approaching the city Archimedes discharged "a piece of rock of ten talents' weight (about 570 pounds), then a second and a third which, striking upon it with immense force and a noise like thunder, broke all its foundations to pieces, shook out its fastenings, and completely dislodged it from its bridge."

Marcellus withdrew for a council of war. New tactics were agreed on, an assault to be made at night, coming up under the walls of the city. The Romans believed that if they could gain these advanced positions, the stones and darts would fly over their heads without effect, since it was observed that the throwing devices were built for long-range operations. But no, the old mathematician had thought of everything, and "long before had framed for such occasions engines accommodated to any distance, and shorter weapons." Thus, "when they who thought to deceive the defenders came close to the walls, instantly a shower of darts and other missile weapons were again cast upon them. And when stones came tumbling down perpendicularly upon their heads and, as it were, the whole wall shot out arrows at them, they retired."

As they retired, "arrows and darts of a longer range inflicted great slaughter, and their ships were driven one against another; while they were not able to retaliate. For Archimedes had fixed most of his engines immediately under the wall; whence the Romans, seeing that indefinite mischiefs overwhelmed them from no visible means, began to think they were fighting with the gods."

Marcellus taunted his engineers. "What! Must we give up fighting with this geometrical Briareus, who plays pitch and toss with our ships, and, with the multitude of darts which he showers at a single moment on us, really outdoes the hundred-handed giants of mythology?"

They didn't give up, but the plan for a sudden overwhelming assault had been countered at every point, and the Romans settled down to a long siege. For three years Archimedes stood them off. So invincible were his engines, that "the rest of the Syracusans were but the body of Archimedes's designs, one soul moving and governing all; for, laying aside all other arms, with his alone they infested the Romans and protected themselves."

Perhaps this invincibility bred overconfidence, or else blinded the Syracuse military command to the possibility of stratagems outside the realm of mechanics. At all events, the Romans felt no obligation to keep their war a physicists' war, and began to look for an opportunity to overwhelm the defenders with guile.

The opening was found in 212 B.C. when they captured a man who had just put to sea from the surrounded city. It turned out that this prisoner was one whom the Syracusans much desired to redeem. There were many meetings between them and Marcellus about the exchange, and the trusting Syracusans even admitted a committee of Romans within their walls to discuss the matter. While there under this truce the sharp-eyed Marcellus spied an outer tower into which a body of men might be smuggled. His photographic mind recorded the architectural layout, estimated the heights and dimensions, and from these details he had ladders and other scaling devices prepared. One moonless night, as Syracuse was celebrating a feast to Diana with much wine and sport, the Romans secretly climbed into the tower. Before dawn they had occupied an adjoining wall with soldiers. As the awakening citizens began to bestir themselves to another day, Marcellus ordered his trumpeters everywhere to sound their loudest notes, and the soldiers made a great tumult, "as if all parts of the city were already won, though the most fortified and the fairest and most ample quarters were still ungained."

These tactics had the desired effect. The people who for three years had withstood the might of the Roman arms with their machines were thrown into panic. Chaos and confusion reigned where before had been discipline, order and confidence; and soon the Romans "obtained also the plunder of the other parts of the city, which were taken by treachery."

Thus fell Syracuse, an early example of what can be done through a war of nerves. The city was looted, and in the melee Archimedes was killed.

THE MILITARY ORIGINS OF ENGINEERING

Note Plutarch's recurrent use of the term "engine." In our diction the word is commonly understood to mean a machine for generating mechanical power: a steam engine, an internal combustion engine, or a railway locomotive. But this usage is modern. Originally all engines were engines of war; and all engineers, military engineers. The engineers of Babylonia, Egypt, Greece, Rome and Carthage were called upon to construct many public works that are now classed as civil engineering, but so great was the preoccupation of governments with war that their design and construction of highways, aqueducts, canals, harbors and other civic improvements were conceived in terms of military usefulness. Even in our time, river and harbor development in the United States is carried on by the U. S. Army Corps of Engineers. The unique jetty system at the mouths of the Mississippi by which their channels are kept clear of sedimentation, the flood-control system of the Mississippi with its vast levees, the extensive system of locks and dams on the Ohio which have been so great a boon to the navigation of that river— these and many other large-scale projects in civil engineering are cared for by army engineers. The army engineers also had an important part in building the first transcontinental railroad.

The center of engineering research in antiquity was the city of Alexandria under the Ptolemies. Its famous Alexandrine Museum was not only an academy or society of scholars but a university. There all existing branches of science were taught and, in so far as they lent themselves to practical uses, were applied. On its faculty were Euclid, Aristarchus of Samos, Eratosthenes and other celebrated scientists. Students came from Egypt, Greece, and even faraway Syracuse. Archimedes was a graduate of Alexandria. It was there that he picked up ideas for those powerful engines which later germinated at Syracuse, for it is related that the museum specialized in the investigation of catapults and other siege engines.

The catapult is older than Alexandria, however. Tradition says that it was introduced about 400 B.C. by the Greeks as an adaptation of the handbow. Later, instead of bending or twisting pieces of wood to provide the propulsive force, engineers devised arrangements of elastic leather, and with these thongs were able to throw 5-pound stones to distances of about 1,200 feet. The Romans improved on the Alexandrine designs and stepped up the power considerably. Their later machines, it is said, were able to throw stones weighing as much as 57 pounds 1,500 feet and more. The ancients also had ballistas, enormous wooden crossbows, with which they shot small stones and darts to even greater distances.

Dampness affects the elasticity of leather, and the early engineers attempted to remedy this defect in their catapults; for war could not wait on the weather. Philo of Byzantium, who lived about the time of Archimedes, proposed two substitutes for leather thongs: compressed air, and springs made of bronze leaf. He wrote a book on pneumatic engines, and designed one such machine for throwing missiles; but there is no evidence that a compressed-air catapult ever was built. Philo pointed to the flexibility of certain swords in support of his idea of springs. In view of our wide use of compressed air today—in air brakes, riveting hammers and other industrial machines—and our even more varied employment of metal springs, it is historically significant that the first proposals of these devices were motivated by war.

Auxiliary to the catapults were mural machines, various forms of battering-rams used to breach and surmount walls. In the siege of Rhodes by Demetrius in 305 B.C., a mural machine which rose to a height of 60 feet was used. It was a tower on wheels and consisted of several stories filled with armed men and with openings on the front side for discharging missiles. All beholders were amazed by its size and mobility. "When it moved it never tottered or inclined to one side, but went forward on its base in perfect equilibrium, with a loud noise and great impetus." This affair was designed and constructed by the Athenian engineer Epimachus. To counter it the Rhodesians engaged Callias of Arados to provide a gigantic crane with a long arm designed to reach over the wall, hook into the enemy engine and lift it away. But the crane proved to be a futile investment, for the machine of Epimachus eluded all attempts to hook it, and the Rhodesians had to fall back on the resources of one of their local engineers, Diognetes. He finally overcame the enemy's tactics by a system of tunneling, whereupon the ground collapsed under the weight of the towering engine, it bogged down and had to be abandoned.

The more eminent and creative mathematical minds looked down on engineering exploits. Although they answered the call of the state in its emergencies, they rated engines as inferior to their theorems, geometric proofs and philosophizing. Archimedes shrank from the title engineer. Plutarch mentions that though his "inventions had now obtained him the renown of more than human sagacity, yet he would not deign to leave behind him any commentary or writing on such subjects. But, repudiating as sordid and ignoble the whole trade of engineering, and every sort of art that lends itself to mere use and profit, he placed his whole affection and ambition in those purer speculations where there can be no reference to the vulgar needs of life."

One wonders if this repugnance for applied science was not rooted in a deeper repugnance. To be an engineer in ancient Syracuse, Athens or Alexandria was to be a military engineer, for there were no others. Therefore it is possible that the early geometers, natural philosophers and other scientists of antiquity disliked to be associated with engineering because they disliked the bloody business of war. The internationalism which characterizes modern science is undoubtedly a flower of slow growth, and yet it is not unreasonable to suppose that even the pioneers of 2,300 years ago had some feeling against chauvinism and for international comity and peace. At all events, there was an early disdain for engineering coupled with outspoken preference for "those purer speculations where there can be no reference to the vulgar needs of life."

As science for science's sake gained momentum, engineering got along as best it could with lesser talent. Indeed, many pursuits of the mind fell into a state of hibernation as Europe lapsed into the intellectual winter which followed the fall of the Roman Empire. In 1163 Pope Alexander III forbade "the study of physics or the laws of the world" to ecclesiastics, which meant, as R. K. Merton has said, "the prohibition of scientific studies to the only persons who were even moderately equipped to pursue them." The search for heresy became a dominating quest, and inexpressible tortures were imposed for the sake of the erring soul. Religious leaders organized military campaigns for the rescue of the Holy Land from a race of heretics whose very name was war. And so the Cross fought the Scimitar with lances and spears, bows and arrows, stones and other missiles, weapons not very different from those of the Fourth-century Constantine.

Then, early in the Fourteenth century, came the greatest military innovation in the history of modern man: the introduction of firearms. Gunpowder was explosive in more ways than one. It revolutionized the profession of engineering, adding new and unheard-of problems of defense, fortifications and supplies. It stimulated the study of chemistry, mining, and metallurgy. It affected political organization; for artillery, by breaching the hitherto impregnable feudal castles, made it possible for monarchs to build nations. Thus firearms gave the first mortal blow to feudalism, and started Western man on his long march from the servile obeisance, intellectual sterility and economic stagnation of the Middle Ages to such rights and liberties as we now enjoy.

ENGINEERING IN THE RENAISSANCE AND SINCE

Military engineering reached a high state of virtuosity in the Renaissance, engaging the attention of such luminous minds as Leonardo da Vinci (1452-1519) and Galileo (1564-1642), among others. Galileo was professor of military science at the University of Pavia, and his important contributions to our knowledge of the laws of motion were derived in part from his studies of the trajectories of cannon balls. Leonardo did not teach military science, but was an active practitioner of it. A glimpse of the range of interests and variety of skills represented by the master engineer of this period is afforded through a letter which he addressed (about 1482) to Ludovic Sforza, Duke of Milan. Leonardo outlines his abilities as follows:

Most illustrious Lord, having now sufficiently seen and considered the proofs of all those who count themselves masters and inventors of instruments of war, and finding that their invention and use of the said instruments does not differ in any respects from those in common practice, I am emboldened without prejudice to anyone else to put myself in communication with your Excellency, in order to acquaint you with my secrets, thereafter offering myself at your pleasure effectually to demonstrate at any convenient time all those matters which are in part briefly recorded below:

1. I have plans for bridges, very light and strong and suitable for carrying very easily, with which to pursue and at times defeat the enemy; and others solid and indestructible by fire or assault, easy and convenient to carry away and place in position. And plans for burning and destroying those of the enemy.

2. When a place is besieged I know how to cut off water from the trenches, and how to construct an infinite number of bridges, mantlets, scaling ladders, and other instruments which have to do with the same enterprise.

3. Also if a place cannot be reduced by the method of bombardment, either through the height of its glacis or the strength of its position, I have plans for destroying every fortress or other stronghold unless it has been founded upon rock.

4. I have also plans for making cannon, very convenient and easy of transport, with which to hurl small stones in the manner almost of hail, causing great terror to the enemy from their smoke, and great loss and confusion.

5. Also I have ways of arriving at a certain fixed spot by caverns and secret winding passages, made without any noise even though it may be necessary to pass underneath trenches or a river.

6. Also I can make armoured cars, safe and unassailable, which will enter the serried ranks of the enemy with their artillery, and there is no company of men at arms so great that they will not break it. And behind these the infantry will be able to follow quite unharmed and without any opposition.

7. Also, if need shall arise, I can make cannon, mortars, and light ordnance, of very beautiful and useful shapes, quite different from those in common use.

8. Where it is not possible to employ cannon, I can employ catapults, mangonels, trabocchi, and other engines of wonderful efficacy not in general use. In short, as the variety of circumstances shall necessitate, I can supply an infinite number of different engines of attack and defense.

9. And if it should happen that the engagement was at sea, I have plans for constructing many engines most suitable either for

attack or defense, and ships which can resist the fire of all the heaviest cannon, and powder and smoke.

10. In time of peace I believe I can give you as complete satisfaction as anyone else in architecture or in the construction of buildings both public and private, and in conducting water from one place to another. Also I can execute sculpture in marble, bronze, or clay, and also painting, in which my work will stand comparison with that of anyone else whoever he may be. Moreover, I would undertake the work of the bronze horse, which shall endue with immortal glory and eternal honor the auspicious memory of the Prince your father and of the illustrious house of Sforza.

And if any of the aforesaid things should seem impossible or impracticable to anyone, I offer myself as ready to make trial of them in your park or in whatever place shall please your Excellency, to whom I commend myself with all possible humility.

Quite in contrast with the earlier natural philosophers, Leonardo preferred to be known as an engineer. His interest in practical applications of science is attested by the preponderance of items of this nature among the 5,000 pages of notes which he left at his death. Included are predictions which came to fulfillment in the twentieth century: the bombing plane, the tank and the submarine. He also described and sketched numerous devices of a non-military nature, and worked out projects in hydraulics, mechanics, city planning and other phases of civil engineering.

But the term civil engineer had to wait another couple of hundred years. It was not until about the time of young George Washington (1732-1799), who was a land surveyor as well as a voluntary soldier, that it came into use. Even then one who wished to obtain formal education in civil engineering must perforce enter a school of military training, for there were no other engineering schools. The famous Ecole Polytechnique, founded at Paris in the days of the French Revolution, and the school at St. Etienne were the chief centers of engineering education in the Eighteenth century, and both were army schools, primarily artillery schools. The first engineering school in the United States was the Military Academy at West Point, established in 1802. It remained an institution for training military engineers until 1866, when it was broadened to include all branches of officer training.

Civil engineering acquired its first habitation in the United States in 1824. Amos Eaton, a country lawyer who was addicted to science, persuaded a rich Hudson valley proprietor to found a school "for the purpose of instructing persons who may choose to apply themselves in the application of science to the common purposes of life." It is interesting to find that this school of science, established at Troy, New York, later chartered as the Rensselaer Polytechnic Institute, made no official use of the term "civil engineering" in its early years. For the words do not appear in any of its catalogues until 1828. In earlier publications the school described its courses in such terms as "land surveying" and "measurements of the flow of water in rivers and aqueducts."

The term civil engineer received official status in Great Britain in 1818 with the organization of the Institute of Civil Engineers, London. In the United States the oldest national organization of engineers is the American Society of Civil Engineers, founded in 1852. And so history repeated itself in other nations: in virtually every place the first to crystallize as a separate profession were the civil engineers.

But as industrialism expanded and invention added new devices to technology, specialties began to separate themselves from the main trunk of civil engineering. First to emerge were mining engineering and mechanical engineering, followed by marine, electrical and chemical engineering. Still more recent are automotive and aeronautical engineering. Later branches from the now massive stem of electrical engineering are communications engineering and radio engineering. Altogether there are more than a score of societies representing separate engineering specialties. Today, when most of these technologies are back at work under the ancestral roof of war, perhaps it is just as well again to call their practitioners just engineers.

HOW WAR HAS INFLUENCED SCIENCE

As science has profoundly influenced the methods of warfare by its contribution of new technologies, it in turn has been affected by war. In the first place, war has provided science with specific problems. History is full of incidents such as the old artilleryman's request of the mathematician for advice on how to point a cannon. That request set Tartaglia to studying the theoretical path of a moving projectile, and out of his studies came the first scientific treatment of the subject. The science of ballistics was born of these efforts, though it needed the experiments of a Galileo, also spurred on by military problems, to bring it to adulthood.

The British physicist J. D. Bernal doubts if the work of the early ballistic theorists gave much help to the warriors, though it did help science. Although their ideas contributed little of value to artillery technique, they proved useful to the development of mechanics. It was left to Isaac Newton (1642-1727), says Bernal in his *Social Function of Science*, "to combine the new ideas of dynamics derived from the problems set by artillery practice with those of astronomy. Astronomy itself was, at this time, in a state of active development in relation to the needs of navigation, and was thus of part military, part commercial, nature. It was not only in astronomy and dynamics that science was linked to war; we owe much of modern physics to the development of vacuum technique and of frictional electricity by Otto von Guericke (1602-1686), quartermaster-general of Gustavus Adolphus in the Thirty Years War, who was able to use his position to carry out large-scale experiments."

Numerous contributions to science were assisted by the fact that the scientist was employed in a military enterprise which afforded him facilities and other opportunities for research. Lavoisier (1743-1794), the chemist who first split water into its two gaseous ingredients and gave oxygen its name, performed his experiments in the laboratory of the State Arsenal of France where he had quarters as a director of the State Powder Company. It was in an arsenal too that Count Rumford (1753-1814) made his great discovery that heat is a form of energy. While directing the boring of a cannon he was impressed with the heat of the iron shavings. So he set up an experiment: surrounded the artillery piece with water, and found that in two hours of continuous boring the friction brought the water up to the boiling point. This experiment in an ordnance shop contributed directly to the overthrow of the old caloric theory and assisted in establishing our modern conception of thermodynamics.

Cannon boring also played a part in the development of the steam engine. The engines of the early Eighteenth century had cylinders so irregular in bore that often there was a difference of as much as a finger's breadth between the piston and the inside of the cylinder. At every stroke of the engine steam escaped in hissing clouds and the power losses were costly. James Watt (1736-1819) corrected this by engaging the services of John Wilkinson, who had a unique drill for boring cannon and whose machine soon demonstrated that it could bore engine cylinders just as smooth and true as it fashioned artillery barrels.

The cannon was in principle an internal combustion engine. There were early attempts to substitute the force of exploding gunpowder for the expansive force of steam in a power machine. None of these efforts was successful, but the gas, gasoline and oil engines that eventually matured from the laboratories into industry owe something to the impetus and lessons of these early ventures.

A close kinship can be traced between the development of firearms and that of many other technologies, including mining and metallurgy, chemistry, machine tools, standardization, the use of interchangeable parts and mass production. Even the sewing machine, that characteristic tool of Nineteenth century domesticity, got its first large-scale use from French tailors engaged to make uniforms for the army. Napoleon III's offer of a prize for an economical armament steel activated Henry Bessemer (1813-1898) to develop the converter process. And right on up to our decade, the higher and ever higher specifications of naval engineers for armor-piercing steel, or for shell-resisting steel, have improved the quality of the metal not only for armament but for a variety of civilian needs. A contemporary example of the influence of war on peacetime technology is the Diesel electric locomotive. This machine was first worked out as a multi-engine Diesel electric drive for submarines in the 1920's and, after meeting the requirements of that highly-exacting naval service, it was applied to land transportation in the 1930's, installed on wheels, and harnessed to the modern streamlined train.

The science of weather forecasting has military origins. In 1854, during the Crimean War, a destructive cyclone swept the Black Sea and inflicted severe damage on the French fleet. The astronomer U. J. J. Leverrier (1811-1877) had recently won world fame by predicting the existence of an unknown planet which was later named Neptune, and, impressed by this achievement, the Emperor Napoleon III now turned to Leverrier for help. If he could predict conditions existing millions of miles out in space, reasoned Napoleon the Little, surely he ought to be able to predict conditions on our own planet. From institutions and individuals that had been keeping records of weather observations over the years Leverrier collected all the data that were available. When the results were mapped, he found that storms followed well-defined paths and their progress across land and sea could be charted. If it were known that a storm was forming in one area, and if the meteorological map of surrounding areas at the same time were known, the probable path of the storm might be predicted. Public applause greeted this discovery. Within a few years meteorological bureaus and networks of observing stations had been set up in many countries, the new invention of the telegraph was widely used to report weather observations, and these early systematic attempts at forecasting laid the foundations on which our modern meteorologists have developed the current theories and practices. One of the results that may come out of the present war is long-range forecasting, for it is known that studies of this problem and trials of proposed systems are being made on both sides.

War sets hard problems, affords the investigator opportunities to test his results in actual practice, is not niggardly with funds; therefore it is not to be wondered at that war gets results from the laboratories. In peacetime research, especially that involving industrial processes, there is often a question how the result may affect existing properties, current models, patents and other vested interests. But in time of war concern over obsolescence disappears. As the advent of the British Spitfire fighter plane rendered the Messerschmitt 109 obsolescent, you may be sure that the German aeronautical engineers sought in their next designs to render all existing fighter planes obsolescent. It is only in such all-out emergencies as war, says E. E. Slosson, that "science has a free hand to show what it can do."

Although science has been molded in innumerable ways by war, it would be false to leave an impression that science is consistently, or even frequently, allowed a free hand in meeting the technological problems posed by the military. The story of King Hiero and Archimedes is almost unique. Certainly its parallel is rarely found in the practice of democratic states. Invariably the state merely calls in the scientist in an advisory capacity. And although the element of surprise, the stratagem of sudden secret attack with novel weapons, is of the very essence of military science, yet history shows a persistent opposition of the military mind to innovation. In 1914 an eminent British scientist offered to organize a special weather forecasting service for the British Expeditionary Force, but the lesson of Leverrier's contribution to the Crimean War effort apparently had lost its impression. At all events, the 1914 offer was rebuffed by officialdom with the rejoinder that "the British soldier fights in all weathers," as Bernal reports it. Before the war ended, meteorology became a recognized arm of the air force and other services, and today meteorologists are rated indispensable to aeronautical operations. The slowness of the Germans to make use of the tank, introduced by the British in 1916, is another example of the characteristic inertia.

This antithesis between military need and military action has been called by Lewis Mumford "the paradox in technics: war stimulates invention, but the army resists it." It is a fact of history that scientists usually have had to take the initiative in making their gifts known to the government. One of the fruitful agencies in promoting interrelations has been the academy of science.

SCIENTIFIC SOCIETIES AND THE STATE

Historically first in the succession of national academies of science stands the Alexandrine Museum. In this instance it was the state rather than the scientists that took the lead. The state was an ambitious monarch, Ptolemy I, successor to Alexander the Great, and apparently he poured unstinted funds into the building up of this institution, for both the adornment and the protection of his kingdom. It is doubtful if any subsequent academy has occupied a position in its age comparable to that of the Alexandrine Museum in the Third century B.C. With the death of Euclid and other superior scholars, its prestige declined; and eventually its last remaining treasure, the great library of 600,000 volumes, was destroyed by Arab invaders. But the tradition of state patronage which Ptolemy inaugurated survived, was perpetuated in the revival of academies after the Renaissance, and seems to be an almost standard attribute of these institutions.

Thus the Royal Society, founded in London in 1660 by a group of experimental philosophers as "a college for the promoting of physico-mathematical experimental learning," took its present name when the King of England "offered to be entered as one of the society." Since then Charles II has been designated as the founder. From his time to the present the Royal Society has been subject to the call of the British government for advice on scientific problems and projects of national importance, including those affecting military and naval affairs.

Six years after the establishment of the Royal Society in England, the Académie des Sciences was formed in France. In this movement, too, the initiative was taken by a group of scientists who had already been meeting informally for discussions and experiments. But Louis XIV at once granted pensions to each member of the academy and provided a fund for the purchase of instruments and supplies for their researches, thus tying the organization to the government. Like its British prototype, it made studies of gunpowder and other matters of military concern. In 1793 the academy was suppressed by the revolutionaries, and there was a lapse of some years, to be followed by revival in 1816 when it was reconstituted as a branch of the Institut National.

In the United States the earliest association of scientists was a group at Philadelphia whose leader was Benjamin Franklin. After several years of informal meetings, it incorporated in 1743 as the American Philosophical Society. The Boston State House had not yet acquired title as "Hub of the Universe," but by 1780 a group of Massachusetts citizens, including John and Sam Adams and John Hancock, organized themselves as the American Academy of Arts and Sciences. The American Association for the Advancement of Science was formed in 1848. It was not until 1863, however, in the dark days of Civil War, that a National Academy of Sciences was set up. It was authorized by Congress under a charter which expressly commits its members to serve the United States government as scientific investigators and advisers.

THE NATIONAL ACADEMY OF SCIENCES

The statement has often been published that President Lincoln established the National Academy of Sciences as a war measure, but there is no actual evidence that the President had anything to do with activating this organization. After the bill creating the academy had passed both Houses of Congress Mr. Lincoln signed it. But the record is clear that it was the scientists, rather than the executive, who conceived the idea and engineered it to fulfillment. As early as 1851 Professor Alexander Dallas Bache was suggesting the need for "an institution of science, supplementary to existing ones, to guide public action in regard to scientific matters." In a public address he argued that it was "a common mistake to associate the idea of academical institutions with monarchical institutions," and outlined a program which foreshadowed much of what was embodied twelve years later in the academy.

Bache was head of the United States Coast Survey. Two of his closest friends were Professor Joseph Henry, head of the Smithsonian Institution, and Admiral Charles Henry Davis, head of the Navy's Bureau of Navigation. They constituted a spontaneous committee of three for the academy project, and often discussed it with other scientists.

Davis, who had only recently been made rear admiral in recognition of his gallant service as fleet captain in the expedition against Port Royal, was distinguished both as astronomer and hydrographer. He was a man of considerable enterprise and drive, continually sparking with ideas. Early in 1863 he read of a select commission which the British War Ministry had appointed to advise it on technical problems, and at once it occurred to him that the U. S. Navy also had technical problems on which expert advice might be helpful. At that time Farragut was operating on the lower Mississippi, Vicksburg still held, and the Navy Department was being flooded with proposals for new devices and other inventions. Why not a commission of scientists to sift through these ideas and advise the navy on their value? Davis confided his plan to Bache and Henry. They fell in with it immediately, and Henry in person submitted the suggestion to the Secretary of the Navy. Secretary Gideon Welles acted promptly. On February 11 he issued an order creating "a permanent scientific commission" and appointed as members Professor Henry, Professor Bache and Admiral Davis.

"We had hardly got through this thing," wrote Davis to his wife, "before the idea flashed upon my mind that the whole plan, so long entertained, of the academy could be successfully carried out if an act of incorporation were boldly asked for in the name of some of the leading men of science from different parts of the country."

He went to work at once to substitute the broader conception of a national academy for the commission, and within a few days had enlisted the support of Professors Alexander Agassiz and Benjamin Peirce of Harvard and Professor Benjamin Apthorp Gould of the Dudley Astronomical Observatory at Albany. It could hardly be said that this group represented different parts of the country, for all of them, including Davis, were from Massachusetts; but they drew up a list of fifty persons, including themselves, to constitute the new organization, and the fifty were representative of various sections and institutions. It is interesting to note that six of the original fifty were scientists connected with the U. S. Army, and five with the U. S. Navy. On February 21, just ten days after the appointment of the commission, Senator Henry Wilson of Massachusetts introduced a bill in Congress to incorporate these fifty into a new body to be known as the National Academy of Sciences. The bill was passed by the Senate on March 3, was proposed in the House the same day by Representative Thomas of Massachusetts and immediately passed, and before midnight it had been signed by President Lincoln. And that is how the National Academy of Sciences came to be.

Its distinguishing feature is the provision, embodied in the bill of incorporation, that the academy, "whenever called upon by any department of the government, shall investigate, examine, experiment, and report upon any subject of science or art." Within a month after it had been organized the new body received five requests from government departments. Three of them came from the navy, and are typical. First, the navy wanted advice on protecting the bottoms of iron ships from the sea water. Next, the navy wanted to know how to safeguard the compass from magnetic deviation on iron ships. The third problem referred to the navy's publication of wind and current charts and sailing directions, and asked whether they were scientifically sound and of sufficient value to mariners to be continued. Then, in the spring of 1864, a gunboat which had been built for blockade duty exploded a boiler on the day she was put into service, killing twenty-eight of the crew; and the academy was immediately asked to investigate and report what engineering defects were responsible.

These four problems, all of which bore upon naval efficiency in the Civil War effort, are representative of the questions submitted to the academy. A review of the long list of inquiries made during its eighty years is a fair index of the progress of technology. Thus, in 1915 the President of the United States called upon the academy for a study of the serious landslides which were threatening the Panama Canal. The resulting report, covering studies of topography, geography, geology, meteorology, seismology and hydraulics, was of direct service to the engineers in remedying the conditions. In World War I days, the academy was asked to assist in developing submarine detectors. In the present war, as would be expected, problems connected with aviation and strategic materials occupy a large place among the subjects referred by government agencies for investigation and advice.

The National Academy of Sciences is by definition of its charter a select group. Originally its membership was limited to fifty persons. In 1870 the membership rule was revised and the limit raised, but a proviso was adopted that not more than fifteen new members be elected in a year, and rigorous standards of election were set up. In his last letter to the academy as its president, written a few weeks before his death in 1878, Joseph Henry counseled: "Great care must be exercised in the selection of members. It must not be forgotten for a moment that the basis of selection is actual scientific labor in the way of original research—that is, in making positive additions to the sum of human knowledge—connected with unimpeachable moral character." At the beginning of 1943 the roster listed 326 members, but recently the academy voted to raise the membership limitation from 350 to 450 and to allow as many as thirty new members per year to be added—an expansion warranted by the rapid increase in the personnel of science in America. Election to membership is generally rated as the highest honor within the gift of United States science, a badge of recognition for exceptional attainment. The academy thus fulfills a role similar to that of the French Institute in France and the Royal Society in Britain.

Over the years the academy has been the recipient of a few gifts of funds to encourage research in particular fields of science, but the total of these resources was small. In 1941 it was decided to organize a special agency to advise prospective donors, and to receive and administer an endowment for research, and the National Science Fund was chartered for these purposes. The hope is that it will serve as a national community trust, whose proceeds will be available for the support of original investigations in all the sciences.

THE NATIONAL RESEARCH COUNCIL

As the War of 1861-'65 provided the conditions which incubated the academy, the War of 1914-'18 imposed problems which led to organization of the National Research Council. This council had its origin in the spring of 1916. The recent German submarine attack on the *Sussex* had added a new strain on German-American relations, deepening the conviction that United States involvement was inevitable. The regular meeting of the academy was being held in Washington at this time, and the members voted to offer the government their services. In other words, the scientists, who were obligated by their charter to respond to the call of the state, did not wait to be called. Innumerable opportunities for preparedness were going to waste, time was being lost, and they appointed a committee to call at the White House.

President Wilson said yes to their offer. He agreed that it would be decidedly helpful if the scientific resources of the country— civilian, naval and military, educational and industrial, private institutions and governmental bureaus—were enlisted and welded into a team for national defense. It was in order to provide a working structure for this wartime undertaking that the academy organized the National Research Council.

George Ellery Hale, famous astronomer and director of Mount Wilson Observatory, was the prime mover in this undertaking, assisted by William H. Welch, physician, of Johns Hopkins, and Ambrose Swasey, engineer, of Cleveland; all members of the academy, of course. The council was not created as an independent body but rather as a branch of the academy—indeed as its operating agency, to which scientific men outside the academy's small membership could be appointed to serve for limited terms on desired investigations. The council thus provided a piece of machinery through which any qualified research man, young or old, could be called for service.

There was an embarrassing handicap at the beginning, however. No funds had been appropriated to support the council, and inasmuch as the academy itself was without operating capital beyond the small income from its annual dues of $10 per member, the new organization began operations on a hand-to-mouth basis. It was the engineers who came to the relief of the scientists and the government in this dilemma. Ambrose Swasey had recently provided a handsome endowment to set up the Engineering Foundation of New York, a joint body representing the national group of professional engineering societies. This foundation now offered to give the whole of its endowment income for a year to the support of the National Research Council and, in addition, the full-time services of its paid secretary, Carey T. Hutchinson. Dr. Hutchinson moved to Washington and became the executive director of the new organization. This timely assistance enabled the council to swing into action at once, and before the year was up arrangements for support of its war-research program had been authorized by the government.

Meanwhile, with the entire personnel of American science to draw upon, the National Research Council was operating an extensive research program. It worked through a series of committees, each focused on a specialty of the natural sciences, the medical sciences and the engineering fields. There were projects in ship camouflage, in submarine warfare, in nitrogen fixation, explosives, gas warfare and other fields of chemistry, in ballistics and other problems of ordnance engineering. In this way a great many laboratory resources were brought into action.

President Wilson was highly pleased with the outcome. In 1918, several months before the armistice, he expressed a wish that the council be continued as a permanent arm of the academy, for service in peace as well as in war. The President issued an executive order to that effect, and the continuity of what had been organized as a temporary wartime agency was assured. Today more than fifty scientific and engineering societies are represented in the membership of the National Research Council, and their contributions through the years have been of inestimable value to the nation.

The council affected academy affairs in another way. It demonstrated the need of building. The academy had been meeting in a borrowed hall, usually in the National Museum, and had office space through the courtesy of the Smithsonian Institution. But now its activities were so many that permanent quarters became a pressing necessity. George Ellery Hale was again the catalyst. He brought the situation to the attention of Elihu Root. And Mr. Root brought it to the attention of the Carnegie Corporation. Root had a keen respect for science. The Royal Society in London was housed in a building appropriate to its importance, and Mr. Root argued that America should do as well by its academicians. He argued the case with such effect before a meeting of his Carnegie colleagues that they appropriated $5,000,000 to provide the building and endow its upkeep and operating expenses. The handsome house of white marble, with its broad classic façade and many commodious rooms for offices and meetings, was designed by Bertram Goodhue. It occupies a block of ground on Constitution Avenue, was opened in 1924, and houses both the National Academy of Sciences and the National Research Council.

A bit of space in this hall of science is dedicated to the engineers. Remembering the generosity which financed the first year's operation of the National Research Council, the academy set aside a room for the Engineering Foundation, including the members of its constituent engineering societies, to serve as Washington headquarters for their affairs and interests. Though primarily utilitarian, this engineers' room has a symbolical significance, recalling that in the sciences the "pure" and the "applied" are mutually dependent, as interrelated "as the tree and the fruit."

When the war clouds began to gather in 1939-'40, the building provided office space for the rapidly multiplying agencies of science mobilized for war. Various activities of the government's Office of Scientific Research and Development were allotted quarters here, including the Committee on Medical Research and certain divisions of the National Defense Research Committee. By 1943 even exhibition halls and corridors had been transformed into offices, and the balcony of the assembly hall was occupied by desks.

GOVERNMENT AGENCIES OF MILITARY AND NAVAL RESEARCH

The arsenals of the United States Army have fostered studies of guns, explosives, and other military equipment and supplies for over a century; and in so doing they have made important contributions to industrial practice. The idea of interchangeable manufacture was early applied to the production of rifles at the Springfield Armory in Massachusetts. Important advances in the hardening of steel, the centrifugal casting of gun barrels and other techniques of metal working were made at the Watertown Arsenal, second oldest among the army ordnance institutions, also in Massachusetts. It was at Watertown, too, that the use of x-rays in the examination of large castings and welds was first applied on an extensive scale— a practice of safeguarding against hidden flaws that has become universal with heavy machine manufacturers. Other arsenals are Rock Island in Iowa, Watervliet in northern New York, Frankford in Pennsylvania, and Picatinny in New Jersey. The Edgewood Arsenal in Maryland is the Chemical Warfare Service's headquarters for research and testing. The Ordnance Department maintains a proving ground of several thousand acres at Aberdeen in Maryland, the center for its research in ballistics, and a Tank Arsenal in Detroit.

Laboratory investigations contributing to developments of both army and navy have been carried on by various outside scientific bureaus of the government, particularly the Bureau of Standards, the Bureau of Mines, the Weather Bureau, the Geological Survey, and the Coast and Geodetic Survey. For example, during and immediately following World War I the Navy Department maintained at the Bureau of Standards a group in radio research, and important advances in communication engineering were made here. The navy's function as timekeeper for the nation involved it early in the business of broadcasting time signals by wireless, and for some years its transmitter at Arlington was the most powerful in the hemisphere.

In 1923 the Navy Department ventured deeper into science by establishing a Naval Research Laboratory at Anacostia, on the banks of the Potomac, a few miles out of Washington. In creating it, Congress outlined the field of activities as "laboratory and research work on gun erosion, torpedo motive power, the gyroscope, submarine guns; protection against submarine, torpedo and mine attack; improvement in submarine attachments; improvement and development in submarine engines, storage batteries, and propulsion; airplanes and aircraft; improvements in radio installations." Not all of these subjects are under investigation at Anacostia. Many have been farmed out to other institutions, and in some instances more than one laboratory is tackling a highly complicated problem, but the list is an enlightening reminder of the sort of secrets that naval engineers have to think about. The use of radio waves for the detection of ships and aircraft is a technology that has been the subject of successful development at the Naval Research Laboratory for a number of years. Its work in this field antedated by several years the British development of radiolocation. And so with underwater sound waves, and how to detect their slightest manifestation and use them to spot submarines—that too is a study in which the Naval Research Laboratory has specialized and produced results.

THE NATIONAL ADVISORY COMMITTEE FOR AERONAUTICS

Although not established until 1915, as the airplane was trying its wings over the European fields of war, this National Advisory Committee for Aeronautics was seeded many years before in the scientific studies of the problem of mechanical flight made by Dr. Samuel P. Langley and by the Wright brothers. Langley's successful experiments with quarter-size models of airplanes—he called them "aerodromes"—had demonstrated by 1896 the practicability of mechanical flight. Shortly after the Spanish-American War he secured government help for his studies. Allotments totaling $50,-000 were made by the Board of Ordnance and Fortifications of the War Department to finance the construction of a full-size aerodrome capable of carrying a man.

Langley was secretary of the Smithsonian Institution, a physicist in the distinguished succession of Joseph Henry; and for his aeronautics he set up a "workshop" in the Smithsonian main building and engaged a young engineering graduate of Cornell as technical assistant. Although Manly, the assistant, designed and built an engine which in light weight and high performance was years ahead of anything else in the field, and although Langley's experiments uncovered many important details of aerodynamics, the actual flight attempts were plagued with bad luck, and ended in a crash in the Potomac in which Manly almost lost his life. The Congress and the press ridiculed the flying machines that wouldn't fly, the government withdrew its support, and the public laughed at the spectacle of another scientific pretense punctured. It was some time before they learned that just eight days after Langley's disaster on the Potomac the Wright brothers rode the air at Kitty Hawk, North Carolina. Climaxing years of gliding experiments and persistent research along original lines, they made the first successful flight of an airplane on December 17, 1903.

Langley abandoned his experiments, and died in 1906, but his associates at the Smithsonian did not forget. They preserved his unsuccessful aerodrome and kept faith in his purpose. Far from abandoning the program, Dr. Charles D. Walcott, who had succeeded to the secretaryship of the Smithsonian, reopened Langley's laboratory in 1913 and appointed an "Advisory Committee for Aeronautics of the Langley Aerodynamical Laboratory" to plan and conduct research. That committee functioned for about a year. Its existence was terminated by a decision of the Comptroller of the Treasury which held that the committee could not be supported by public funds since it had not been established by law. Dr. Walcott continued his efforts to have such an agency established by law, but it was not until World War I was several months old that he was able to convince Congress that aeronautics deserved government support. At last, in 1915, the legislation was passed, and the National Advisory Committee for Aeronautics was established. As authorized by Congress, it was to "supervise and direct the scientific study of the problems of flight, with a view to their practical solution" and to "direct and conduct research and experiment in aeronautics."

How well it has done this job is in large measure the history of American aviation during the last quarter century. No other United States agency, either private or state, has played so large a part in the development of aeronautics. All that Congress was willing to risk on the committee at the beginning was $5,000 a year for five years, "or so much thereof as may be necessary." But as research began to justify itself in results, appropriations were stepped up until they reached more than $19,000,000 for the fiscal year 1942.

The first research station for the committee is appropriately named the Langley Memorial Aeronautical Laboratory, and is located at Langley Field, near Old Point Comfort, Virginia. It represents today a capital investment of $20,000,000. Here one finds an odd assortment of buildings, each shaped to its engineering need: a vast sphere, a towering perpendicular, enormous rectangular sheds, and long, meandering, tubular buildings that turn at right angles and bend around corners and constitute the wind tunnels. One of these wind tunnels is so huge that a pilot can "fly" a full-size airplane, with the plane mounted on stationary balances and the air the moving element.

Under the pressure of current wartime needs Congress was persuaded to allot funds for a considerable enlargement of the research plant, which now fills every available space at Langley Field. So the work has recently been expanded in two centers: Cleveland, Ohio, where a branch establishment costing $18,000,000 has been erected, and Moffett Field, California, where the investment is $16,000,000. This California branch has been named the Ames Aeronautical Laboratory in honor of Professor Joseph S. Ames, celebrated physicist and one-time president of Johns Hopkins University, who served many years as chairman of the committee. The latest type wind tunnels to propel the air at almost unbelievable speeds have been provided, including a 16-foot tunnel powered with wind at 600 miles per hour, a supersonic tunnel through which air will hurl at 1,400 miles per hour, and two 7-by-10 tunnels. There is also a full-scale tunnel, measuring 80 feet wide by 40 feet high, the largest in the world. The laboratory in Cleveland is devoted primarily to engine research, whereas at the Ames and the Langley laboratories studies are focused chiefly on aerodynamic and flight problems. Langley also conducts research in hydrodynamics, in structures, and temporarily in engine problems.

The National Advisory Committee for Aeronautics is a joint board of civilian and military technologists. Its success is credited in large measure to this joint form of organization, which was unique at the time it was constituted. There are fifteen committee-men: two from the U. S. Army, two from the U. S. Navy, two representing the Civil Aeronautics Authority, one each from the Bureau of Standards, the Weather Bureau and the Smithsonian Institution, with six members chosen from the ranks of aero-nautical engineering and related sciences. Appointments are made by the President of the United States. The chairman is usually a civilian, the present one being Professor Jerome C. Hunsaker, emi-nent aeronautical authority of the Massachusetts Institute of Tech-nology.

As the bombing planes of the Luftwaffe dived upon Poland in the dark September days of 1939, and the irrepressible war of ideas became at last a physical war of weapons, American defense had no better prepared or more closely integrated scientific resource than this National Advisory Committee for Aeronautics. Its staff consisted of more than 800 technicians. Its equipment for research was modern, and if not complete was more nearly so than that of any other laboratory in the land. Its relations with the aeronautical industry and with the army and navy were wholesome, stimulating and productive. Its relations with other research institutions were close and co-operative. Above all, it was a going concern capable of stepping up its research and developmental program almost over-night. And because of the preponderating weight of aviation in the new warfare which Europe was engaged in perpetrating, the com-mittee became at once a key institution in the American movement for rearmament, preparedness and national defense.

CHAPTER III

The Office of Scientific Research and Development

It is physical science that makes intelligence stronger than brute force.

—Thomas Henry Huxley, ESSAYS

ONE of the members of the National Advisory Committee for Aeronautics—its chairman in 1939 when the German dictator began his raid of Europe—was Vannevar Bush. Dr. Bush was also president of the Carnegie Institution of Washington, which is the parent body of several laboratories and other outposts of science. The Carnegie group includes such varied institutions as the Mount Wilson Observatory in California, the Geophysical Laboratory and the Department of Terrestrial Magnetism in Washington, the Embryological Laboratory in Baltimore, the Department of Genetics on Long Island, and the Nutrition Laboratory in Boston, with an archaeological branch in Yucatan and magnetic observatories in Peru and Australia. From his administration of these research centers, so different in their methods and materials of study and yet so integrated within the central organization of the Carnegie Institution, Dr. Bush was well acquainted with what could be done through scientific research, and particularly through co-ordinated scientific research. His experience on the National Advisory Committee for Aeronautics had demonstrated what could be done in a single field of engineering that was highly strategic to national defense. And yet in other fields, equally critical and important to American preparedness for the inescapable war, so little was being done, and what was being done was so loosely organized.

As Bush talked with his friends in the laboratories he found that other men of science were concerned over this situation—deeply, anxiously concerned. Frank B. Jewett, president of the National Academy of Sciences, was one of these. But the academy could not take the initiative on any problem; it must await the call of the government, was restricted to a purely advisory service, and moreover had no funds for war research. The same restrictions applied to the academy's subsidiary body, the National Research Council. Three others who consulted with Bush and Jewett on the dangerous lack of integration between scientific resources and national emergency needs were James B. Conant, president of Harvard University; Karl T. Compton, president of Massachusetts Institute of Technology; and Richard C. Tolman, a dean of California Institute of Technology. It was too far to commute from California, so Tolman got leave of absence from his post in Pasadena and transferred to Washington. Bush and Jewett are engineers, Conant is a chemist, Compton and Tolman are physicists. These five men became the unofficial spearhead of American science in what was rapidly maturing as a world emergency. Soon their function was to be made official.

AN ORGANIZATION WITH POWER TO INITIATE
AND FUNDS TO SUPPORT WAR RESEARCH

In June of 1940, as Hitler's war machine was racing westward across Holland and Belgium, President Roosevelt's Council of National Defense issued an order setting up the National Defense Research Committee and appointing these five scientists as members. In form the new committee was modeled after the National Advisory Committee for Aeronautics. There was one member from the army, Brigadier General G. V. Strong; one from the navy, Rear Admiral H. G. Bowen, and one from a government civilian bureau of science, Commissioner C. P. Coe of the Patent Office, in addition to Bush, Compton, Conant, Jewett and Tolman. The committee was allotted federal funds and authorized to undertake researches on "instruments and instrumentalities of warfare."

In 1941 the organization was broadened, though the essential pattern was not changed, by appointment of a co-ordinate Committee on Medical Research and the creation by Presidential decree of a new agency, the Office of Scientific Research and Development. This office was ordained as the top authority of American wartime science, embodying and integrating the two committees. President Roosevelt named Bush director of the new over-all agency, which immediately took its place in the alphabetical hierarchy of Washington as OSRD, and at the same time President Conant of Harvard and Dr. A. N. Richards of the University of Pennsylvania Medical School were appointed chairmen of the committees.

Through this office with its two operating committees a vast program in the natural and the medical sciences has been forwarded. Within Dr. Conant's National Defense Research Committee the scientific problems to be investigated were classified under four general headings, and four divisions corresponding to these were organized. Eventually, as the work expanded and problems in other fields developed in importance, it became necessary to reorganize, and toward the end of 1942 this was done by setting up eighteen divisions in place of the original four. Similarly, within Dr. Richards's Committee on Medical Research, various subdivisions on war medicine and surgery have been organized, utilizing previously existing committees of the National Research Council. In most instances the divisions within the two committees are broken down into still more specialized sections, and altogether more than 1,000 of the leading scientists and engineers of the country were enlisted within this departmentalized organization. They come from universities, industrial laboratories and professional practice, from large institutions and small, some from private laboratories, and they represent all parts of the nation. Many of these men serve without remuneration on a part-time basis; others are on the government pay roll while on leave of absence from their home institutions. But in every case they were chosen for their individual qualifications, and serve as individuals.

Through these groups of experts every scientific technique or specialty that offers a prospect of contributing to the winning of the war has been canvassed. Those proposals which are accepted for laboratory investigation and development are organized as government research projects.

In a few fields of study special laboratories have been built to carry on the research. For example, the division concerned with problems of submarine warfare found it necessary to provide their investigators with subsurface experiment stations and to install highly specialized equipment. But such cases are exceptional, and for the most part the projects have been cared for by established institutions which are already equipped and manned for first-class scientific research.

The arrangement between these institutions and the government is on the basis of a no-profit-no-loss contract. The Office of Scientific Research and Development selects the university, college, institute, or industrial or private laboratory that is best prepared to undertake the particular problem designated for investigation. It then enters into a contract by which OSRD agrees to finance the research to its conclusion. At the end of 1942 the number of contracts in operation totaled more than 2,000 and employed between 6,000 and 7,000 scientists in 280 institutions.

In some instances, when the problem is the development of a novel type of weapon involving new techniques which require the combined efforts of many highly competent investigators, the project has been intrusted to a single institution instead of being divided among several. Usually the place chosen is the one that has the men and equipment that provide the best available nucleus for the research, and then workers from other institutions are assigned there to complete and round out the team. In one case of this kind, when a bold problem involving advanced studies of electronics was to be investigated, the top physicists, engineers and mathematicians of twenty-five laboratories scattered from coast to coast were brought together in one university. There they were organized as a closely knit group, under a young and dynamic leader, and for months they lived with their problem, worked at it and, it is fair to say, mastered it to a degree that twenty-five scattered independent research centers could hardly have attained in double or triple the time.

SECRECY IMPOSES COMPARTMENTALIZATION

Virtually everything that is done by the Office of Scientific Research and Development, and by institutions under its contracts, is highly confidential. The guiding principle is that secret matters are to be held carefully within compartments, and no member of the Washington organization, or of the research teams in the various laboratories, is informed of projects and their details except to the extent that is necessary to enable him to function in the work committed to him.

And this brings up the question, often asked, why the organization needs to be constituted on a national and vertical basis, why it cannot be decentralized geographically. "The necessity for secrecy and compartmentalization is the reason," explained Dr. Bush. "In many cities it would be quite possible to form strong technical and scientific groups locally, composed of men who would put in part of their time, in the evenings and week-ends, on technical matters connected with the war. These groups could represent many sciences and many types of engineering, and they would be composed of decidedly effective individuals. However, this scheme would not be compatible with necessary restrictions on the work of OSRD. It would hardly be possible to assign one subject to each group of a locality. Neither would it be possible to give to such a group the knowledge of the entire range of development of weapons, which would be essential in order to use effectively the diverse characteristics such a group would have. Hence we have felt, though reluctantly, that such groups could not be utilized within our organization."

The regimen of war research has had a curious effect on the atmosphere of many universities, transforming what used to be so open and hospitable into centers of walled secrecy. In some institutions whole groups of buildings have been placed out of bounds, as far as the public, including the students and faculty, is concerned. Guards patrol the approaches to see that only those who hold passes are admitted. In one, where a group of several hundred is working as a team in a highly crucial field of investigation, it is customary to hold a weekly conference in a near-by auditorium. Before each meeting the building is searched from roof to cellar by federal agents, who also guard it with unrelaxed vigilance during the conference period. A newspaper man visiting one of the large industrial laboratories was impressed with the fact that even high executives of the company were barred from entering. Another manufacturing company, occupied with the development and production of a secret weapon, engaged a publicity man to function in reverse: instead of promoting publicity his responsibility is to keep facts about the confidential device from getting into the press.

"RESULTS IN COPPER AND IRON"

During its first twelve months, ending June 30, 1942, the Office of Scientific Research and Development spent $37,000,000. Its report to Congress showed that 100 devices, formulas and methods which have been developed through these government-supported studies were already in use by the army and navy. By that time the federal agencies had placed orders with industry for many hundreds of millions of dollars worth of equipment and materials which either did not exist or whose military value was unknown until the scientists mobilized their forces. This record is remarkable, as any industrial research director would agree. Ordinarily it takes at least three years, and usually five or more, from an idea in the laboratory to its use in industry. Under this intensive, highly compartmented but co-ordinated and adequately supported plan of attack, problems have been solved in a matter of months and, as one of the scientists put it, "results are taking form in copper and iron." By January, 1943, the office was making expenditures at the rate of about $100,-000,000 a year.

A fundamental reason that this new agency has been able to do what it is doing lies in its possession of power of initiative. The National Academy of Sciences and its National Research Council are by their charter advisory bodies and, as Dr. Jewett described them, are "in the position of a doctor waiting for patients." But the Office of Scientific Research and Development has both authority and funds. It can initiate research. After it has devised a new implement of war it can submit its results directly to the War and Navy Departments.

Another factor which has contributed to success is the policy of picking brilliant investigators in frontier fields of science and intrusting difficult problems to them. The use of nuclear physicists to investigate the application of radio to weapons is an example. These are the chaps, most of them young, who have been building cyclotrons and other novel electronic devices, who have been hurling subatomic projectiles through the vacuum, smashing atoms, transmuting the elements, discovering new isotopes, exploring the borderland where physics overlaps chemistry. Such work of necessity calls for new techniques, stimulates the imagination, and tends to eliminate the pedestrian thinker; so in these fields daring young men of science were to be found, and they have been put to work, and their labors have issued in new and powerful instruments of war. Physical chemists also are frontiersmen, and it is interesting to find some of the knotty problems of medical research being assigned to these borderland investigators.

Beyond its responsibility for organizing American science for war, the Office of Scientific Research and Development has a co-ordinating function. Its membership includes with civilian scientists representatives of the army and navy, and on questions of the use of scientific research in the war effort it speaks for the President who created it. Not only the top organization but each division of the National Defense Research Committee and the Committee on Medical Research has attached to it army and navy men as liaison officers. They tell of the needs and problems of the armed forces, join in the councils, sit around a table, talk it out; and the success of the war research program owes much to this close tie-in of civilian, army and navy scientists on the technical problems of weapons. In its original organization, however, the office had no part in councils on strategy.

In the spring of 1942, following the establishment of the Joint U. S. Chiefs of Staff, this situation was changed. The organization of the Joint U. S. Chiefs of Staff was itself revolutionary, for it provided a mechanism for issuing orders jointly by army and navy. One of the first acts of the new body was to appoint a Joint Committee on New Weapons and Equipment, assigning to it responsibility for recommending policies regarding new weapons of both army and navy. To this Joint Committee on New Weapons and Equipment the chiefs of staff appointed an admiral, a general and a civilian, Dr. Bush; and they named Bush chairman of the committee.

Then, for the first time in United States military and naval history, a civilian scientist was brought into the war councils on strategy; not simply as a guest or a consultant, but as chairman, executive, leader. He is there, in the highest deliberations of the military and naval command, as the spokesman of American science.

OTHER AGENCIES FOR THE COLLABORATION OF SCIENCE IN WAR

The Office of Scientific Research and Development has been able to draw upon many resources for special services and other cooperation. In first place stand the National Academy of Sciences and its National Research Council, and the liaison between the new office and these older organizations is close and helpful. In effect, the national academy is the parent of the OSRD, for the group which activated the latter were all academy members, and one of them, Dr. Jewett, was its president. The academy provided OSRD with its leading personnel and has been called upon repeatedly to serve in an advisory capacity on various technical problems. The National Research Council, through its already organized committees on medical and surgical matters, provided OSRD with personnel for its Committee on Medical Research. And both this Committee on Medical Research and the National Defense Research Committee are housed in the building of the National Academy, though the headquarters of OSRD are in the building of the Carnegie Institution of Washington.

Research in problems of flight remains the province of the National Advisory Committee for Aeronautics, but the Office of Scientific Research and Development has carried on studies of weapons to be used in aircraft, and in all such and related projects there is close collaboration between the two organizations. The research activities of the army and navy, centered in their arsenals, proving grounds, experiment stations and specialized laboratories, are integrated with the general program through the presence of army and navy members in OSRD.

Among the new wartime agencies is the National Inventors Council, formed in 1940 under the leadership of Charles F. Kettering. Models, sketches, ideas, suggestions of new weapons and ways of fighting the war pour into Washington by the thousands, addressed to the army, navy and other departments. The council was established to sift through these offers, pick out whatever gives promise to be workable and pass it on to the proper authorities. In the 14 months of operation prior to Pearl Harbor the council received inventive suggestions at the rate of 2,300 per month. After Pearl Harbor they poured in at the rate of 7,000 per month. For military reasons, says the council, it is not able to reveal the number of these ideas which were found sufficiently important to pass on to the military and naval experts but, the statement adds, "it is larger than the number that received consideration in any previous war."

Irritation has been expressed by some inventors who, after submitting a carefully worked out idea or device, have been unable to learn the outcome of their offer. Unfortunately, the authorities in charge of the development and use of "new instruments and instrumentalities of warfare" cannot inform a man whether his idea is new, whether it is considered valuable, whether it is being used. The imperativeness of secrecy, the policy of compartmentalization, forbids any report at all. "If this principle were not adhered to," said Dr. Bush, "the enemy might find out a great deal simply by putting in suggestions and thus learning the general state of the art and the status of development of various military weapons."

Close relations exist between the Office of Scientific Research and Development and the various professional societies of scientists and engineers. The American Institute of Physics, which co-ordinates the activities of five specialized societies of physicists, has been useful in cushioning the shortage of physicists. Henry A. Barton, director of the institute, estimates that there were only about 7,000 physicists in the United States when the war began, and the matter of distributing them among many highly technical war-research projects, at the same time not crippling the necessary industries and teaching institutions, has been itself one of the war problems. The institute has been active in the movement to increase university, collegiate and school facilities for education in physics. It is estimated that the projected army and navy programs involve the task of imparting some working knowledge of this science to more than 200,000 persons in the services annually, and in 1943 a shortage of physics teachers was imminent.

Finding the right worker for a war-research job is a task that has been facilitated in thousands of instances by the National Roster of Scientific and Specialized Personnel. This is a systematic listing of all the technically trained men and women of the United States. The roster was established in Washington in 1940 under the direction of President Leonard Carmichael of Tufts College, and with the setting up of the War Manpower Commission in 1942 became part of that federal agency. By 1943 it listed more than 500,000 names, including natural scientists, social scientists, and other specialists. Each person is catalogued on a card which records not only his professional field of work but additional occupations in which he has had experience, his command of languages, first-hand knowledge of foreign lands and other qualifications which might add to his usefulness. The Office of Scientific Research and Development has its own committee on scientific personnel; the National Research Council has a corresponding committee, and these work in close co-operation with the national roster. Between them they have aided in solving many a ticklish manpower problem.

THE THREATENED SHORTAGE OF SCIENTISTS

Toward the end of 1942 the War Production Board created an Office of Production Research and Development. This was conceived as an agency to serve wartime industry in much the same way that the Office of Scientific Research and Development was serving the War Department and the Navy Department. But before launching the new organization there was a question as to just how many scientists would be available to serve it. So the War Production Board called upon the National Academy of Sciences for a canvass of all the research establishments of the United States, to ascertain their actual status in regard to war research.

The returns from this canvass were astonishing. It was found that the university laboratories had only 28,000 hours per week of research workers' time not already engaged in war work. Reckoning on a forty-hour week, this is equivalent to the services of 700 research workers. Moreover, most of this available time was part time, which means that the men available were already occupied to some extent with war problems.

Among industrial laboratories the canvass found that only 2 per cent were entirely free of war research, and less than 20 per cent of those reporting had as much as half their facilities available. Most of these were small laboratories. Reckoning up the returns, it appeared that all the laboratories which were 100 per cent available totaled under 650 scientists, and those that had more than 75 per cent available could muster fewer than 900 persons for war research. The total for both universities and industry was relatively so small that the National Research Council committee which made the survey suggested that "special effort should be made to keep the small remaining balance of research manpower available for emergency use as new needs arise."

In view of the results of this canvass, it may seem strange to find protests against inactivity. Yet there were such protestants as recently as 1943—capable scientists who complained that they were unable to find opportunities to use their special talents in the national war effort. This is particularly true of biologists, chemists and geologists. Some, after volunteering their trained abilities to various government agencies, have been bitterly disappointed at finding their offers declined or postponed. It is also true that some colleges and other institutions have felt that they were neglected in the selection of laboratories to be used for war-research projects.

Any waste of brain power is unfortunate of course, both in its effect on morale and in the loss of the potential service of workers, but there is no evidence of favoritism or willful discrimination on the part of authorities who assign war problems for research. Certain institutions have been chosen to perform certain lines of investigation because they already possess the specialized equipment needed, or because they have the appropriate research personnel, or for geographical reasons. And if biologists, chemists and geologists find that they are less in demand than the physicists, it can only be repeated again that this is a physicists' war.

Important calls have been made on geologists in connection with the location of strategic minerals; biologists have been given assignments in fields of agricultural, medical and nutritional research; and numerous problems in explosives, metallurgy, plastics, protection against gas poisoning and other fields of chemistry have been turned over to chemists as war tasks. But there are many thousands of chemists—they constitute the largest specialized group of physical scientists in the United States—and there are not enough formulated war problems in chemistry to employ them all. In the vast emergency in which such specialties as ballistics, electronics, communications, aeronautics and other engineering applications of the laws of physics have been used by the enemy in efforts to overwhelm us, it does not seem strange that our war-research problems and our war-research personnel should be concentrated mainly in these fields.

THE LIAISON BETWEEN BRITISH AND AMERICAN SCIENCE

The executive order which established the Office of Scientific Research and Development did not limit its service to the United States. The order provided that the director should also initiate and support such research as might be requested by countries receiving aid under the lend-lease act; and of course this included Great Britain.

In the spring of 1941, with the passage of the lend-lease act, British and American science moved quickly into active collaboration. There had been close personal relations before this, an exchange of visits between unofficial scientific representatives of the two nations, but now the partnership became official, direct and productive. An office of British science was opened in Washington, with a secretary of the Royal Society in charge; and a corresponding branch of the American Office of Scientific Research and Development was opened in London. There has been the fullest flow of information between the two groups. And with the exchange in knowledge there has been an exchange of problems. Several originating in England have been passed on to the United States for investigation. Similarly, British science has undertaken investigation of other problems of joint interest. The partnership with British science includes Canada, Australia and New Zealand; and, although representatives of American science are not maintained in those nations, co-operative relations exist in the exchange of war problems and research results.

British organization has been slow to evolve a top agency (with integrating functions and executive authority) comparable to the American Office of Scientific Research and Development. Some of the English scientists have been outspoken in criticism. In the summer of 1940 a group of twenty-five, all of whom, according to their publisher's claim, "speak with authority in their own fields," wrote *Science in War*. This book asserted that the scientific resources of Britain were being only half used. A second edition, printed the following November, granted that since the first publication "some favorable changes have taken place in the use of our scientific resources," but insisted that "many things still remain to be done." In the British scientific press and other mediums there has been complaint of a lack of co-ordination in British war research, with the army, navy and air force each maintaining its separate scientific staff. An important step toward co-ordination was taken in 1942 with the appointment of a select board of three—a physicist, an engineer and a chemist—to serve as scientific advisers to the Ministry of Production.

American science, so far removed from the center of active warfare and providentially allowed a full two years of probation before the blow fell on Pearl Harbor, cannot assume any attitude of superior wisdom. Nor has it. Many scientists have acknowledged and challenged our American sins of omission and commission. Dr. E. U. Condon of the Westinghouse Research Laboratories, speaking in 1942 at the dedication of the new Stuart Laboratory of Physics at Purdue University, referred to the shameful decade of the 1930's when people lived in insecurity, with much unemployment and little hope of professional advancement, neglecting and wasting natural resources, including scientific talent and inventiveness.

"Like fools we watched while our present enemies bent every effort toward the mobilization of their universities and their industries to prepare the means that would crush us as a free people," said Dr. Condon. "In 1934, when Hitler started to rearm, many of our physicists were unemployed, and our young people could see little opportunity for a career in science. By 1936 the armament program had progressed so far in Germany as to require speed-up in the universities, such as we now have, in an attempt to supply the vast numbers of technical men which modern warfare requires. But we slept on, seeing in this not a marvelously co-ordinated effort to conquer us, but simply viewing it as a distant anti-intellectual attack on their universities. As late as 1940, even in 1941, there were those who argued against taking steps to resist these murderers of Lidice—because to do so would call for disturbing our way of life, and upsetting the calm detached pursuit of knowledge in our universities!"

It was peace when there was no peace—an artificial and obviously false neutrality. Suddenly the enemy struck. The nation we had appeased, whose weapons had been forged of our steel and powered with our fuel, attacked a key fortress. This time there could be no mistaking whether we were their target or no. The rain of bombs on Pearl Harbor mocked our era of expediency, and even our diplomacy was infuriated by the treachery of this raid. Only force could speak now. And so America took its place in the battlefront of another world war.

CHAPTER IV

Force, Force to the Utmost

There is therefore but one response possible from us:
Force, force to the utmost, force without stint or limit.

—Woodrow Wilson, ADDRESS OF APRIL 8, 1918

WAR's technological foundation is physics. It is possible, to be sure, to pack enormous energy into a few crystalline granules by hitching nitrogen into unwilling wedlock, and this is a job for the chemist. But in order for the t.n.t. to be effective in combat it must be sealed up in physically correct parcels—shells, bombs, torpedoes or mines—and these must be delivered to the enemy by means of guns, airplanes, submarines or other physical conveyances. War may be waged by chemical, biological or psychological means, but there is hardly a procedure that does not depend in some way on physical tools, physical techniques or physical principles. So physics is the military scientist's first line. Whatever else is done is usually in addition to, in extension or reinforcement of, some basic physical weapon.

WHAT IS PHYSICS?

Physics is the science of forces and their interaction with materials. Historically it grew out of the study of bodies in motion. It has to do with the pressure of expanding gases, the inertia of moving projectiles, the pull of gravitation, the pulsation of air in sound waves, the radiations known to us as heat and light and their response to mirrors, lenses and prisms, the surge of electricity, the attractions and repulsions of magnetism. All these are concerns of physics. The strength of materials too is a subject for the physicist's measurement, and their behavior under the influence of pressure, impact, weight, sound, heat, light, electricity and magnetism. Devices used to transmit energy or to convert it into work, such as levers, pulleys, wheels, pistons, valves, electromagnets and vacuum tubes—as well as those used to convert one form of energy into another, e.g., the gasoline engine, the microphone, the artillery piece—are likewise products of physical experimentation.

Despite its basic place in industry, our science is only hazily conceived by the average citizen. One reason for the public's widespread ignorance of its function, and even of its very name, lies in the fact that not all who are physicists call themselves by that name. The weather man is a physicist, for meteorology is the physics of the air. Astronomy, man's first systematic study of nature, is now dominated by astrophysics. Almost all engineers are physicists. Those who specialize in the physics of steam power call themselves mechanical engineers. Those who put their physics to work in the design and construction of automobiles are known as automotive engineers. Those who specialize in the physics of wireless communication are radio engineers. Even chemical and metallurgical engineers, whose basic subject is chemistry, are increasingly called upon to apply physical techniques in their specialty.

Early in 1940 a conference of army, navy and industrial leaders met in Washington to discuss problems of national defense. When the importance of mobilizing physicists was mentioned, some of the conferees discouraged the idea. They could see no need for "men who dabbled only in atoms," and questioned how such persons would be useful on concrete problems whose immediate solution was required for the defense of the nation. This episode reflects a fairly common attitude, for which the scientists themselves are not blameless, but it was surprising that men of leadership should be so narrowly informed.

"The rather general belief that physicists are interested only in atoms probably has arisen because the progress in atomic and nuclear physics is so spectacular that newspapers print news in this field to the almost complete exclusion of news of any other work of the psysicist," commented the *Journal of Applied Physics*. "As a result, the painstaking care which the physicist has used in the establishment of precise standards of temperature, in the analysis of internal friction in vibrating rods, in the exact specification of color, in the development of optical instruments, in the design of electrical measuring instruments, and in innumerable other projects of the greatest immediate importance, has escaped the attention of those who are not directly concerned with the progress in physics."

Nor are the atom chasers to be dismissed. From their highly theoretical and unconventional studies of electrical discharges in gases and in vacua have come not only new techniques but many items of knowledge now in practical use, contributing directly to improved instruments of detection, communication and control. Electronics will be discussed in a later chapter, but here let us look into a few of the more massive contributions of physics to the prosecution of war.

ARTILLERY AND OTHER GUNS

About a fourth of a mile was the best effective range of artillery fire in the days of Leonardo da Vinci. The 16-inch guns of a modern battleship can drop their shells at distances of 20 to 30 miles, which is approximately the range of the 190-ton coast-artillery guns used to defend important harbors and bases. But the record for distance is still held by the Paris gun, the "Big Bertha" of 1918 with which the Germans shelled Paris from a hidden spot 75 miles away. It is possible that a gun of even longer range could be constructed today, but the bombing airplane, "a gun that can shoot thousands of miles," has made these giant artillery pieces obsolete. Not only can it transport a bomb farther than any conceivable gun could shoot a shell but the plane can deliver a heavier charge of high explosives.

In order to lob its projectile across 75 miles of ground, the Paris gun was restricted to a shell weighing 228 pounds. Of this only 22 pounds were explosives; so it isn't to be wondered at that 140 days of intermittent firing killed only 256 Parisians and inflicted relatively trivial property damage. Compare the air attack on Hamburg in the summer of 1943, when R.A.F. planes dropped bombs weighing as much as two tons each, dumping 2,300 tons in a single hour and completely devastating large areas of the city.

The only advantage that the Paris gun had over the bombing plane was speed, for its projectile traveled the 75 miles to Paris in three minutes, whereas a plane would need to go 1,500 miles per hour to match that velocity. Indeed as the shell emerged from the muzzle of "Big Bertha" it was moving a mile a second, but air resistance and gravitation immediately began to put their brakes on and after 25 seconds, when the projectile had reached an altitude of 12 miles, it began to drop, meeting denser air, varying wind currents and changes in temperature; all of which affected its course and determined what part of Paris, if any, it would hit. The barrel of this gun weighed 200 tons, including its detachable steel lining. Each time the gun was fired the erosion caused by the intense heat and chemical action of the explosion, and the sudden friction of the moving shell, removed some of the inner surface and increased the diameter of the barrel by about fifteen-thousandths of an inch. Beginning with a diameter of 8.2 inches, the muzzle had enlarged to 9.2 inches after 66 shots were fired, and that was the stage at which the old lining was removed and a new one installed.

This problem of overheating and corrosion is a long-standing vexation to the ordnance engineer, perhaps even more so now than in 1914-'18. For today it isn't only the occasional "Big Bertha" or other heavy piece that is subjected to an excessive toll of muzzle wear and tear, but thousands of antiaircraft guns, antitank guns and other rapid-fire pieces. Some antiaircraft guns send their shells upward at velocities which carry them to heights of six miles and more. There are machine guns which can fire hundreds of bullets a minute, guns in which the explosive pressure within the barrel reaches 20 tons to the square inch. In order to generate this pressure the gun must be heavily charged with the propellent explosive, which means that you kindle a larger fire within the barrel. Special alloys permit temperatures which would not have been endurable twenty-five years ago. Some rapid-fire guns are water-cooled and others have vanes for air cooling, but despite these facilities it sometimes happens that a machine gun will be burned out after a few minutes of firing. Antiaircraft guns have been known to require renewal or relining after a single night of intensive use.

Overheating is caused not only by the calories released by the burning of the explosive but by the sudden friction of the projectile against the barrel. Most guns are rifled: the inside of the barrel is grooved in a spiral form. As the explosion of the propellent gunpowder forces the shell through, this rifling cuts its groove into a softer band of copper which is built into the hard steel casing of the shell. Thus the departing projectile is given such a mighty twist that it literally screws its way through the air as it speeds to its target. This spiraling motion prevents the projectile from tumbling end over end, keeps its nose forward and contributes directly to the range and accuracy of the shot.

Various efforts have been made to stabilize the flight of projectiles without rifling. One of the developments is a smooth-bore gun whose projectiles are fitted with rear fins. Because of this construction the tail of the missile offers a little more air resistance than its front end, and the effect of the slight drag is to keep its nose pointed forward in flight. The projectile carries a soft encircling metal skirt which insures a close fit and prevents the explosive gases from escaping between barrel and shell. It is reported that, under some conditions, accuracy of fire is better with this weapon than with rifled guns. Even a smooth bore, however, may suffer from the corrosive effects of exploding gunpowder.

Another innovation is a gun with a tapered bore. The diameter of the barrel is largest at the breech end, where the charge is fired, and this gun too is supplied with a specially designed projectile surrounded by a skirt of soft metal. As it pushes through the narrowing barrel the skirt is crushed or sheared off, leaving only the solid bullet of armor-piercing steel. This arrangement provides the expanding gases at the moment of explosion with a large area to press upon, gives a tremendous push which is enhanced by the tapering bore, and the emerging bullet, now stripped to its solid streamlined slug, leaves the muzzle at an extremely high velocity.

THE LAWS OF MOTION

Artillery fire provides a striking demonstration of the three laws of motion, first enunciated in 1686 by Isaac Newton. Because he made use of them to explain the movement of the moon around the earth, and of the planets around the sun, Newton's laws are associated in the public mind with celestial mechanics. But they were derived directly from Galileo's studies of the behavior of pendulums, rolling balls and moving projectiles, and are the foundation of the artilleryman's science of ballistics. All calculations of range, trajectory, forces of impact and other details of behavior of gun, projectile and target are based primarily on these fundamental principles.

First Law of Motion: *Every body continues in its state of rest, or of uniform motion in a right line, unless it is compelled to change that state by forces impressed upon it.*

Projectiles move through space according to this law of inertia, their curved paths being determined by the twin forces of air resistance and gravitation affecting the original velocity with which the missiles emerged from the gun barrel.

Second Law of Motion: *The change of motion is proportional to the motive power impressed, and is made in the direction of the right line in which that force is impressed.*

The operation of this principle is familiarly illustrated, for example, in the influence of wind on shellfire. The range of a gun, which is primarily determined by the explosive force of its charge, depends on the velocity and direction of the wind at the moment.

Third Law of Motion: *To every action there is always opposed an equal reaction; or, the mutual actions of two bodies upon each other are always equal, and directed to contrary parts.*

When a gun is fired the force of the exploding gases acts to push the shell forward and, at the same time, tends to push the gun backward. This force on the gun gives rise to the familiar behavior known as recoil.

RECOIL

Recoil bothered artillerymen from the earliest days, marring the accuracy of aim and often causing other confusions. An example of what used to happen is drawn from the history of the siege of Port Arthur in 1905. The Russians had installed a battery of wheeled guns on the side of a hill, and each time one was fired the recoil sent it rolling down the slope, with its gunners chasing frantically after to catch the runaway and drag it back into position.

Modern artillery pieces are mounted on cradles so arranged that as the gun is fired the barrel slides back under the force of the recoil. Springs or compressed air then return the piece to position automatically. The French 75-millimeter cannon, famous introduction of the 1914-'18 war, had a secret device called a "recuperator" which controlled the compressed-air operation of the recoil mechanism. With this improvement the speed of fire for field artillery was increased from the usual one or two rounds a minute to twenty, though the rapid heating of the barrel reduced the rate in practice to about six a minute. Recoil cradles are used only for artillery. In automatic rifles and machine guns the force of the recoil is harnessed to operate the gun—it ejects the cartridge, reloads and fires, in a continuous sequence, as long as the gunner's finger is on the trigger.

With the increase in fire power which mobile warfare has called forth, there has been a marked increase in the amount of recoil which a gun and its mount must sustain. In order to hit fast-moving tanks, and even faster-moving airplanes, a gun must send its projectiles forth at tremendous velocity; and this means a heavier charge of propellant than was formerly necessary, a more powerful explosion at each firing and a heavier recoil. Then, in order to increase the probability of a hit, the shots must be fired in swift succession, and this means more of these heavier kicks per minute. Some of the antitank guns now in use are so powerful that if built according to 1914-'18 standards they would jump from their mountings. New designs provide a means of conducting the emerging gases backward from the tip of the barrel in a way that provides a partial compensation for the recoil.

The recoil effect may become very noticeable when guns are fired from an airplane. In the British Hurricanes of the type engaged in the Battle of Britain it was found that when all eight machine guns were firing—and they fired forward from positions in the wings—the effect of their combined recoil was to slow the plane's flight by 30 miles per hour. More recent types carry even heavier fire power. The recoil from certain installations of fighter-aircraft guns is equivalent to the pull of a 5,000-horsepower engine—and no single-motored plane has that power. So tremendous is the recoil that if the forward firing of all the guns were continuous the plane would stop in the air and then move backward even though the propeller were pulling forward at full strength. This never happens, of course, because aircraft guns are rarely kept in action longer than a few seconds. Their targets, the enemy planes, move out of the field of fire so rapidly that a few seconds is all the time available for a spurt of effective gunnery. What the aeronautical gunners are continually striving for is to put a vaster punch, and more punches, into these few seconds.

ROCKET PROJECTILES

One device for increasing the punch without adding guns of prohibitive weight to the aircraft is the rocket. Like artillery-fired shells and other bombs, these projectiles may be set to explode within a given time or on contact. An advantage lies in the fact that by means of the rocket principle a projectile equivalent to a three or four inch shell can be launched without the aid of a heavy artillery piece. For the rocket does not depend on one sudden thrust of exploding gunpowder to get the energy to carry it to its target. Instead, it travels under its own power, stored within its jacket in the form of a rapid-burning fuel. The backward discharge of fumes from this continuous burning provides the force which pushes the rocket forward. The gases emerge from the tail in the form of a jet and, again thanks to Sir Isaac's third law, the rocket moves forward in reaction to this jet. Aircraft projectiles of the rocket type can be larger and heavier than those fired from such cannon as it is possible to mount in planes. Moreover, unlike the artillery shell whose momentum and hitting power decrease with each instant of flight, the self-propelled rocket gathers velocity as it moves. Rocket bombs discharged downward on ships and ground objects may hit with greater force than bombs which are merely dropped, for the added impetus from the jet reaction adds to the acceleration of gravitation.

The rocket is a weapon of which interesting reports have come from the battlefield. On the ground it has been used with devastating effect against both tanks and stationary fortifications. This was officially disclosed early in 1943 by Major General L. H. Campbell,

Jr., chief of the U. S. Army Ordnance Department, in a public statement regarding the bazooka, an American introduction of the present war whose unrevealing name masks a rocket-projecting device of tremendous power. General Campbell described the bazooka as "revolutionary in design" and asserted that its projectile will penetrate armor, drive through masonry walls, shatter bridge girders, and "perform other seeming miracles."

In one of the tank battles in North Africa an American soldier fired his bazooka at six enemy tanks. Although he missed his target, the projectile hit a large tree, and so completely demolished the tree that the German tank commander surrendered, astonished at the size of the projectile and its explosive power. On another occasion in the North African campaign, a single fort was giving the American troops considerable trouble. Though small it was strong and powerful until one American soldier cut loose from the landing party, waded ashore with his bazooka, and with one well-planted shot so smashed the fort that its commander surrendered. "Carried in the hands of a soldier," said General Campbell, "the bazooka can destroy any enemy tank on the battlefield. It is so simple and yet so powerful that any foot soldier using it can stand his ground with the certain knowledge that he is the master of any tank which may attack him." Reconnaissance squads, scouting parties, tank hunters, raiders and other advance groups make use of the new weapon, which is of such light weight that two soldiers running can easily carry it.

The rocket has established itself as a valuable supplementary weapon. Meanwhile, projectiles that are discharged from guns, bombs that are dropped, torpedoes that are propelled by a self-contained mechanism, and mines that are anchored or set afloat in the sea continue to be the principal missiles of mechanized war. They are the modern equivalents of the Archimedean stones, darts and arrows.

THE NEWER MISSILES

They vary in size from the rifle bullet, of a quarter-inch diameter, weighing less than half an ounce, to the demolition bomb, of 12-foot length and longer, weighing 4 tons. Although many of them correspond in designation to missiles known in the first world war, there is hardly one which has not been improved in some important detail, utilizing new developments in metallurgy, explosives, aerodynamics and other technologies.

Many of the newer types of projectile, especially those fired from antiaircraft and antitank guns, are calibrated in the metric system. This is a consequence of the historic influence which French artillery has exercised on British and American ordnance design. The reader can readily convert metric dimensions into the more familiar English terminology if he remembers that it takes about 25.4 millimeters to equal an inch. Thus, the French 75-millimeter gun fires a shell which is slightly less than 3 inches in diameter. American artillery nomenclature is somewhat mixed at the present time. In general, the heaviest shells are rated in inches. The largest naval and coast-defense projectiles are still the 16-inch, and we also have the 14-inch and the 12-inch. Below that come the 240-millimeter high-explosive shell and many others, both high-explosive and armor-piercing, in a numerous sequence down to the 37-millimeter. But, in addition to the projectiles whose diameters are usually given in millimeters, the United States forces are also using 3-inch shells and some other small ones rated in inches. Caliber refers to the diameter of a gun barrel, measured between opposite points on the "lands" or elevations of its rifling, and is in fractions of an inch. Thus 50 caliber means a diameter of .50 or one-half inch.

It is a truism of ordnance engineering that a gun is no better than its projectile. Shells are scientifically designed as to size, shape, thickness of casing and amount and position of explosive charge, each detail considered with reference to the purpose of the projectile. The shrapnel shell, which caused most of the wounds in 1914-'18, has nearly disappeared. Instead of shrapnel, in which the shell carried a large number of half-inch balls which were scattered by the explosion, the artillerymen today are using such things as fragmentation shells. These are designed to break into the maximum number of destructive pieces when they burst. They are used primarily against troops, and have thicker walls and a smaller charge of explosive than other types of high-explosive shells.

High-explosive shells are so named because they are charged not with gunpowder, cordite, or any other propellent but with one of the quick-detonating chemicals, like t.n.t. Shells with thin walls and heavy charges are used for demolition purposes, when the object is to wreck a building, bridge, or other ground construction. Such shells accomplish their purpose by concussion or blast. Antiaircraft shells, though smaller, are more sturdy. They range from 37 millimeters in diameter (weight 1¼ pounds) to 105 millimeters (33 pounds). They are designed to burst into wing-tearing, fuselage-piercing fragments, for mere concussion is simply another wind to the firmly welded airplanes of today. Some of the antiaircraft shells are equipped with fuzes sensitive to the slightest touch of wing or other solid part, and explode on contact. Indeed it is said that the touch of a raindrop will discharge some. Others have time fuzes, activated by a watchlike mechanism and set to explode at a given altitude. Some of these shells are so powerfully charged that any plane within a radius of 50 feet of the explosion is almost certain to be hit by a metal fragment.

Armor-piercing projectiles are built to penetrate steel. They range in size from the solid 37-millimeter bullets used to fight tanks to the huge shells of 16-inch diameter used to attack battleships. The latter, which weigh more than a ton, carry a substantial charge controlled by a fuze timed to explode a few seconds after the hit. These 16-inch projectiles have noses of the toughest steel; they are capable of piercing 16 inches of armor plate, after which the explosion can inflict maximum destruction, and one well-placed shot is sufficient to sink a battleship. All the varieties of modern projectiles are carefully streamlined, and correct aerodynamic principles are followed to make them cleave the air with the minimum of resistance. In some instances the shape that will be most effective in piercing steel armor is not the best shape for boring through the atmosphere; so the armor-piercing projectile is tipped with a streamlined windshield of aluminum or other soft metal which crumbles or pulverizes when it hits, leaving the naked point of steel to finish the job.

BOMBS

Shells are fired, but bombs are dropped and depend on gravitation to bring them to their targets. A hand-thrown grenade, such as was common in the trench warfare of 1914-'18, is actually a bomb. But in modern parlance the term is usually reserved for the aircraft-carried projectile. Though there are many kinds, most aerial bombs can be classified under three headings according to type of action: explosive bombs, incendiary bombs and gas bombs.

Gas bombs have been used sporadically by the Japanese in attacks on China, and of course they were early resorted to by the Italians in their campaign against the Ethiopians. Strange as it may seem, no gas bombs were used in World War I. The Germans initiated chemical warfare in 1915 by opening cylinders of chlorine in their frontline trenches on a day when the wind was blowing toward the enemy. Later both sides loaded shells with gas and dropped them into opposing lines by artillery fire. But today military munitions include large stores of bombs whose purpose is to spread gas, and, as we know from the warnings issued by war leaders on both sides of the conflict, the preparations for aerial gas attacks are considerable. Gas bombs are made with thin walls and carry small charges of explosive, enough to burst the container and release the gas which constitutes their principal load. The standard bombs of this type (some of which may also be used to generate smoke for purposes of concealment) weigh from 30 to 550 pounds.

Incendiary bombs, loaded with yellow phosphorus, thermite and a tarsoaked fabric, were dropped from German Zeppelins in 1914. The British retaliated with 6½-ounce parcels of thin steel filled with thermite which were thrown from airplanes. Other types were developed by both sides in 1918, though too late to be of effective use. But one of these 1918 creations, the German elektron bomb, is the prototype of the incendiaries which the Luftwaffe used by the thousands in their 1940 and 1941 attacks on British cities. Its principle is followed in most of the aerial bombs now used to spread fire. This weapon was called an elektron bomb because its casing was an aluminum-copper-magnesium alloy for which the German trade name is "elektron metal." It is loaded with thermite, a granulated mixture of pulverized iron oxide and powdered aluminum which readily burns on ignition and attains a temperature of 5432° F., and in the process sets fire to the elektron casing which also burns. The combustion of the metal casing is a very important contribution to the effectiveness of this incendiary missile. The original bomb was of one kilogram (about 2 pounds, 3 ounces), but most of the fire spreaders dropped in the present war range from 2 to 100 pounds.

A combination bomb was introduced by the Germans in raids on England in 1942. It is designed to set fires in the usual way, but has attached to the incendiary compartment another loaded with high explosives controlled by a time fuze set to go off some minutes after the incendiary starts to burn. The explosion is calculated not only to scatter fires but to go off in the face of the fire fighter, and the British have named this German introduction the a.p.i., or anti-personnel incendiary.

Explosive bombs closely parallel explosive shells in function. There are fragmentation bombs, armor-piercing bombs and demolition bombs. Fragmentation bombs are used to attack troops, airplanes on the ground, and other materiel which is vulnerable to a burst of steel fragments. These bombs are usually small, in weight from 25 to 75 pounds. Armor-piercing bombs are designed for air attacks on battleships and fortresses; like their sister shells of the 16-inch class they are contained in heavy casings which penetrate steel and then explode. Demolition bombs depend on concussion to get their results and they come in a variety of sizes, from the 100-pounders used against light constructions to the 8,000-pounders which blast entire city residential blocks.

Aerial bombs are fitted with tail fins to stabilize their position in falling and keep their noses pointed downward. In addition, the nose end of some bombs has a small paddle wheel in its tip, with vanes like a propeller. This is a safety device which controls the fuze. For, as the bomb falls, the air twirls the paddle wheel and it in turn unscrews the mechanism which frees the firing pin and sets it for action the instant the bomb strikes. In some delayed-action fuzes, the firing pin ignites a mixture of slow-burning powder which takes two to ten seconds to burn through and detonate the charge of t.n.t. In some time fuzes the firing pin is held under tension by a spring. This spring is supported by a strip of metal adjacent to a small glass vial of acid. When the bomb hits the impact breaks the glass and the spilled acid begins to eat away the metal strip, thereby eventually releasing the firing pin. By regulating the thickness of the metal strip and the strength of the acid it is possible to delay the detonation of the bomb for hours or even days, according to the will of the bombardier. Sometimes chance interposes an even longer delay. In the summer of 1942 a bomb which had been dropped in May of the previous year suddenly exploded in the Southwark district of London, killing 19 persons and wounding 59. This quiescence of a full year was probably a freak occurrence rather than the result of fuze setting.

In their 1940-'41 raids on London the Germans used a type of demolition bomb which became known as a "land mine." It weighed a ton or more (almost all t.n.t.) and was dropped with a supporting parachute which slowed its speed of descent. The fuze was set to explode about 10 seconds after the landing, and the blast of these huge parcels of hair-triggered explosives was terrifying and destructive.

Later the land mine was supplanted by a new weapon: an extra long tubular bomb fitted with large tail fins which slowed the fall somewhat. Because of their shape these bombs were called "aerial torpedoes." The giant block-busters of the R.A.F. were also torpedo-shaped in their early designs.

TORPEDOES

But don't let the name confuse you. It is only in its long tubular shape that the aerial torpedo has anything in common with the marine torpedo. This latter is in reality a miniature automatic battleship, complete with power plant, steering gear, mechanical crew and cargo of high explosives. And yet it is a missile, a sea-going projectile. During the first world war the torpedo sank some 2,000 ships totaling around 6,000,000 tons. In the present war such fortresses as the British plane carrier *Ark Royal*, the American plane carrier *Lexington*, the Germans' invincible *Bismarck*, and the crucial *Prince of Wales* and *Repulse* (whose early loss left Singapore open) were victims of the torpedo, along with hundreds of lesser warcraft and merchant vessels which have felt its fatal sting. Of all the missiles that have been invented since the boy David struck down the mighty Goliath with a pebble, the torpedo is the most ingenious, the most complicated, and perhaps the most successful in doing the work for which it is designed.

Despite its high record of ship sinkings, the torpedo of 1914-'18 was an erratic, fumbling, unpredictable mechanism which was still in the developmental stage of its engineering. Several German submarine boats were blown up by their own torpedoes. Moreover, the World War I torpedoes gave off such a stream of bubbles that they betrayed their presence well in advance and often pointed the enemy's lookout to the location of the mother submarine. Sometimes the torpedo would circle uncertainly, often it rose to the surface, and occasionally one was seen to leap out of the water. A German U-boat commander of 1918 survived to tell the marvelous story of a British torpedo, suddenly launched against him as he was cruising on the surface. His sub was a perfect broadside target, there was no time to submerge or turn, the torpedo was plowing straight for him with its frothy wake of bubbles, when amazingly it leaped upward like a porpoise, slid over the smooth sea-level deck of the U-boat and dropped unperturbed into the water on the other side.

The modern torpedo is larger, more heavily powered, more precisely controlled. It travels faster, has a wider range and deals a heavier blow than its ancestor of 1914-'18. It is 24 feet long, a straight tube 21 inches in diameter, and probably no other weapon packs in equal space so many applications of physics and related sciences. The prow end is the warhead, a compartment loaded with 600 pounds of the most destructive high explosive available, and it is tipped with a contact fuze which detonates the charge a moment after the projectile hits. Behind the warhead is a steel tank of compressed air held at high pressure. Next are smaller containers of water, fuel oil and lubricating oil. Then comes the "engine room," with its mechanical "crew" (a gyroscope and other secret devices) which controls the navigation of the torpedo and holds it to whatever course is indicated by the dial set before the weapon is launched. The 400-horsepower engine is driven by a mixture of compressed air, hot gas and steam. It whirls the twin propellers which revolve in opposite directions; for a lone propeller would cause the torpedo merely to roll over and over like a rotating barrel and get nowhere. Also at the stern end are the rudders, vertical for direction and a horizontal one to keep the course at the determined depth. The usual depth for torpedo travel is 15 feet, which is about right for inflicting a serious blow below the water line.

All in all, some 3,000 parts go into the construction, many of them as finely wrought and as precisely meshed as the parts of a watch; therefore it is not strange that the torpedo is war's most expensive missile. Each costs from $10,000 to $12,000. And when one misses there is an internal mechanism which opens its flood gates and causes it to sink within a few minutes. This is done not only to remove a navigational hazard but because each warring power believes its torpedo embodies valuable secrets.

The modern torpedo travels fifty and more miles per hour and its 3,000-pound mass gathers such momentum that even if it carried no explosive charge its blow is sufficient to knock a hole in a heavily constructed cargo ship. Its range is about five miles, and mechanical control is such that the torpedo does not have to be pointed at its target. After the dial has been correctly set, it can be launched in any direction, will turn and circle into the designated course, and then make a bee line for the unsuspecting target. Both engine and rudders are piloted by the whirling gyroscope—a mechanical brain which never misunderstands orders, never forgets directions, never tires or grows anxious, and never falters in its control.

Although the torpedo is self-contained to a degree that few weapons can parallel, it is completely dependent on human direction to set its controls and get it into the water. Torpedoes were first launched from surface vessels, and are still, but it is the submarine which has made the most frequent and effective use of them. So much is this so that torpedo warfare has generally meant submarine warfare, though submarines also carry guns of caliber up to 5 inches and in surface raids often make powerful use of them.

The submarine is one of the youngest of the numerous types of warships, but perhaps it has embodied more improvements in the last twenty-five years than any other naval vessel; except, possibly, the new types of boats designed to fight submarines. Many technological improvements which have contributed conspicuously to air warfare have also contributed in varying degrees to submarine warfare. Because of their stealth, subs can execute surprise attacks that rarely fall to the lot of surface warships. In the 1942 fighting in the Pacific, the U. S. submarine *Seawolf*—operating as "a lone wolf"—sank a Japanese cruiser, a destroyer and a transport, and damaged two cruisers, a transport and other vessels.

SUBMARINE CHASERS AND SUBMARINE SPOTTERS

Against the submarine naval war is being waged not only with destroyers, depth charges, and mines both anchored and floating, but with a new kind of patrol boat whose distinctive characteristics are high speed and exceptional maneuverability. It can turn in such a short radius that a submarine hasn't time to use the escape tactics which occasionally enable one to elude a destroyer. Although much smaller than destroyers and carrying less than half as many men, these sub-chasers do all that a destroyer can do in hunting submarines. They carry depth charges, machine guns, light artillery, and are equipped with supersensitive acoustical and electrical apparatus for detecting their quarry. Under normal weather conditions a sub-chaser can stay out on U-boat trails for as long as two weeks, then rush into port, refuel, restock and leave in 24 hours for another patrol. The key item of equipment, the engineering innovation which gives the new vessel its high speed and ready response to the rudder, is the "pancake engine."

Various stories are afloat as to the origin of the curious name of the pancake engine, most of them apocryphal. The truth is that the name arose quite incidentally in an early planning conference of the design engineers. They had arrived at the idea of installing the crankshaft vertically, instead of in the more usual horizontal position, and then stacking up the cylinder units around this vertical shaft. "Yes, stack 'em up like pancakes," agreed one of the consultants. Thus the name "was a natural, and probably nothing could have stopped it," relates Lieutenant Commander W. D. Leggett, Jr., "but we frankly encouraged it as a term which gave little or no information as to the characteristics of what was at that time our most confidential Diesel development."

Rear Admiral H. G. Bowen has told of the navy's acquirement of this engine, a high-powered lightweight Diesel of radical design which came out of the fertile brain of Charles F. Kettering, research director for General Motors. In July, 1937, when Bowen was engineer-in-chief of the navy, word reached his headquarters in Washington that Kettering had something new; so he journeyed to Detroit to look over the batch of pencil drawings which were all that then existed of the invention. At that time few people in government had any apprehension of the war that was already brewing in Europe. But "the design looked good" to the Admiral, who "was positive that Boss Kettering's dream was worth $250,000." He allotted that amount from naval engineering funds to the development, although some skeptics were saying that an engine of such description could never be of use to the navy. What happened is history, very recent history, which can be reported as yet only in general terms. As Admiral Bowen phrases it: "This unwanted baby, conceived in 1937, arrived in 1942 to help us solve a submarine menace never dreamed of in 1937."

The pancake engine, a giant for power and speed but a dwarf in its space requirements and weight per horsepower, made possible the sub-chasers which were rolling out of the shipyards in droves by the summer of 1942. At the same time a special school, set up in an old wharf in Florida to provide intensive 30-day training courses for picked men to serve on the sub-chasers, was rolling out its graduates.

Aircraft are used in antisubmarine warfare, for it was discovered during World War I that from the sky the hull of a submerged U-boat appears as a distinguishable spot in the water. The U-boat designers have sought to make their craft less conspicuous, but in a smooth sea complete camouflage has proved unsuccessful, and a considerable number of U-boats have been accounted for by airplane spotters. A principal assignment of the Coastal Command of the Royal Air Force is to hunt German submarines. These U-boats generally operate in groups, "wolf packs" the Nazis call them, and often are directed to British convoys by scouting planes of the Luftwaffe. Coastal Command aircraft are instructed to attack and sink them when they can, and if a detected U-boat or wolf pack cannot be directly bombed to keep it below the surface, where mass attacks on convoys are more difficult. Through performance of this second function, even though the submarines are not hit, the British aircraft are able to dislocate the submarine time-tables, reduce their surfacing to the minimum and thereby slow their speeds, often enabling the threatened convoy to escape.

One of the episodes of the Battle of the Atlantic was the capture of a German U-boat and its entire crew by a British bomber. The air pilot forced the submarine commander to surrender. Then for 11 hours this Coastal Command plane, assisted by another which came to relieve it, held the Germans captive until a British naval surface ship could arrive. The navy took off the prisoners, put a prize crew aboard and brought the U-boat intact into port. You may be sure that every detail of its construction and equipment was searched for the much-vaunted German "secrets."

Still another antisubmarine agency is the dirigible airship. A backhanded testimonial to its value has been received from the enemy. In the summer of 1942 Admiral Karl Doenitz, commander of the German submarine forces, made a report in which he said: "Operations in American waters are by no means an easy matter. . . . The United States dwarf zeppelins unquestionably have a definite defense value." The "dwarf zeppelins" are the blimps, the small lighter-than-air non-rigid type of dirigibles which are sustained by the noninflammable helium gas. The name is of British origin, and is derived from the fact that originally two types of nonrigid dirigibles were built, designated as "A-limp" and "B-limp." B-limp survived the final tests and was adopted, and eventually the hyphen dropped out. These small dirigibles have a cruising speed of about 60 miles per hour, carry depth charges, and are able to idle their engines and hang over a suspected area of sea, or drift with the wind in a continuous patrol of submarine-infested waters. Their underhung gondolas give an unobstructed view of the sea over a wide field. The disadvantages are slow speed and a relatively large bulk which make the blimp an easy target in case the enemy submarine is defended by airplanes.

But there is a type of balloon which the airplane has found exceedingly annoying. This is the barrage balloon, the large sausage-shaped gas bag anchored by means of cables to boats at sea or to motor trucks or stationary winches on land. Early in the war the British set up a barrage of these balloons over the Dover cliffs, in front of London, the Thames Estuary and other places thought to be in danger of air attack. A few German planes were destroyed by collision with the cables. As recently as January, 1942, for example, a German night bomber sought to pass between two barrage balloons; its starboard wing struck one of the cables and was sliced off, and the plane crashed. But it is rare that the enemy pilot will risk an encounter with the steel anchor wires, and the principal effect of the balloon barrage is to drive him to higher altitudes. In *Berlin Diary* William Shirer tells of a German airman returned from an attack on England who "related that they approached London at a height of from 15/16,000 feet, dived to 10,000 feet and released their bombs at this height—too high for accurate night bombing. They did not dare go below 7,000 feet, he says, on account of the barrage balloons."

These tethered gas bags continue to be an important arm in the defense of ships, factories, cities and shores against low-flying air attack. But they can be regarded as only part of the complete protective system which includes aircraft warning systems, antiaircraft artillery, and patrol, pursuit, and other fighter planes.

GUNS GET WINGS

The airplane has been described as a mobile gun mount, but it was not such at the beginning of its military use. In 1914 both the German and the British-French high commands regarded their air forces as primarily for reconnaissance, to spy out objectives and the disposition of troops in enemy areas and to check the accuracy of artillery fire. No planes were armed, but British pilots were instructed to take along some sort of weapon. First they carried revolvers, then a loose rifle; later the rifle was "mounted" by lashing it to a strut, and eventually machine guns were installed. But the utility of the guns was narrowly limited, for they could be fired only in unobstructed directions. The latest and fastest planes were those in which the propeller was placed in front of the pilot, and eventually a French airman, Garros, discovered that if the propeller was made of tough metal he could risk firing a machine gun between the whirling blades. Only 7 per cent of the bullets struck the blades, and the slanting moving surfaces threw them off without suffering serious injury. Garros's invention might have given the Allies an early advantage, but unfortunately his plane was forced down on German territory and the captors turned it over to Fokker for examination.

This Anthony Hermann Gerhard Fokker was a Dutchman, born in Java, who had established a small airplane factory, airfield, and pilots' training school in Germany just a year before the outbreak of war. Fokker had tried to sell his services to various countries, Holland, England, Russia, Italy and Germany, all without success until 1913 when he won a German military competition and was given an order for ten planes. With the outbreak of war he became Germany's principal consultant on military airplanes, and it was routine for the captured Garros device to be referred to him. He immediately rejected it as too crude, not worth imitating. What was needed, he reasoned, was a precision device, something that would control the gunfire automatically, so that bullets were discharged only between the blades, without any trusting to luck to miss hitting them.

When the problem was thus analyzed, says Fokker, the solution came to him "in a flash." Why not gear the gun control to the propeller mechanism, and make the rotation of the propeller fire the gun? Then no matter what the speed of the engine, the rate of gunfire would be limited to the same speed, bullets would be released only between blades, and every bullet could be counted on to move unimpeded.

Four days later Fokker returned to the German air command with a working model of his synchronized machine gun. Military conservatism ran true to form and insisted that the thing was impracticable. Finally the military challenged him to go up with his invention and shoot down an enemy plane. He protested his neutrality, his civilian status, but they insisted, dressed him in the uniform of a lieutenant, and sent him aloft. In his autobiography, *Flying Dutchman*, which Fokker wrote in collaboration with B. Gould, he gives a graphic account of this experience:

While I was flying around 6000 feet high, a Farman two-seater bi-plane, similar to the ones which had bombed me, appeared out of a cloud 2000 or 3000 feet below. That was my opportunity to show what the gun would do, and I dived rapidly toward it. The plane, an observation type with the propeller in the rear, was flying leisurely along. It may even have been that the Frenchmen didn't see me. It takes long practice and constant vigilance to guard against surprise air attack, for the enemy can assail one from any point in the sphere.

Even though they had seen me, they would have had no reason

to fear bullets through my propeller. While approaching, I thought of what a deadly accurate stream of lead I could send into the plane. It would be just like shooting a rabbit on the sit, because the pilot couldn't shoot back through his pusher propeller at me.

As the distance between us narrowed, the plane grew larger in my sights. My imagination could vision my shots puncturing the gasoline tanks in front of the engine. The tanks would catch fire. Even if my bullets failed to kill the pilot and the observer, the ship would fall down in flames. I had my finger on the trigger. . . . I had no personal animosity toward the French. I was flying merely to prove that a certain mechanism I had invented would work. By this time I was near enough to open fire, and the French pilots were watching me curiously, wondering, no doubt, why I was flying up behind them. In another instant it would be all over for them.

Suddenly I decided that the whole job could go to hell. It was too much like "cold meat" to suit me. I had no stomach for the whole business, nor any wish to kill Frenchmen for Germans. Let them do their own killing.

The Germans were not so squeamish, and they did do their own killing, using the synchronized machine gun with devastating effect. The technique, as Fokker described it, was to drop out of the sun in a dive, pull up underneath the unprotected enemy plane, and "simply sew the opposing airmen in a shroud of bullets." The inventor added that "the courage of the French and English in facing such disheartening odds seemed almost superhuman to me."

But the odds did not remain overbalanced. Soon one of the Fokker-equipped planes was brought down behind the Allies' line, and it was not long before French and British planes were equipped with guns that fired unerringly between the propeller blades.

Current practice in gun placement has gone far beyond this. Guns are now installed in the wings, in the fuselage, and in the nose of the plane, and all may be fired at the same time by the pilot's pressing an electric switch. Certain types of fighter planes mount a cannon over the engine, and fire their shells through the hollow propeller shaft. Other guns are mounted in turrets. These turrets are built of bullet-proof glass or transparent plastics, giving a view over a wide field. Despite the resistance of the air against a gun barrel protruding from a plane moving 300 to 500 miles per hour, the turret gunner is able to manipulate his weapon with the aid of hydraulic or electric drives. These powerful mechanisms turn the turret and elevate or lower the barrel.

Turret gunners have ballistic problems of a high order of complication. Suppose, for example, the gunner in the waist of the plane has to fight off an enemy bearing on his left. His own plane is moving forward at 400 miles per hour. But this velocity is affected by a wind of known or unknown velocity, and the relative direction of the wind is changing as the plane maneuvers. Then, too, every burst of fire from his gun has its recoil, and this affects the motion of the plane. The plane's velocity moreover contributes a forward motion to the sideward-moving projectile. At the instant it leaves the gun barrel, the missile is traveling forward with the plane at 400 miles per hour and simultaneously moving outward at its muzzle velocity. A further uncertainty arises from the fact that the rifling in the gun barrel gives the emerging bullet a clockwise spin, and the effect of this on a burst of fire to the left causes the projectiles to drop in their flight. This behavior, known as the "Magnus effect," results from the spinning of the projectiles, and if the gunfire is directed to the right it tends to cause them to rise. The effect is similar to that which causes a spinning baseball to curve from its normal path. Finally, the degree of downward or upward swerve depends on the velocity of the plane. Here are enough variables to keep a differential analyzer busy continuously, and no gunner could possible figure where to point his barrel so that a shot fired from his moving platform would hit the moving target.

Tracer bullets are the practical man's answer to this dilemma. These are bullets coated with a phosphorus preparation which ignites as they speed through the air. By having every fifth cartridge in the belt carry a tracer bullet, the burst of gunfire is made visible: it is like a long straight line of light. Thereby the gunner can see where his fire is going, judge whether he is reaching the enemy or not and guide his gunnery accordingly.

The Hurricane fighters in the Battle of Britain carried eight machine guns, but by 1942 a new model known as the Hurribomber mounted ten guns. One of the deadliest fighters then in use—and it scored especially well against German aircraft in the Middle East—was the twin-engined British Beaufighter with four cannon in its nose in addition to "several" machine guns. The story is told of a head-on encounter between a Beaufighter and a German Dornier bombing plane, in which the British pilot fired a quick burst from all his forward guns. The concentrated fire shattered the Dornier, which broke into fragments, and, as reported by Air Marshal F. J. Linnell in *Flying*, "the Beaufighter, its pilot temporarily blinded by a dazzling shower of sparks, actually flew, at 300 m.p.h., through the place in the sky where the Dornier had been only a second before."

With increase in firepower has come increase in armor. One of the advantages which the British possessed over their German adversaries at the beginning of the present war was bullet-proof glass and sections of steel armor. It was impracticable, because of weight, to protect the plane throughout, but plates of tough steel were placed where projectiles were likely to do the most harm. How well these patches of armor served is attested in experience after experience. A British Coastal Command fighter plane returned one day from a reconnaissance flight during which it had had an encounter with enemy aircraft. As the pilot dismounted he began to rub his head. The plane was okay, he said, everything was okay, except that he had picked up a splitting headache. When the mechanics went over his ship, to ready it for the next flight, they found a deep dent in the armor shield behind the pilot's head, the imprint of a Messerschmitt bullet!

The Germans made little effort to armor their planes in the early months of the war, apparently thinking that rate of climb and maneuverability, which would have to be sacrificed to the extra weight of steel, were the better alternatives. But this judgment was reversed by the test of actual fighting, and after the Battle of Britain steel armor became standard equipment on the European fronts. The Japanese, however, left their Zero fighters unarmored, and while these planes are very lively they are very vulnerable, and are easily destroyed by a few hits.

One device which the Germans had at the beginning of the war, a protection that far excelled the steel plate which the British first used to surround aircraft fuel tanks, was a rubber compound spread like a blanket all over the outside of the reservoir. If punctured by a bullet, the hole in the resilient covering immediately sealed itself and fire was prevented. The British were not long in adopting the self-sealing fuel tank.

The military planes of today are so ruggedly built and so well protected that they are able to endure gunfire that would have been devastating to the craft of 1939. This is particularly true of the huge bombing planes. An experience to illustrate this comes from an engagement in which eight Flying Fortresses battled a pack of twenty to twenty-five German Focke-Wulf 190's over the North Sea. Six of the German planes were shot down; all eight Fortresses returned to their bases, but one had been mangled. An enemy shell had reached its cockpit, killing the co-pilot and injuring the pilot; other enemy projectiles struck two of its four engines, and the big bomber was hit in other places; yet she kept aloft, dealt tremendous destruction to her attackers, and despite all this punishment landed successfully at an English base.

FASTER AND HIGHER

In 1913 the international Schneider Cup race was won by a plane flying 45.75 miles per hour. In 1914, just on the eve of the war, the winning speed was 86.8. There were no more races until 1920, when the fastest flyer did 107.8 m.p.h. By 1926 the winner had reached 246.5; the 1931 winner reached 340, and airplane speeds since this last Schneider Cup race have continued to rise. In 1933 the maximum speed was 424 miles per hour; by 1939 it had reached 469; and during the war, combat planes have been flown at speeds exceeding 500 miles per hour.

Many considerations affect aircraft speed. The shape of the ship and the smoothness of its exterior surface are one; the design of the propeller is another; the altitude at which flight is made is also a factor; and crucially important is the relationship between total weight and the capacity of its power plant. The power plant which propelled the Wright brothers' first flight at Kitty Hawk in 1903 was a four-cylinder gasoline engine of twelve horsepower. That engine weighed 144 pounds, an average of 12 pounds per horsepower. Today we have engines of 2,000 horsepower whose "dry weight" (i.e., exclusive of auxiliary equipment) is only a little over 2,000 pounds, and larger engines averaging less than a pound per horsepower are in the laboratories.

Dry weight for a liquid-cooled engine is a hypothetical term, for an internal-combustion engine will not operate very long without a cooling system. Liquid cooling, because of the fluid contents, requires pumps, extra plumbing, thermostats and other auxiliaries. The metal fins used in air-cooling systems weigh only about half as much as the liquid-cooling extras.

But weight is not the only consideration. A radial-type air-cooled engine may waste power through its greater drag, requiring as it does a strong flow of air over its cylinders and presenting a large surface offering resistance to this flow. Not only can a V-type liquid-cooled engine be built long and slim, and be buried in the body of the plane, but liquid distributes the heat over the cylinders more evenly than fins. Both British and German designers gave the preference to liquid-cooled engines for their Hurricanes, Spitfires, Messerschmitts and other high-speed fighters, and limited their use of air-cooled engines to the slower bombers, transport planes, and the like.

Meanwhile, in the United States, the arguments for air cooling had prevailed to such an extent that by 1936 both army and navy, as well as the commercial air lines, had standardized air-cooled engines. Reasons for this preference were lower weight and greater simplicity. For the liquid-cooling system has more mechanism, more parts to get out of order, and is more vulnerable to puncture by gunfire. Even its advantage in streamlining was overcome. The National Advisory Committee for Aeronautics plunged deep into this problem in the Langley Field wind tunnels. By 1941 it was able to report that through scientific ducting and cowling, the drag of the radial air-cooled engine could be made as low as that of the best V-type liquid-cooled airplane installation. "Recent technical progress has enabled American airplane builders to demonstrate airplanes with larger air-cooled engines at speeds exceeding 400 miles per hour," says Jerome C. Hunsaker, "and there now appears to be nothing to choose, as to speed, between the two types of engines when each is properly installed."

These developments of air-cooled power systems have been of utmost value to the U. S. armed forces, and are widely applied in all types of aircraft; nevertheless, several American fighter planes are using liquid-cooled engines. An example is the famous Lightning, the

P-38, whose versatile performance in the Battle of Tunisia is one of the sagas of the war. It was a Lightning, powered by its two liquid-cooled engines, that made the record vertical dive over England in the summer of 1943—a straight downward plunge of nearly five miles, in which the diving speed attained was greater than the velocity of sound, 750 m.p.h.

The military and naval plane needs not only speed but also high ceiling. Indeed, if it is properly proportioned as to wing surface and engine power, it can travel faster in the thin air of the upper atmosphere than it can in the thicker medium below. But this thin air creates a problem, not only for the pilots and other crew members who must breathe it but for the engine whose combustion is just as dependent on air as it is on fuel. Engines are built to burn fifteen parts of air to one part of gasoline, and at sea level the atmospheric density is such that its pressure pushes air into the carburetor at an adequate rate. As a plane rises from the ground the air density decreases steadily, but for the first three or four thousand feet the thinning is not serious enough to interfere with the functioning of the motor. At 20,000 feet atmospheric pressure is less than half that at sea level; therefore the amount of air which the carburetor will receive at each gasp is less than half of what the engine needs to develop full power.

An early invention to correct this deficit was the supercharger, an air pump driven by gearing from the engine. This device pumps so fast that the air is compressed to sea-level density even at heights of 17,000 feet. In order to go higher it was found necessary to add another stage to the process; that is, to install a second supercharger which takes the air as compressed by the first stage and pumps it to still higher density. The pumping is not accomplished without cost, however, for as much as 150 horsepower of a 1000-horsepower engine may be used in driving this type of supercharger.

Later invention has greatly increased the efficiency of super-charging by substituting a turbine for the gear-driven mechanism to drive the pump. In the turbo-supercharger, which is used in the Flying Fortress and other high-altitude aircraft, the blast of exhaust gas as it escapes from the engine is conducted through a turbine which it whirls at 25,000 revolutions per minute and more. In the process, air is sucked into the supercharger and forced into the carburetor at such velocity that sea-level density is provided at heights of 25,000 feet. By adding another supercharger to the first stage, the same pressures can be provided at yet higher altitudes. Inasmuch as the turbine spins faster as the air density grows thinner, its supercharging effect increases at higher altitudes, where the need for it is greater. Also, the turbo-supercharger makes no serious drain on the power of the engine, since it simply uses the discharged gases.

ENGINES, PROPELLERS, ROCKETS

The airplane engine, despite its progressive attainment of lower weight per unit of power, is far from perfect. One third of the energy released by its burning fuel is carried off as heat by the cooling system, another third is wasted through the exhaust fumes, and what is left drives the propellers. Designers have been busy for years trying to develop an engine which would exceed this ratio of efficiency. Efforts have been made to apply the turbine principle to aircraft propulsion, having the explosion of the gasoline twirl a rotor instead of push a piston, but the design still remains a project rather than a practical achievement.

The propeller is more efficient than the engine which drives it. Under favorable conditions it converts more than 80 per cent of the engine's power to useful thrust. One of the recent developmental features is an automatic device which controls the pitch, the angle at which the blade cuts the air. For each speed of rotation there is a pitch of maximum efficiency, and this ingenious automatic control directs electric or hydraulic motors which shift the angle of the blades according to the needs of the moment. In this way the propeller's pitch and the engine's rotational speed are kept in tune during flight according to the speed pattern set by the pilot.

How propellers can be designed to utilize the output of a 4000-horsepower unit is a current question. The blades cannot be indefinitely lengthened; for the longer the blade, the higher is the relative air speed of its tip. And as the tip speed approaches the velocity of sound—1100 feet per second—shock waves are set up which generate a serious drag. Adding more blades has been tried, but four blades appear to be a practical limit. A more promising alternative is to mount two propellers on the same shaft and rotate them in opposite directions, an arrangement which has aerodynamic advantages.

It has been found possible to add a little push to the pull of the propeller by utilizing the exhaust gases of the engine. If these waste fumes are conducted in a rearward direction through nozzles which expand the hot gases to atmospheric pressure, the expansion increases their kinetic energy and the result is jet propulsion. It has been found that for planes flying 400 miles per hour and more the emerging gases impart a forward thrust which adds from 10 to 12 miles per hour to the speed. For planes of less than 300 miles per hour the exhaust ejector has no appreciable value.

The Italian engineer Campini has combined an engine installation with jet propulsion in an interesting way. In this plane the engine is buried within the fuselage and used to drive a compressor which sucks air into the nose of the plane through a large circular vent. By burning gasoline in the compressed air stream, a jet is thrown out at the rear which drives the aircraft forward. Two planes of this type were completed in 1941, and in December of that year one flew successfully the 168 miles from Rome to Milan in a little less than an hour. No attempts at high speed or high altitude were ventured at this trial, and its designer says that his type of plane will show superiority only in operations faster than 248 miles per hour.

Both the Axis and the Allies have used rockets as auxiliaries to boost the pull of aircraft propellers. As early as the Battle of Britain it was learned, from German planes shot down, that the Heinkel 111K was equipped with two rockets. They were calculated to assist the plane at the take-off and up to two or three thousand feet, after which the 1,300-horsepower gasoline engine carried on. A similar scheme has been used by the British.

If exhaust gases, accelerated air jet and auxiliary rockets can boost the speed of planes, why not install a super-rocket or battery of rockets and depend entirely on jet propulsion? This, at one stroke, would do away with all rotating parts, eliminate lubrication problems and make supercharging unnecessary. It is not a new idea. Rocket propulsion has been an interest of aeronautical engineers for years, and experiments with it were under way prior to the outbreak of war. In 1929 Fritz von Opel flew a short distance in a plane that was entirely powered by rockets burning gunpowder; but the flight was precarious, only fifty feet above ground, and the aircraft was damaged in landing. By 1935 rockets of 60 to 70 pounds had been made to travel at 700 miles per hour, but the attainment of such speeds with a rocket-driven airplane is yet to be announced.

Last year the National Advisory Committee for Aeronautics published an English translation of a scientific paper by the German engineer Eugen Saenger, giving the calculations for rocket planes, fueled with gasoline to be burned with liquid oxygen. The entire fuel of a fighter plane of this type would be consumed in one half-hour of flight, according to its designer, but in the thirty minutes it would travel 500 miles, partly under rocket power, partly gliding. Even more startling accomplishments in speed and range are claimed for a large bomber similarly powered. Although Herr Saenger's paper was originally published in the German periodical *Flug* nine years ago, there is no evidence that Herr Hitler found it possible to make practical use of its computations.

Meanwhile, radical proposals in aircraft design have been explored: such developments as planes without tails, the so-called "flying wing," and other constructural innovations to reduce head resistance and economize power or increase speed.

COMBAT PLANES

Aircraft types are almost as numerous as their makers, and may be classified according to size, according to horsepower, cooling system and number of engines; according to whether they take off from land, from a ship's deck, or from water; according to the particular service for which they are designed. For purposes of war there are training planes, observation planes, combat planes and transport planes. In addition to huge aircraft driven by high-powered engines (for the transport of troops, tanks, and other matériel and supplies), some transport use has been made of gliders which are towed by a plane and then cast off to descend singly when the destination is reached. For purposes of combat there are fighters and bombers.

Fighter planes have three primary functions. First is the purely defensive job of intercepting and attacking enemy bombers, or shooting down enemy fighters which accompany enemy bombers. Second is the job of co-operating with the ground army, either in offense or defense, to attack ground troops, guns, tanks, transport vehicles and other surface objectives. And third is an offensive task of longer range, that of accompanying their own bombers in flight and protecting them against enemy interceptors. This last responsibility is somewhat analogous to that of the naval destroyers which escort a battleship. In the May, 1942, raid on Cologne, for example, it is reported that 1000 British bombers were escorted by 250 fighter planes. Each of the fighter functions has its specialized requirements as to the combination of speed, range, maneuverability and firepower which will best serve its tactical purpose; and so the fighter forces have interceptor planes, attack planes, and escort or "destroyer" planes.

Bombing technique also specializes, and here too the aircraft have become highly differentiated. First we find the light and medium bombers, usually powered with single or twin engines and designed to carry loads of bombs a few hundred or a thousand miles, drop them and scurry home. Some naval planes carry marine torpedoes in place of bombs, and attacks on enemy ships are made by dropping these self-propelled missiles into the water from a low height.

European geography favored the development of the short-distance bomber, but with the extension of the war to whole continents, and eventually to every continent, the importance of the heavy bomber capable of carrying large loads thousands of miles was demonstrated. American strategy particularly has emphasized this second type, the heavy high-powered craft for long-range bombing; hence the advanced development in the United States of such giants as the Flying Fortress and the Liberator, each powered by four engines. The British, who at the beginning of the war preferred short-range two-engine bombing planes, now have their long-range four-engine Stirling, Halifax and Lancaster bombers.

Bombing in daylight is more precise than bombing at night, simply because targets that can be seen are more easily hit than those whose location in the darkness must be reckoned from charts and maps or uncertainly glimpsed by means of flares. But daylight bombing is precise and successful only if the bomber is able to avoid the bullets and shells of interceptors and the bursts of anti-aircraft fire—defenses which took a costly toll of the Heinkels and Dorniers in the Battle of Britain. As a result of that first great air battle, both the Germans and the British gave up daylight bombing and timed their raids to hours of darkness. Thereby they lessened their losses, but also lessened the accuracy of their attacks; and air raids on both sides became an affair of less discriminate and less effective spreading of explosives and incendiaries over selected areas.

But the heavy bombers can fly high, some of them above 35,000 feet; above the range of most antiaircraft guns, above the ceiling of many of the fighter craft. Because of this, and because of their sturdy construction, they are able to risk the hazards of sunlit skies; and with their introduction on the European battlefront daylight attacks against the enemy were resumed. By the autumn of 1942 these raids were moving with almost clockwork routine. Factories, docks, shipyards, and other chosen targets were being hit squarely on the nose from planes moving in level flight above the defenses. A special optical and computing device for aiming the missiles contributed directly to the percentage of accuracy of this high-level bombing. For it is not enough to see an objective. The bombsight tells when to loose the bomb so that all the forces acting on the missile will combine to deliver it on the target, at the same time making allowance for the course and speed of the plane.

There is still another way to promote accuracy of bombing. It makes use of the third type of bombing plane, the dive bomber. The technique of dive bombing was invented and perfected by the U. S. Navy back in the 1920's, but the Nazis appear to be the first to use it in warfare. Here it is the aircraft rather than the bomb that is aimed. The plane is directed downward at a steep angle from a height of many thousands of feet, and at a certain preferred distance above the target the bomb is released. This preferred distance may be anywhere from 2,000 to 2,600 feet. At the time of release the pilot pulls his plane out of the dive, levels off into the horizontal, and climbs as rapidly as he can back into the upper skies. Meanwhile the bomb which was traveling with the plane, continues at the same angle.

Dive bombing has been used with particular success in naval

operations. A vessel may zigzag to avoid the attack of a high-level bomber, and certainly the chance of hitting a moving target from the upper altitudes is slight. But the pilot of a dive bomber, with his eyes fixed on the target through the telescopic sight, can follow its weavings to the moment of bomb release. Then the missile is so close to the objective that there is no time to zigzag. The surest escape from a dive bomber is to hit the pilot or deflect his plane before the bomb is released.

The dive bomber is more vulnerable to antiaircraft fire than the level-flight bomber, since every instant of his dive brings him nearer to the defensive guns. Also the pilot's blood circulation is subjected to stunning inertial strain, particularly in the centrifugal act of pulling out of the power dive and leveling off for the climb. Finally, the high-level bomber has this advantage: a bomb dropped from 26,000 feet will hit harder than one carried down by a dive bomber and released at 2,600 feet—simply because a plane cannot be allowed to dive at a speed so great as that attained by a bomb dropped from a high altitude.

32 FEET PER SECOND PER SECOND

It was Galileo—that Seventeenth-century genius who could never accept statements of the behavior of nature on mere say-so, but insisted on testing the phenomena to see what nature itself would answer—it was this Italian physicist who discovered that the pull of gravitation is equal for all freely falling bodies. When the effect was measured, the acceleration proved to be 32 feet per second per second. That is to say, if an object is released from a stationary position in free space, it will be dropping toward the earth at a velocity of 32 feet at the end of the first second, 64 feet per second at the end of the next second, 96 feet per second at the end of the third second, and so on, adding 32 feet per second to its velocity for each second of its descent. This is true of every kind of object, irrespective of size, shape, or weight. It applies equally to falling bombs, falling airplanes, falling parachutes, and falling feathers— provided they are freely falling.

In that proviso is the catch. In order for an object to fall freely it would have to fall in a vacuum, and our atmosphere is not a vacuum. It is not even a uniform medium, since its density decreases with increasing altitude. For all practical purposes, however, air resistance to a streamlined bomb is not appreciable for the first few hundred feet. Through a fall of 1000 feet it begins to be noticeable, and on bodies falling from several thousand feet the retarding effect is quite marked. This is because air resistance increases with the square of the velocity. Thus a bomb falling at the rate of 200 feet per second has only double the velocity of one of equal size falling 100 feet per second, but it meets with four times as much air resistance, and one falling 300 feet per second meets with nine times as much.

The longer it falls the greater is the dragging effect of the air, until finally a stage is reached at which this retardation balances the weight of the bomb. Then, no matter how much higher you climb to drop your missile, nothing will be added to the momentum of its impact. The "terminal velocity" has been reached. The terminal velocity of a 550-pound bomb is 918 feet per second (more than 600 miles per hour), which is about the velocity with which it hits when dropped from 36,000 feet. Even when dropped from 20,000 feet its impact velocity is 880 feet per second. From these considerations it is clear that bombing from higher altitudes than those now navigated by our heavy bombers would add nothing to the force of the impact.

For the first second after the bombardier has pulled the release, the free bomb tags along with the plane as though unwilling to part from the maternal apron strings. This is only temporary, however, and soon it is falling in a long parabolic path whose curvature depends on the speed at which the plane was moving at the instant of release, the altitude and other factors. Thus, if the plane was moving 250 miles per hour at a height of 26,000 feet when the bomb was released, the bomb's inertia or tendency to continue with the plane would cause it to sweep over about 14,800 feet of ground before it hits; if the plane's velocity were 375 miles per hour, the range of the bomb would be about 21,000 feet. If the plane were moving in level flight at only 10,000 feet altitude, the bomb's range would be much shorter—about 9,000 feet for 250 m.p.h. speed, about 13,300 feet for the 375 m.p.h. speed.

In addition to the speed and the altitude of the aircraft, accuracy of bombing requires that the effect of air resistance on both the forward and downward movement of the missile be reckoned, and also the direction and velocity of the wind and their effect on the bomb. To determine and compute these elements in the course of flight, and fix on precisely the right moment to release the bomb, is a task beyond human brain power—but it is not beyond human brain power to invent, design and construct an optical instrument which will do the job. Such is the Norden bombsight. Men entering the bombardiers' school for training are required to take a special oath to guard its secrecy. As the Flying Fortresses and other American bombers approach Berlin and other enemy centers, the bombsight tells our bombardiers just how many miles out in the country bombs are to be released in order to hit particular spots of military importance within the cities. The device is a mechanical guesser, for it is impossible to know precisely all the factors of every layer of the atmosphere at a given moment, but the bombsight has already established a distinguished record for accuracy in placing its parcels of destruction on the intended objectives.

LANDSHIPS

While the development of aerial bombing has been transforming war into a three-dimensional performance, in which not only missiles but human beings are subjected to the laws of ballistics, the development of the tank has wrought a revolution of another kind. The tank has been described as a "mobile trench," bearing in mind its introduction as a means of breaking the stalemate of trench warfare. But today's tank is more than a trench on wheels, more than a roving fortress. For it is an offensive weapon, an instrument of attack, whereas trenches and forts are primarily defensive. Its operations are better likened to those of naval vessels.

Indeed it was in a navy department, the British Admiralty, that the tank idea first got official hearing; and the record shows that, from 1914 on, its constant friend and principal advocate in the British Cabinet was Winston Spencer Churchill, then First Lord of the Admiralty.

The father of the tank was a British army officer, Colonel Ernest Swinton. Within a few weeks after the beginning of World War I he had fixed on the tank as a means of restoring the initiative to the offense. Colonel Swinton became a gadfly on this subject. He was swatted again and again, but always managed to return with his idea of a bullet-proof steel motorcar, armed with rapid-fire guns and mounted on caterpillar treads. Two American inventions are responsible for this weapon—one through its creation of the trench deadlock, the other in providing the antidote—as Liddell Hart has pointed out in his *History of the World War*:

The trench deadlock was due above all to the invention of an American, Hiram Maxim. His name is more deeply engraved on the real history of the World War than that of any other man. Emperors, statesmen, and generals had the power to make war, but not to end it. Having created it, they found themselves helpless puppets in the grip of Hiram Maxim, who, by his machine gun, had paralyzed the power of attack. All efforts to break the defensive grip of the machine gun were vain; they could only raise tombstones and not triumphal arches. When at last a key to the deadlock was produced, it was forged from the invention of another American, Benjamin Holt. From his agricultural tractor was evolved the tank —an ironic reversal of the proverbial custom of "beating swords into plowshares."

Swinton's suggestion, which was submitted to the Committee of Imperial Defense in London on October 20, 1914, found a willing listener in Colonel Maurice Hankey, the committee secretary. Thereafter, while Swinton pushed the idea at General Headquarters in France, Hankey worked for it in England. The authorities at G.H.Q. said at once that they were not impressed. Lord Kitchener in London was equally cold. But at the same time that he submitted the idea to Kitchener, Hankey sent a memorandum to Prime Minister Asquith. This chanced to reach Churchill.

At that time Churchill's Admiralty Office had certain detachments of its Royal Naval Air Service operating on the Belgian coast with armored cars, and the problem of propelling these wheeled vehicles across broken ground was causing difficulty. Swinton's suggestion of caterpillar tractors appealed instantly to Churchill. He wrote to the Prime Minister supporting the idea, and Asquith referred Churchill's letter to Kitchener. This was in January, 1915. It just happened that Swinton was in London and, gadfly-like, had called on Kitchener the day before. Thus prodded, or stung, Kitchener passed the proposal on to his director of mechanical transport. The director couldn't see anything in it, and so reported.

But Churchill was not going to give up just because the army was unwilling to experiment. In February he appointed a committee of the Admiralty. This body, which came to be known as the Land-ships Committee, conducted a number of studies, and though not conclusive these served to keep the subject alive in government circles until finally, in the summer of 1915, Swinton reached the ear of the Commander-in-Chief. Haig authorized the building of an experimental landship, and the eager gadfly hurried to England to get the model started.

By September "Little Willie" had been constructed, but Swinton found it lacking. A larger machine was attempted, and in February, 1916, "Mother" was ready for inspection. On the proving grounds she trundled across eight-foot trenches with ease and repeatedly climbed a five-foot vertical face. Very good! As a result of these trials forty machines of similar design were ordered; later the order was increased to 100. Crews started training in a secret inclosure in England in the summer of 1916. And as the big steel hulks under their tarpaulin covers began to be loaded on railway cars for the channel ports, and on ships for France, it was said that they were "tanks." In their wrapping they looked sufficiently like water reservoirs for the designation to be accepted, and tanks and crews arrived at the battlefront with their secret intact.

These first tanks were ungainly structures of a rhomboid shape. They waddled like heaving, overheavy, mechanical dinosaurs. The terror of the Germans at their first appearance has been recorded, but unfortunately their use in that engagement was premature. The crews had not completed their training, the number of tanks was meager and insufficient, the carefully prepared tactical plan for using the new weapon in a surprise attack without the preliminary warning of artillery fire was ignored. In consequence, the few machines that lumbered across no man's land at the Somme in September, 1916, became the targets for concentrated gunfire; gasoline reservoirs were punctured, flames were started; it was a tragic fiasco.

There were other battle trials in 1917 in which the landships gave a better account of their power in attack, but it was not until August 8, 1918, that the new weapon was used according to the plan of those who had conceived it, who had developed it and who believed in it. On that day 456 tanks were loosed before Amiens at daybreak in a thick ground mist, and as they swept forward, crashing through barbed-wire entanglements, rolling over trenches, crunching down barricades, the artillery barrage and infantry advance followed. The staff at German General Headquarters was surprised at breakfast. The puffing, creaking, irresistible machines rolled deeper and more terrifyingly into the enemy lines. It was then, according to General Ludendorff, that German morale cracked. "August 8th was the black day of the German army in the history of the war," he said. And when army representatives appeared before leaders of the Reichstag, they explained: "The enemy made use of tanks in unexpected large numbers; in cases where they suddenly emerged from smoke clouds, our men were completely unnerved."

One may speculate on the possible outcome, on how many months and perhaps years the struggle might have been shortened, if instead of its premature use in September, 1916, the new weapon had been saved by the British command for an initial surprise attack of massive proportions, with complete infantry and artillery coordination, according to the design of its sponsors.

Among the curious quirks of military history is the slowness of the German command to catch on to the potentialities of the landship. At the time of the armistice in 1918 the Kaiser had only fifty tanks. Hitler's advisers learned well the lesson of "the black day" of August 8th, and in their plan the tank was second only to aircraft among the new weapons. When war began in 1939 the landship at once assumed an influential role in the German offensive. Invariably it was used as a closely articulated weapon, in combination with the air force, the artillery, and follow-up tactics of motorized infantry.

Even in 1918 the British had begun to differentiate tank design in three types. There were heavies for use against barricades and strongly fortified trenches, mediums for overriding ordinary trenches, and whippets for quick work in battle attack. Since then specialization has provided landships for every conceivable function in land warfare. Nor are the armored vehicles confined to the solid ground. Some are amphibians, able to cross a stream or take off from barges. One of these light "alligator types" has a speed of 10 miles per hour in water and 25 on land, and can navigate swamps and marshes at 10 miles per hour or faster. There are giant tanks, heavily armored and heavily armed, weighing 57, 90, and even 100 tons; some of them capable of traveling 30 miles per hour, which is the usual speed of medium tanks. The mediums range in weight from 20 to 30 tons. Some carry as many as seven men to a crew.

The American medium tanks, christened General Grant and General Lee at their baptism of fire in the desert fighting in Africa in 1942, are both of 28 tons' weight. Each was originally armed with a 75-millimeter gun in addition to machine guns, and about the only noticeable difference between them is the turret. Their exterior lines presented a beveled surface designed to deflect the enemy's shots. Instead of being riveted, the armor plates were solidly welded. Peepholes for gunners and drivers gave way to periscopes. The inside walls were padded with a soft synthetic material. Airplane motors of the whirlwind type were adapted to the propulsion of these massive hulks of steel.

ANTITANK

Having said as much for tanks, one must add that by 1943 the reputation of the tank for invincibility was shattered. The landship had met its match, and more than its match, in some of the new antitank weapons. Both on the Russian front and in North Africa the use of ground mines, backed up by antitank guns of concentrated high-velocity firepower, proved to be a devastating combination in encounter after encounter. Such spectacular stories were coming back from Tunisia regarding the tank-smashing power of the American secret weapon, the bazooka, that the U. S. Chief of Ordnance made a public announcement of the performance of this rocket projector. At about the same time Hanson W. Baldwin was writing from Egypt to the *New York Times* that "the tank has now been put more or less into the position that the cavalry was in in the First World War, when it came up against the machine gun"; and in Washington the Under Secretary of War was telling the House Committee on Military Affairs that "the changing needs of war come along and show that we do not need any more of a certain weapon, but on the other hand we need far more than we had originally estimated of another weapon."

So in the spring of 1943 tank production was being cut down, the manufacture of certain types had been discontinued or was being tapered off, while the production of certain guns was being accelerated. Reports from North Africa credit the 105-millimeter gun with considerable success as an antitank implement; mounted on the chassis of a General Grant tank it has proved to be a weapon of high mobility and tremendous firepower. In place of the famous 75-millimeter gun, a new artillery piece which fires 3-inch shells was also in high favor. The pursuit of Rommel from Egypt to Tunisia was greatly aided by two other types of antitank guns, one firing a 2-pound shell, and one a 6-pounder. The latter was particularly effective against the Germans' massive Mark IV tanks.

An important element in this development, both of tanks and of antitank guns, is the new metallurgy. Without the modern processes for alloying steel with toughening ingredients, tank makers could never have endowed the landships with their vast capacity for taking punishment. Similarly, without new steels able to endure the heat and the tremendous pressures imposed by the heavier charges and higher velocities of modern artillery fire, the gunmakers would have been critically limited.

TOUGHER STEEL AND HOTTER STEAM

But it isn't only in the heavier charges of its explosives and the sharper and more massive blows of its missiles that modern war makes harder demands upon metals. In many critical places other than the gun, heat imposes conditions which would have been beyond the endurance of any available metal a few years ago.

For example, an extreme high-temperature spot in combat aircraft is the turbo-supercharger, that little giant whose whirligig action in concentrating the thin air of the upper levels was mentioned earlier in this chapter. The airplane engine's exhaust gases strike the rotor of this machine at a temperature of more than 1000° Fahrenheit. One of the problems is to provide a metal which will stand up without softening, buckling, or brittling.

Steam engineers have struggled with this problem for years. Ever since Carnot in 1824 recognized "the moving power of heat" as the true principle of the steam engine, pointing out that engine efficiency depends on the difference between the temperature of the live steam entering it and that of the spent steam, engineers have sought to increase the span of heat change between the two ends of the cycle. Their triple rule has been to generate steam at a temperature as high as can be controlled, to keep the engine as hot as the steam which enters it, and to cool the exhaust steam to as low a temperature as can be economically managed. The principal limiting factor has been the strength of materials. For steam must be generated in boilers, and conducted to the engine through pipes or other vents; and the question always is how much heat and pressure can be sustained by boiler, conduit and engine.

Ordinary steel loses its strength rapidly if heated above 700° F., and a dozen years ago steam engineers viewed the 700°-750° range as a practical ceiling for industrial practice. Gradually it was found that the addition of small quantities of other metals—nickel in some experiments, chromium in others, molybdenum in still others— would enhance the heat resistance of steel. By such means stainless steel alloys were produced which permitted the confinement of steam at 800°, then 900°, and by 1942 a commercial steam power plant in the United States was using the vapor at 940° under a pressure of 2300 pounds to the square inch.

Turbines are the power makers for these high-temperature installations. As the torrid blast reaches the turbine, hitting it with the speed of a rifle bullet, the spinning vanes literally extract energy from this caged tornado. The machine becomes so hot that its metal glows a dull red in the dark. The rotor is built on an expanding scale: the vanes (small at the entering end of the machine) grow larger at each advancing stage, more extended, providing more surface against which the steam expands, until at the end of the cycle the exhaust vapor drops into the condenser's vacuum at 80°. This installation, with a thermal efficiency of 33½ per cent, holds the performance record for a steam plant.

Still higher outputs of power are being obtained from a two-vapor system. In this, heat is first applied to boil mercury and the mercury vapor raised to 1000° is used to drive a turbine; after which the spent mercury vapor at 480° is still hot enough to boil water, thereby generating steam to drive a second turbine. In this dual mercury-steam engine an efficiency of 37½ per cent is attained.

The practical test for rating a steam engine is the amount of electrical energy that can be generated by a dynamo in proportion to the amount of fuel burned to drive its engine. In 1919 the utility plants of the United States averaged about 3 pounds of coal for every kilowatt hour that pulsed over the transmission lines. By 1925 the average had been brought down to 2 pounds. By 1940 it was a trifle under 1.7 pounds. Today the average is a little under 1.37 pounds. For the top dozen plants, the twelve most efficient steam producers in the United States, the present toll of fuel is .85 pound for each kilowatt hour; and for the mercury-steam plant it is .65.

This progressive sequence of engineering attainments contributes in an important way to America's role as the arsenal of the democracies. For of course the production of steel and other metals, of guns, tanks, planes, ships and other weapons and munitions, is directly dependent on electrical power; and electrical power means primarily steam power. Despite the important new hydro installations in the Tennessee Valley, at the Grand Coulee, and other ambitious river harnessings, the erection of new steam plants has kept pace with the water-power developments. According to a report by the editors of *Power*, the plant resources for the public supply of power in the United States at the beginning of 1943 totaled 46,000,000 kilowatts. New installations then under construction or on order will provide an estimated additional 5,300,000, most of which should be in operation before the end of 1943. This means that the American power-generating plant will mount to slightly over 50,000,000 kilowatts and remain there for the duration. About two-thirds of this is steam driven, and (because of the seasonal variation in water-power production) fully 70 per cent of the electricity actually delivered each year is born of Carnot's "moving power of heat."

One of the direct effects of the advances in steam engineering is higher-powered, faster and more efficient cargo and naval vessels. A ship necessarily imposes its own restrictions on the designer, restrictions as to space and factors of safety, and for various technical reasons marine engineering practice follows a few years later the experimental results which are first demonstrated in central power stations and industrial plants on land. But the climb of temperature and pressure in land installations is directly reflected in marine installations. In World War I a ship using steam at 550° F. and 200 pounds pressure to the square inch was rated a high-temperature high-pressure plant. Today marine engines operating at 750° and 600 pounds are common, and there is at least one U.S. ship designed for 850° and 1200 pounds.

THEY FIGHT WITH ELECTRICITY

Nowhere on land will you find mechanical power concentrated to such a degree as on a modern warship. Steam, applied through compact but powerful turbines, propels the vessel and also drives dynamos to generate electricity. The electricity is used to operate the turrets and guns, energize the radio and other communications, and provide power, heat and light for a variety of services. On a modern naval aircraft carrier, for example, there are gigantic elevators which deliver planes to the fighting deck; and only electrically-operated, electrically-controlled elevators could move so swiftly and stop so precisely. It has been calculated that the generators on a single large fighting ship produce enough electricity to light a city the size of Seattle or New Orleans; yet the entire power-generating plant and the entire power-consuming clientele are packed into a steel-clad space no larger than a city skyscraper.

The navy fights with electricity. And so do the air force, the tank corps, the artillery, the infantry. At the heart of many modern weapons is an electric spark, or a circuit of conducting wire, often a wire-wrapped magnet, and everywhere is the versatile lamp of our western Aladdin—the magic electron tube.

CHAPTER V

Electric Warfare

Is it a fact—or have I dreamt it—that by means of electricity the world of matter has become a great nerve vibrating thousands of miles in a breathless point of time?

—Nathaniel Hawthorne, HOUSE OF THE SEVEN GABLES

WHEN the first world struggle with Germany began in 1914, only two planes of the British air arm were equipped with radio transmitters. The rest of the squadron used pocket flashlights to communicate with the ground. And to warn a fellow plane of danger during flight, about all that a pilot could do was to dip his wings or perform some other frantic stunt of signaling. Electricity served the engine—its spark was necessary to ignite the gasoline in the cylinder; but beyond that electricity entered very little into the operation and navigation of the fragile flying machines of August, 1914, with which the Royal Air Force began its great tradition.

Today's aircraft are as highly electrified as the modern battleship. The latest fighters, bombers, and observation planes are equipped with radio sets for transmitting and receiving messages over a wide range of frequencies. They use both radio telephony and radio telegraphy. They have direction finders to feel their way in the darkness, plane finders to warn of unseen enemy aircraft, electric altimeters to determine height above ground, and the pilot's finger on an electric button fires his guns. Other electric devices operate the turrets, and turn the turret guns against the massive drag of air swirling past at hundreds of miles per hour. Electrically-heated clothes protect the airmen from the below-zero cold of the upper levels. A sensitive "feeler" measures the formation of ice on the wings and automatically turns on a de-icing mechanism to remove the hazard before it becomes dangerously heavy. Then there is a robot which can take over the pilot's responsibility as the big bomber approaches its target. Instructed by the infallible bomb-sight, this electrical brain insures that no eagerness, anxiety, fatigue, or other frailty of human nerves and muscles will mar the steadiness of flight in the critical moments before the release of the bomb. As the night-flying plane turns homeward, above the clouds, lights off and the land blacked out below, electrical aids to navigation guide its course and bring it safely out of the cloudy sky down to the foggy ground and set its wheels unerringly on the home runway. There are more than 200 instrument dials and controls in the cock-pit of the American heavy bomber, and most of them are electrical.

Many of these devices in the plane would be of limited value without a reciprocal device down on the ground; and so we find the airfields and other ground services also electrified. Within the fighting tank, amid the deafening din of its gunfire and rat-a-tat of the enemy's bullets, tank driver talks with tank gunner over telephones clamped to their heads; and one tank communicates with its fellow tanks by means of staticless ultrashort-wave radio. Slung over their shoulders like knapsacks, infantrymen carry "walkie-talkie" sets which enable them to converse over distances within the limits of the horizon—portable kits that ought to make future "Lost Battalions" highly improbable.

An index to the current importance of radio techniques to the war effort is furnished by the magnitude and operations of the U. S. Army Signal Corps. This branch of the army is now requiring of the electrical manufacturers a larger annual output of radio sets, tubes, batteries, and related equipment than was required in peacetime by all the American civilian radio needs, including those of the hundreds of broadcasting stations, thousands of experimenters, and the 29,000,000 radio homes. And with the tremendous multipli-cation of mechanisms has come a corresponding increase of personnel to man the mechanisms. As a comparison, to suggest the size of this specialized arm of the military, General James G. Harbord has said that the Signal Corps now probably numbers more officers and men than served Napoleon at Waterloo, a greater army than Grant had in the Wilderness battles, more than Pershing led into the Argonne. The present war is a war of communications, and its mightiest messenger is electricity.

"THE STEED CALLED LIGHTNING"

The telegraph began it. Emerging from the laboratory in the 1840's, the telegraph was the first electrical invention to receive commercial application; and when the Crimean War broke out soon thereafter, engineers lost no time in turning it to military use. The files of an old journal carry quaint drawings of plumed soldiers plowing a trench into which the insulated wires were laid, and the army telegrapher's wagon made its appearance in the Crimea in 1854.

After a brief interval of peace, "the steed called lightning" got back into military harness on April 13, 1861. That day a telegram brought President Lincoln the fateful message of the fall of Fort Sumter. The telegraph, aided by the press, spread the news overnight, and telegrams poured into Washington offering volunteers. A few weeks later, as General McClellan advanced into western Virginia, a telegrapher with a portable installation in a wagon accompanied him, and that was the beginning of the federal army's extensive system of field telegraphy. It strung wires right up to the battlefront. By November of that first year the U. S. government had built 1,137 miles of telegraph line for military use, and by the end of the war the extensions totaled 15,000 miles. On the Confederate side other men of the wires also rendered valiant and often crucial service, though there were fewer of them and less mileage.

After Appomattox, the value of the telegraph to the hard-pressed nation of the '60's soon lost its purse appeal. By 1885 the Secretary of War was advising Congress that "the conveyance of military orders or intelligence by telegraph is not a proper subject for the existence of a bureau within the War Department." The Signal Corps was reduced to a state of near-starvation, and was actually restricted to an annual pittance of $3,000 by 1898 when the United States suddenly found itself at war with Spain. Only through the prompt action of the commercial telegraph, telephone, and electrical manufacturing companies was the army supplied with equipment, electricians and other trained personnel sufficient to establish and maintain communication between Washington and General Shafter's headquarters and the various units in Cuba. The telephone first entered military service in this Spanish-American War, though its reach was puny compared with present telephonic distances.

The Russo-Japanese affair came along in 1904, and by that time radio had been born. It was still a feeble and uncertain infant, but half a dozen crude systems of transmission and reception had been originated, and most of these were in use by the navies, armies, news correspondents and other observers in and around the war zone. The Russians had a German type of equipment, but no outsiders ever learned what system the Japanese were using. Their smiling little men told the press that the Japanese scientists had been experimenting with radio since 1896, and the information stopped there. The Czar's forces found their German sets quite useful, and after the Japanese had surrounded Port Arthur the Russians within the besieged city continued to rasp out wireless messages to their army on the other side of the enemy and to receive instructions and news. This was the first demonstration of that kind of magic, and it thrilled the world.

By the time of the first world war great changes had come. The radio had acquired its three-element vacuum tube. The telephone, by using vacuum tubes as amplifying repeaters at appropriate intervals, had spanned the North American continent with conversation from coast to coast. And the telegraph had learned how to send six messages over a single wire. These and many other new electrical ingenuities were pressed into war service in 1914-'18.

The navies on both sides made radio their principal medium of sea communication from the beginning, while on land the wired services, and particularly the telephone, reigned almost supreme. Telephone wires were strung right up to the front-line trenches. Not content with using Mr. A. G. Bell's invention as a means of mere communication, the Signal Corps developed a practice of crawling into no man's land under cover of darkness and planting the business end of a listening post as near as possible to the enemy's line. This "business end" was a copper plate buried an inch or so below the surface of the ground. By the mystery of electromagnetic induction it picked up pulsations from telegraphs and telephones in its vicinity, occasionally also getting some of the messages that were going by radio. Insulated wires led from the copper plate back to the dugout, where vacuum tubes amplified the pickups, and telephone apparatus converted them into audible sound waves.

The Germans employed similar schemes of eavesdropping, and various stratagems were used to outwit and confuse them. An amusing example of counter-eavesdropping is cited by Alvin F. Harlow, in his history *Old Wires and New Waves*. It occurred in a sector where the opposing lines were close together and enemy listeners were getting entirely too free with Allied messages. So an American commander resorted to this novel scheme: He assigned, to take charge of the telephone service in the critical area, a group of A.E.F. soldiers who were members of an American Indian tribe; and he instructed them to phrase all messages and other telephonic conversation in their Choctaw or other native tongue. Whether or not the German linguists were able to crack this "code" has never been published.

Before the end of World War I, the recently-fledged wireless telephone was turned to naval and army use, but for the most part radio confined itself to the dots and dashes of telegraphy. Each side of the conflict had its secret code, and at intervals each changed the system to throw the enemy off the scent. Early in the war, however, the Allies came into possession of the German code by accident. It happened in January, 1915, when a derelict U-boat was cast up by the sea on the Yarmouth shore of England. The submarine was intact, but all its crew were dead inside, and in the captain's tin box was found a book containing the code. Thereafter whenever a U-boat was sunk a British salvage ship hurried to the scene; if the wreck could be reached deep-sea divers searched its hull, and often they brought up the captain's box with its confidential contents. By such means the Allies kept fairly up to date on German changes.

There was another circumstance, fortunate for the Allies. Shortly before the war a British corporation had acquired the radio compass from Italian inventors, and this was now developed into a direction finder. Each intercepted broadcast from a U-boat, surface ship, or other enemy source not only gave away the information which its coded signals were intended to conceal but it told the direction from which the message had come. From cross bearings received at two or more direction-finder stations, the Royal Navy was able to plot the position and movement of every ship within hearing, and the prompt sending of destroyers accounted for many a German loss. After 1916, however, these listening-in tactics were less productive, for the Germans had caught on, and thereafter they greatly restricted radio communication from units at sea.

A receiving set may also give away its presence by the mere act of operating. For as it receives it also automatically rebroadcasts on a weaker wave, and many an unsuspecting ship, in the very act of picking up a wireless message, has thereby revealed its position to the sensitive detector of a prowling U-boat. This circumstance made the submarine's work easier until the engineers learned to equip naval and other marine radio receivers with a protective screen.

It is also possible to throw an electrical camouflage around a transmitting station to prevent it from betraying its whereabouts, or to cause it to indicate directions that are confusing and thus make it a misleading beacon. This is particularly the case in areas where there are numerous broadcasting stations, as in the United States coastal regions. With proper engineering service it should be unnecessary for radio stations to go off the air at times of approaching air raids. It is then that they are most needed, for purposes of warning the population against the threatening danger and to direct air-raid precaution and defense procedures.

Thus radio can reveal and betray, or it can conceal and serve; it can serve the offense, or it can be turned to purposes of defense; it's all a question of the use that man makes of electronics.

ELECTRONICS

Here we enter the most glamorous realm of contemporary physics. It is a field of discovery so fertile, already so fruitful of applications, so rapidly extending its scope and multiplying its yields under the stimulus of military demand that it is profoundly changing the face of the future. This does not mean an automatic, self-directing, foolproof attainment of human perfection. Electronics may win the war for us, but only with the collaboration of competent and courageous soldiers, sailors and airmen. It may contribute to the winning of the peace and to the stabilization of world society on a humane basis, but again only if men make intelligent and wise use of its resources. In twenty years, from the feeble radio of 1918 to the world-wide broadcasting of 1938, electronics transformed the globe that Magellan took more than two years to circumnavigate; shrank it to dimensions smaller in terms of communication than his native Portugal; inoculated its inhabitants with the power of instantaneous communication. Here was something that mystics, holy men, magicians, clairvoyants and other unusual personalities had claimed as a supernatural gift, in favored individuals, in special times and places; in fasts, trances, dreams, through discipline and extreme self-denial. Now, as though an invisible barrier had suddenly lifted to reveal what was there all the time, the magic of instantaneous communication became a universal faculty available to the poorest inhabitant. By 1938 technology had installed a vast network of radio services encircling the earth, making it possible at last for the ancient prophecy to be fulfilled, "Nation shall speak unto nation." But when nation spoke to nation, its most momentous message of that year came out of Munich.

Electronics has been widely advertised during the war years as a new science; its name has been bandied about in commercial broadcasts and other advertisements as "the bright new word of the future," but in actual fact this "new science" is as old as x-rays. Indeed it was foreshadowed a century ago by Faraday in his idea of the electromagnetic field. The theoretical studies of James Clerk Maxwell and the experiments of Henrich Hertz laid the foundations, on which the cathode-ray investigators built. Sir William Crookes and Sir Joseph J. Thomson were followed by Marconi, Fleming, Richardson, de Forest, Langmuir, Arnold, Armstrong, and other experimenters, mathematicians, inventors and engineers. The only thing that is new about electronics is the accelerated pace of its development in the last few years. Never has a technology moved so rapidly from the laboratory into the factory and up to the battlefront. Electronic devices which at the beginning of the war were still in the experimental stage are now in practical, everyday use. Instruments that were delicate in construction and finicky in performance have been made rugged and dependable, able to operate in all climates and under the violent demands of battle service.

Ordinary electrical engineering, such as developed the telegraph, telephone, dynamo, electric light, and power applications, was concerned with the flow of electrons in wire circuits. Electronics is concerned with the flow of electrons in empty-space—the space within the vacuum tube; for the science derives from this invention. The thing that makes the difference between electronics and ordinary electrical engineering is what happens to the electric current in empty space.

ELECTRONS IN THE OPEN

The mathematical theory of the vacuum tube is among the most complicated in the entire domain of physics, but the fundamental idea of the device can be briefly and simply told. Away back in 1883, when he was working on the electric lamp, Thomas A. Edison used to seal an extra wire into his experimental lamp bulbs. He used this wire to test the degree of evacuation, to make sure that he had a good vacuum within the tube before turning current into the light filament. In the course of these experiments Edison found that when the light was turned on a weak current of electricity flowed from the incandescent filament across the half inch of empty space to the wire. It was not until years later, after his patent had expired, that scientists were able to explain this "Edison effect" as a flight of electrons from the hot filament to the wire. Soon vacuum tubes were made for the express purpose of studying this flight of the still unknown electrons. The two ends of a wire circuit were sealed into a glass bulb, the air was pumped out, the current turned on, whereupon the electrons would flow through the vacuum from one wire end to the other. This performance greatly excited the curiosity of the early experimenters, for it brought the electrical particles out into the open where they could be subjected to outside forces, where their behavior could be tested and observed.

What came out of these studies was revolutionary. Things could be done to the current as it leaped across the empty space, results achieved that were not obtainable after the electrons were back in the metal. Among other results, for example, it was found that the stream would swerve out of its path under the influence of outside electrical or magnetic fields. In recent years this discovery has been put to work in oscillographs, television, panoramic radio, and other applications in which the weaving stream is made to write a message or paint a picture.

A far-reaching step in development came with the introduction of a third element into the tube, another wire terminal meshed into the form of a miniature gridiron which was placed between the two original wires. It turned out that a very slight electrical impulse imposed upon this intermediate grid could be made to regulate the entire flow of current across the vacuum, a current that might be hundreds of thousands of times greater. Thus a little power would control a very large amount of power. If the imposed impulses came in a certain pattern, the regulated current would pulsate in exactly the same pattern, indeed would reproduce it precisely, but on an enormously enhanced scale.

Here was a magic wand for which the wireless industry was yearning. Like the wand of the fairy godmother, it could do many things. First, it could pick out of the ether the weak pulsations of travel-worn radio waves and translate them into current; so it served as a detector. Next, it could magnify these picked-up pulsations, raise them to any degree of amplification, and at the same time preserve their precise pattern down to the finest detail; so it could be used as an electrical lever. Moreover, it could send as well as receive, for by a reverse operation the vacuum tube became an oscillator, a generator of radio waves; and so it was pressed into service as a transmitter.

It was these three capabilities that won the vacuum tube its pre-eminent place. Even if it had remained an implement only for radio communication its level of usefulness would be far above that of most inventions; but it has branched out into a multitude of fields, and today is serving long-distance telephone lines, electric power lines, electric furnaces, automatic machines, medical and surgical practice, and many other applications. After the electromagnet, no other electrical device has influenced human habits and served human needs in so many ways.

Certain types of tubes were found to work best if their vacua contained an inert gas, such as nitrogen or argon, at low pressure. In other types the gaseous state is supplied by the vapor from a few drops of mercury, which are inclosed within the evacuated bulb. These latter types are the mercury arc rectifiers, which change alternating currents into direct currents. The term "electron tube" has come into use as the comprehensive designation to include both the vacuum tubes and the gas tubes. The modern electron tube is highly specialized to a variety of uses, and today there are close to two hundred different types. Virtually every one is serving the war effort in a critical place, either in a munitions factory on the industrial front or in a weapon on the fighting front—some of them in many places on both fronts.

ELECTRONICS IN WAR INDUSTRIES

In the steel industry, for example, certain photo-sensitive vacuum tubes function as electric eyes to keep watch on the furnaces and other receptacles in which steel is cooked. Both the Bessemer process and the open-hearth process are safeguarded against waste of time and material by installations of these photo-sensitive devices. In the Bessemer process there is a moment when the heat has reached the critical stage; it is announced by the change in color of the plume of flame which flares up from the roaring converter, and it used to be necessary for an expert to watch for this moment of color change and then swiftly shut off the blast of air. Not only has the electric eye released these watchers for other work but it makes no mistake, is never too slow or too fast. In the open-hearth process, by which the better grades of steel are made, the highest possible temperature is essential to good production; and yet it must not be so hot as to melt or crack the furnace. Here again the electric eye is serving as an infallible thermostat.

After the steel has been cast, and the heavy billet is swung into the mill to be rolled into sheets, an electric eye catches sight of the red-hot mass as it emerges from the rollers, trips the machine to reverse and gives the piece another rolling, and so repeats the process until the billet has been flattened to specification. Other electric eyes control the cut-off saws which trim the sheets into the required lengths. In most of these services the photo-sensitive tubes serve as triggers to control power vacuum tubes which in turn activate the mechanisms.

If the steel is being shaped into a shell casing, electron tubes assist in hardening it for battle service. The tubes used here are oscillators. The shell casing is placed within the field of influence of these generators of electromagnetic waves, the waves induce high-frequency currents in the steel, its surface particles are violently agitated by the invisible pulsations, and the resulting heating effect produces a hard tough skin. This electronic tempering process is a vast improvement over the methods formerly used; it takes only a few seconds, and inexpensive grades of steel lend themselves to its treatment.

After the shell is made, an electronic chronoscope is available to measure its explosion time and muzzle velocity in thousandths of a second. The pressures generated within the gun barrel during the firing of the shell are recorded by another electronic device. There are also electronic means of determining the time required for a gun mechanism to operate, the blow-out time of fuzes, explosion time of explosives, and reaction time of the gunner.

Many of these devices were available earlier, though their use was the exception rather than the rule. The effect of the emergency has been to make more common, and in some instances to make standard, practices that before the war were found in only the most advanced industrial plants. Consider, for example, the recent performance of the x-ray tube, an electronic device now widely employed in industry to test the quality of castings and other metal parts. According to St. John and Isenburger, authors of *Industrial Radiology*, the best industrial x-ray apparatus available in 1928 required 3 hours and 30 minutes to take a photograph through a four-inch-thick steel casting; by 1938 equipment and technique had improved to the extent that it was possible to photograph through the four inches of metal in 20 minutes; whereas in 1942, with the giant tubes and appropriate photographic films then available, the same thickness was penetrated and sharply photographed in 1 minute. These progressive gains in speed are largely the result of improvements in x-ray tube design which permit the use of higher electrical pressures to generate the radiation. Fifteen years ago the most powerful x-ray apparatus available to industry was limited to 250,000 volts, whereas today x-ray tubes energized by 1,000,000 volts are in use in certain American industrial plants, each capable of photographing effectively through as much as eight inches of steel. Just what the upper limit of thickness for industrial x-ray photography may be nobody knows, but in 1943 the General Electric Company had completed the installation of a machine capable of producing x-rays of 100,000,000 volts, and it is hoped that this apparatus may answer the question.

With the tremendous explosive pressures at which engines and guns now operate, and the stresses to which such parts as turbines, propellers, aircraft wings and armor plate are subjected, x-ray examination for hidden flaws has become of critical importance. Magnetic methods of examination are used in some instances, and also the electron microscope has recently demonstrated its ability to spot invisible defects if they are not too far below the metal surface.

On the battlefront electric devices serve the fighting forces as ears, eyes, fingers and muscles. Sometimes they seem to take the place even of brains, and perform difficult operations with a speed and accuracy beyond the power of ordinary brains. Most of these services can be classified under three main functions: communication, detection, and control.

COMMUNICATION

The U. S. Army Signal Corps uses a variety of means for military communication: flags, blinkers, rockets, homing pigeons, wired telegraph, teletype, telephone; and radio telegraph, telephone, facsimile, and television. And of course there are men trained to "carry the message to Garcia" when other communications fail or their use for any reason is not expedient. But despite the wide range of its varied facilities, more than 90 per cent of the Signal Corps personnel are specialists in the ways of electricity.

The privacy of the wired message gives it preference in all situations which permit the stringing of wires. And linemen operate in the war zones to a far greater extent than the outsider would believe possible. Communication wires have been unreeled through jungles and forest, along stretches of desert, dragged over mountain passes, and the rugged insulation even permits them to be dropped across rivers. Wherever wire service can be provided, it is the chief medium of getting the military message through. But for distance and celerity radio can of course far outdo the lineman, and the swift mobility of modern warfare is as much a gift of the vacuum tube as it is of the internal-combustion engine. Certainly air warfare, tank warfare and other motorized warfare could not proceed at their present pace without radio. In naval warfare radio has been the principal arm of communication since World War I.

Radio has been greatly facilitated by the progressive harnessing of shorter and yet shorter electromagnetic waves. In the 1920's, when broadcasting first popped out of the laboratories, short waves were regarded as of no commercial value, though the laboratories were experimenting with them. The types of apparatus then available were best adapted to the generation of signals ranging from a wave length of about 20,000 meters to one of 200 meters and a little less. Early studies had indicated that the longer the wave length, the farther the signal would travel on a given input of power. So the longest waves—those of around 20,000 meters, about 12 miles from crest to crest—were assigned to the transoceanic stations. The bands next in order of wave length were reserved for government, ship-to-shore, and other marine uses. What was left was available for the commercial broadcasters, but these stations showed no interest in waves shorter than 200 meters, which were reputed to lose strength rapidly; so the federal authorities assigned them to the amateurs.

There were several thousand of these enthusiasts in the United States, each with his self-made experimental set, and they were anything but happy at being shoved off at what seemed the dead end of the radio rainbow. Nothing could be done about it, however; so they made the best of the situation by prospecting even shorter waves, trying those of 175 meters, 150, 125, 100. And soon—marvelous it seemed to them!—they were conversing with one another over continental distances. It was found that the energy required to send long waves a few miles would send 100-meter waves thousands of miles.

In this quite accidental way the practical value of the short waves was opened up. But they were not left in undivided possession of the amateurs. Certain bands of the short-wave spectrum were set aside for aircraft communication, some for police, fire, and other local uses, and still other wave lengths for point-to-point, trans-oceanic, and various governmental communications. By 1932 the entire range between 200 meters and 100 meters had been mapped out for use by various services.

Although the amateurs, according to popular radio history, were the first to make practical use of short waves for communication, investigators in research laboratories had been experimenting with these and even shorter wave lengths for years. When they ventured into the no man's land beyond the 10-meter frontier, vacuum tubes had to be redesigned to produce satisfactory ultrashort-wave signals; for as wave lengths decrease in size the vibrations of the waves increase in frequency, and the generators in ordinary use were not able to oscillate fast enough. The maximum obtainable frequency of vibration is related to the time of flight of the electrons through the vacuum tube, and various stratagems were tried to shorten this transit time. In some tubes the positive charge on the receiving electrode was increased, so that it would attract the electrons more powerfully and thus pull them faster across the space. In others, the electrodes were placed closer together, thereby reducing the distance of flight in the vacuum. The outcome of these and other efforts was the generation of radio waves measured not in meters but in centimeters.

Earlier experimenters with short waves had found them possessed of many of the characteristics of light, and now these optical properties showed to an even greater degree in the waves shorter than one meter. They could be reflected at angles by flat mirrors and concentrated into beams by concave mirrors, and by means of lenses the radio beam could be focused into a narrower, more intense beam. The extremely short waves were called micro waves.

The range of signals available for radio communication thus became classified into a graduated spectrum whose boundaries we may roughly define as approximately of these dimensions:

Long waves—ranging from 30,000 meters to about 187 meters
Medium waves—ranging from 187 meters to about 30 meters
Short waves—ranging from 30 meters to about 10 meters
Ultra short—ranging from 10 meters to about 60 centimeters
Micro waves—ranging from 60 centimeters down to heat waves

MICRO WAVES

One of the first public demonstrations of micro-wave communication was in March, 1931, when engineers of Le Materiel Telephonique of Paris and of the International Telephone and Telegraph laboratories of Herndon, England, set up experimental stations on opposite sides of the English Channel. In the presence of and with the participation of a group of scientists, government officials and industrialists, they talked between Calais and Dover on a wave length of 18 centimeters. The waves were projected and received at each end of the transmission with identical apparatus mounted on tall steel towers. The most conspicuous feature was two 10-foot parabolic mirrors, one for sending and the other for receiving, which were so placed on the towers that they exactly faced the two similar mirrors on the opposite shore. The sending mirror concentrated the radiation and projected it horizontally in a beam which was caught at the other station by the receiving mirror, which directed the signals into the receiving antenna. Particularly remarkable was the power economy, for the transmission across about thirty miles was made at an expenditure of only half a watt.

"The conversations exchanged between Dover and Calais were of high quality, well up to the standard of the best telephone transmission," reported the editor of *Electrical Communications* in a contemporary account of the experiments. He speculated on possible uses of micro waves—or micro rays, as the English call them. "Apart from their obvious applications in a world-wide communications network, such as that of the International System, a ray which is not affected by weather conditions such as fog and rain will very greatly extend the usefulness of lighthouses, especially at times when they are now least effective and are most needed due to poor visibility. For maintaining secret communication between aircraft and land, and between ships of a fleet at sea, the micro ray offers fruitful possibilities. Other valuable applications will be the landing of aircraft in darkness or fog, and dependable means for ships to locate one another in foggy weather. In the field of television, also, the micro ray should permit developments which are not practicable with the wave lengths hitherto available."

At that time a program of research was under way at the Massachusetts Institute of Technology, directed at the problem of air-craft navigation in fog. The investigations had tested the possibilities of signaling the fogbound pilot by means of sound waves, light waves and radio waves, and settled on short-wave radio as offering the best prospects of success. By 1940 this research group was working with micro waves of 50 centimeters wave length, and the director, Professor Edward L. Bowles, was moved to report to *The Technology Review* that "The shorter the wave length, the more effectively the beam may be controlled and directed by a directive device of a given over-all size. Since for vessels, and particularly for aircraft, apparatus must be relatively small, here is further reason for effort to reach shorter and shorter useful wave lengths."

Shorter and still shorter wave lengths have been provided, thanks largely to three independent inventions which came out of three American physics laboratories in 1939. They provide a current example of what has often happened in science: the simultaneous discovery or development of the same idea by separate investigators working independently. At Stanford University the inventors called their device the "klystron," first announced in *The Technology Review* of February, 1939. Very similar was an "ultrahighfrequency power amplifier of novel design" announced by the RCA Radiotron laboratories in the February issue of *Electronics*. And in the same month came the *Proceedings* of the Institute of Radio Engineers with an account of a "velocity-modulated tube" just developed at the General Electric laboratories. Although certain details were peculiar to each device, all three were alike in their ability to generate very short radio waves by a process of breaking up a stream of moving electrons into groups, bunching them in their precipitous flight through the vacuum into separate regiments, so that, in the picturesque phrase of the editor of *The Technology Review*, they "are made to do the goosestep." These goose-stepping electrons have generated one-centimeter waves and even shorter ones; radio waves about as wide from crest to crest as the diameter of a pencil; waves with a frequency of 30,000,000,000 per second. A clock ticking off seconds would take more than 940 years to swing its pendulum as many times as a one-centimeter wave vibrates in a single second.

The extension of radio communication into the short, ultrashort and micro wave bands has opened up a truly enormous region of frequencies. It remains true, of course, that these waves do not conform to the curvature of the Earth. But within this limitation there is room here for directional broadcasting, television and facsimile transmission. A British authority has suggested that after the war Europe dispense with long waves, and utilize short waves for international broadcasting and ultrashort waves for local broadcasting.

THE USE OF FM RADIO

Another advantage of the ultrashort waves is the opportunity they afford for the extension of the high-fidelity staticless radio developed by Professor Edwin H. Armstrong of Columbia University. This is the frequency-modulation system, or FM, as it is familiarly called. The basis of all radio communication is a carrier wave of uniform frequency and uniform amplitude which flows through the system whenever the circuit is on. In ordinary radio the tones of the human voice, music, or other sounds to be communicated are imposed upon these uniform carrier waves by a modification of their amplitude. That is to say, the waves are made to swing out wider or shrink narrower to represent the pattern of the imposed sound, but the number of their vibrations per second remains the same throughout. In Professor Armstrong's system the order of modification is just the opposite. The amplitude does not change, but the imposed differences in sound are represented by changes in the number of vibrations per second. Thus it makes use of frequency modulation, as contrasted with the old amplitude modulation. Electricity is so amenable to discipline that it does not matter what pattern of electrical change is used in transmission to represent the pattern of sound change put into the microphone. All that is necessary is to keep track of the order and magnitude of electrical change—whether of amplitude, as in the amplitude-modulation system, or of number of vibrations per second, as in the frequency-modulation system; for if you know and control the electrical pattern you can change it back at the receiver into a counterpart of the original sound pattern.

The fact that FM radio utilizes changes in the frequency of the wave vibration greater in magnitude than can be produced in nature makes it most adaptable to the ultrashort waves; for their high frequencies provide a wide range through which the frequency changes may operate without overlapping and interfering with neighboring broadcast bands. There are various technical reasons why frequency modulation reduces static, both that of the lightning crash and that of the electric motor and other man-made interferences, and why it at the same time permits reproduction of sound waves on a high level of fidelity. Marked progress in demonstrating the fidelity and reach of FM radio has been attained by several high-power stations in the United States, using the ultrashort (but not micro) waves for frequency-modulation broadcasting. These stations have been able to furnish service up to three or four times the horizon, and daily experience is showing that the ultrashort signals pass through buildings and even massive structures. "In fact," says Professor Armstrong, "they penetrate buildings better than the ordinary broadcast waves. It is a startling experience to drive into a tunnel or under a bridge or the 'elevated,' and find the solid FM signals coming through unimpaired after all trace of regular long-wave broadcasting has disappeared."

FM radio seems destined for tremendous development in the postwar years. Meanwhile the army and navy are making considerable use of the system, particularly for communication with tanks, planes, and other motorized and electrified vehicles and weapons.

Micro-wave communication possesses a high degree of privacy. This derives from the fact that these shorter waves permit a transmission to be confined into a narrow beam whereby a message may be directed at a point and be received only in that direction. Also the tubes and other apparatus for micro-wave transmission and reception can be built extremely compactly and of light weight, and can be operated with relatively small power—properties which make an installation easily portable, well adapted for use in airplanes, tanks and jeeps, and on the backs of infantrymen.

The range of micro-wave communication is bounded by the horizon, however. Unlike the long, medium and short waves, it will not travel around the curve of the Earth. In order to gain a wider horizon the transmitter must be elevated, and the higher it is above the ground the farther its signals will reach. These very, very short waves are similar to light also in that they will not pass

through solid objects, like mountains, buildings and other constructions. In the 1931 communication between Calais and Dover on
18-centimeter waves, mentioned earlier in this chapter, it was
found that when people walking along the Dover cliffs chanced to
intercept the micro-wave beam, very large sudden changes showed
up in the strength of the received signal. "A similar effect occurred
when ships were crossing the line of the beam at a certain distance,"
reported one of the French engineers.

This response of the micro waves to interception by opaque
objects, and especially their property of bouncing back from reflect-
ing surfaces, gave radio a high utility in the service of aircraft
detection and warning. What these properties meant to the British
in the first year of the war has been widely extolled by Lord
Beaverbrook and others in their public praise of the radiolocator,
"the golden cockerel" of the Battle of Britain.

Radiolocation had also been the subject of prolonged research
in the United States, but army and navy control of these investigations zealously guarded them from publicity. Apparently the first
public acknowledgement of American work in this field came from
Vannevar Bush early in 1943, in an address before the American
Institute of Electrical Engineers:

It has been publicly known for a long time that when Germany
started its all-out air attack on Britain in the summer of 1940, the
attack was repelled not only on account of the magnificent equipment and fighting qualities of the R.A.F., but also because the
British had and effectively used certain radio warning devices which
took the surprise out of the Germans' attacks and assured that their
bombers were promptly met by fighter squadrons. It is also known
that the British had this device because of the effective work of a
group of British scientists and engineers over a considerable period
of time. I am also very glad to be able to state that at the same time
our own army and navy had equally effective devices for this
purpose, well developed and in hand. This had been accomplished
during years of peace, in spite of the fact that this country had
failed to support its military departments to an extent which
rendered research and development in peacetime possible on anywhere near an adequate scale. In particular, I know personally of
the early work in this field by a small group of keen naval officers,
and there were undoubtedly other groups at work elsewhere. I am

looking forward to the day when due tribute can be paid to those officers who very early saw the possibilities of devices of this sort and worked assiduously to the end that they might be practically available. I also wish to emphasize strongly that this work was done long before Europe went to war, still longer before there was any such thing as the National Defense Research Committee. Certainly, since its advent, NDRC has worked along these same lines. It has been proud to collaborate with the army and navy in so doing, and to work in partnership for the further development of devices on which they had already pioneered, and to share in all the various possibilities flowing out of that early work. The full story of this development, when it can be told, will involve many scientists and engineers, and its roots go back for many years.

Actually, the roots go back more than twenty years, to 1922.

RADAR—"RADIO DETECTING AND RANGING"

In 1922 an American experimenter chanced to notice that communication from a radio station was interrupted when a solid object moved into the path of its signals. This accidental observation was the starting point for a systematic research. A transmitter and receiver were set up on opposite shores of a river, and it was found that passing boats interfered with reception. In 1925 a related discovery was made: not only did the intervening object interrupt the signals, but its surface operated as a mirror. Thereafter transmitter and receiver were installed in the same location, and as one projected a beam of waves, the other picked up the reflections. By 1930 it was possible to detect reflections from a passing airplane; by 1934 a satisfactory method of measuring the distance of the plane had been developed. A U. S. Navy officer in 1940 coined the term "radar" from the initials of "radio detecting and ranging." The word spells the same either forward or backward, and seems an apt name for this amazing device whose waves bounce back at the same speed with which they move forward.

There was a radar installation at Pearl Harbor on the "date that will live in infamy." It told of the approaching Japanese planes, but its warning was not needed. The official account of this neglect is contained in the reports of the commission of inquiry, headed by Justice Owen J. Roberts, which President Roosevelt appointed to visit Hawaii and find out the facts. Among the facts, which were published in Senate Document 159 of the 77th Congress, are the following:

1. The army was responsible for the installation and operation of "an aircraft warning system for the detection of waterborne and airborne craft at a distance from the coast."

2. Although permanent installations of this detection system had not been completed, "certain mobile equipment had been installed at temporary locations," it "was being operated intermittently throughout the day for the purpose of training personnel in its operation," and after November 27th it had been operated each morning from 4 to 7 o'clock by order of the commanding general.

3. In accordance with this order, the system closed at 7 a. m. on the fateful Sunday, December 7th, and our story would end here but for the persevering interest of a Signal Corps sergeant. He was being instructed in the mysteries of aircraft detection. As the official report tells it: "A noncommissioned officer, who had been receiving training, requested that he be allowed to remain at one of the stations, and was granted leave to do so. At about 7:02 a. m. he discovered what he thought was a large flight of planes slightly east of north of Oahu at a distance of about 130 miles. He reported this fact at 7:20 a. m. to a lieutenant of the army who was at the central information center, having been detailed there to familiarize himself with the operation of the system. This inexperienced lieutenant, having information that certain United States planes might be in the vicinity at the time, assumed that the planes in question were friendly planes, and took no action with respect to them."

It was not until 7:55 a. m. that the Japanese raiders reached Pearl Harbor. The sergeant got his indication of them at 7:02, fifty-three minutes before they struck. He reported his finding to the "inexperienced lieutenant" at 7:20, thirty-five minutes before they struck. A great deal of alertness, preparedness, interception and other defensive measures might have been crowded into those thirty-five minutes, if only the warning of the farseeing radio eye had been used.

The refusal to give any credence to the possible seriousness of the signal is of course only part of the general picture which the commission characterized as "dereliction of duty." The admiral in charge of the fleet, said the commission, "assumed that the aircraft warning system was being fully operated by the army, but made no inquiry after reading any of the messages of October and November from the War and Navy Departments as to what the fact was with respect to its operation." As for the general, and the use he made of his resources, the commission reports that as early as November 27 "there was sufficient partially trained personnel available to operate the aircraft warning system throughout twenty-four hours of the day, as installed in its temporary locations. An arc of nearly 360° around Oahu could have been covered."

Fortunately, the lesson of this tragic negligence was well learned. Today there is no one so set in the old ways, or so inexperienced in science, that he does not have a healthy respect and even admiration for the aircraft warning system. The noncommissioned officer, Sergeant J. L. Lockard, was recalled to Signal Corps headquarters at Fort Monmouth, New Jersey, given the opportunity of additional training, and was graduated from the Officer Candidate School in July, 1942. As a mark of recognition for his attention to duty at Pearl Harbor, he was commissioned a lieutenant one day in advance of the remainder of his class of 855 new Signal Corps officers.

Meanwhile, at a press conference on April 23, 1942, Secretary of War Stimson spoke of the extension of the army's aircraft warning system. "We have a lot of detectors," he said, "and are working hard to increase that number. We are establishing listening posts as rapidly as possible along our coasts"; and, referring to his visit of inspection to one of the Signal Corps stations, Mr. Stimson said, "I looked through the warning instruments and saw the electrical indication of a plane which I believe was sixty miles away." The Signal Corps, he added, "are very busy in our schools studying radio, electronics, and the application of radio to our new system of detection—what you might call the electric eye—which can see 100 miles or more, and which works at night as well as day and through fogs and clouds to locate enemy vessels and planes."

In addition to radio, other warning systems were devised in prewar days and details of them have been published. In one, an apparatus sensitive to heat rays is used; the detector senses the presence of an unseen plane or ship by the heat from its engines.

In another system, television is the medium of detection. The fundamental principles of these devices are well known, for they have been widely published in scientific and engineering publications, but the particular applications and refinements attained in the program of war research are of necessity confidential and secret.

SUBMARINE SOUND DETECTION

The location of underwater craft presents a different problem from that of air or surface craft detection. Radio waves do not penetrate the sea so easily as they do the air. The water does transmit sound waves very distinctly, however, and it is practically impossible for the highly complex machinery of a submarine to operate without generating sounds. Therefore, the science of submarine detection is largely concentrated in the field of acoustics, using microphones, vacuum-tube amplifiers and other electronic devices.

Submarines first became a problem in World War I, and it was not long before warships and merchant vessels were equipped with "hydrophones" to detect their sounds. These were simply a rugged form of microphone, impervious to sea water, installed on the side of the ship at an appropriate distance below the waterline. When properly mounted and suspended on a vertical axis, the instrument served as a direction finder, inasmuch as a picked-up sound is at its loudest when the diaphragm is turned broadside to the source and weakest when edgewise. Also, by attaching two hydrophones at different places on a ship, a binaural effect was attained, and it was possible to locate the direction of origin of the sound from the difference between its times of arrival at the two electric ears. Before 1918 the sensitivity of the hydrophone was greatly increased by improvements in the then newly developed vacuum-tube amplifier, and the U-boat trick of remaining on the bottom with engines off and all mechanisms hushed was often insufficient to assure escape. There are stories of the hydrophone picking up the tense nerve-racked voices of the trapped crew as they quarreled in their hide-out on the sea bottom.

The real problem of the hydrophone is one of selectivity. For the underocean is full of noises, though the layman's imagination may picture it as a vast submerged world of silence. The task of detection is mainly one of identifying, out of the myriad sound waves traversing the waters, the telltale vibrations generated by a U-boat or its occupants.

The hydrophone listens for sounds originating in the submarine, but there is another method of detection which generates its own sounds and then determines the presence and direction of submarines by the reflected echoes. This method was introduced in World War I, and was developed to a high state of efficiency by Professor Paul Langevin of the College de France, Paris. Working at a laboratory set up for him at the arsenal in Toulon, Professor Langevin devised a method of projecting high-frequency sound waves in a narrow beam, and then sweeping the undersea with this sound beam somewhat as the aircraft warning systems now sweep the skies with a radio beam. If the sound beam encountered a submarine its echo bounced back and could be picked up by microphone. Other Allied physicists and engineers contributed in important ways to the development of the supersonic echo locator, and, as in the case of the hydrophone, the end of World War I found this device a highly sensitive antisubmarine weapon.

In the score of years between the two world wars tremendous advances were made in acoustical engineering and in the application of electronics to this technology, stimulated in large measure by the well-financed demands of radio broadcasting, sound movies and the telephone industry. New devices and new knowledge of acoustics and electronics were therefore available for countering the renewal of submarine warfare which was unleashed by Germany in the first week of World War II. Both the British Admiralty and the U. S. Navy Department had devoted considerable study to the improvement of their systems of detection. The British device, known as "asdic," was tested under war conditions in spotting the operations of outlaw submarines during the Spanish Civil War, and it was rushed into service against German U-boats in September of 1939.

Asdic gets its name from the initials of the Antisubmarine Defence Investigating Committee, a group of scientists organized by the British Admiralty several years ago, whose researches are responsible for this highly effective and still highly secret detector.

Meanwhile, the Germans have not stood still in their technical development of the U-boat. "German submarines are greatly improved since the first World War," reports a memorandum of the U. S. Navy Department. "Present boats are more sturdy in construction, can descend to depths beyond 500 feet, and withstand easily depth charges which are not exploded either by contact or very close aboard." Not only are the modern U-boats more rugged and resistant to attack, but they are "equipped with extremely efficient newly-invented underwater sound devices which permit discovery and bearing of any merchant surface vessel within ranges of five miles. The same equipment permits a submerged submarine to keep accurate track of the position of attacking destroyers or submarine chasers. . . With such information it is comparatively easy to dodge depth-charge attacks, particularly as these new devices have great maneuverability and small turning circles. At submerged speeds of less than three knots, the noise of the submarine's own machinery cannot be detected by listening devices."

In the United States, in addition to the well organized group at the Naval Research Laboratory which has been working on submarine locators for many years, the Office of Scientific Research and Development has been giving considerable attention to the development and improvement of antisubmarine weapons through a division of its National Defense Research Committee.

THE OUTDOOR CARPET SWEEPER

Sometimes the danger to be looked for is not a rapidly moving object like an airplane, nor yet a vibrant noise-producing object like a submarine, but a stationary, silent, hidden weapon. Such are the ground mines. These were a World War I introduction, but have been used on a far greater scale in the present struggle; particularly against tanks and motorized forces, but also against infantry, guerrilla warriors and other personnel.

A typical antitank mine is a pie-shaped package of destruction about sixteen inches in diameter and four inches thick. The crust of the pie is thin steel; its filling ten pounds of t.n.t. The weight of a passing tank or other motor-driven vehicle will detonate the charge, and there are more sensitive mines which go off under the weight of a man. These hair-triggered parcels are buried an inch or two in the ground, covered over with leaves, sod, sand or other characteristic material to simulate undisturbed terrain, and in some defensive areas they have been sown by the thousands. The explosion of one mine may set off others by resonance.

The first problem of the antimine engineer or sapper is to locate the mine field. It may be a beach, a country road, a pasture, the slope of a hill, the main highway into a town, any surface over which tanks or troops are likely to pass. One way of going about the detection is to prod the suspected ground with a bayonet or other sharp implement for the feel of metal. Less risky is the use of the electromagnetic locator, which is now fairly common equipment on both sides of the conflict. This device, a mounted coil which is pushed over the ground like a long-handled carpet sweeper, can sense the presence of metal by electromagnetic induction. It picks up the sudden surge of energy that results whenever an electromagnetic field is moved into the proximity of iron, steel, or other conducting metals. Faint currents are set up in its antenna, are magnified by vacuum-tube amplifiers, and the end effect of passing the sweeper over the buried steel casing of a mine is a buzz or click in the earphones of the operator. Once the death trap has been located, the task of uncovering it without disaster, finding its detonator and disarming it, still remains a major problem. But, after a region has been prospected by the locator, the "delousers" at least know where to look for their treacherous quarry, and where not to look.

CONTROL DEVICES

Systems of electrical control function in almost innumerable ways in warfare. They are in the airplane, in the tank and other ground equipment, and in the warship. It is even possible to operate ships by remote control, directed only by radio. Away back in 1931 the U. S. Navy made a demonstration of this kind off San Diego, when the destroyer *Stoddert* was sent to sea without a human being on board. Her course was set and her steering wheel controlled by radio. She was speeded up from six to fifteen knots, to twenty knots, to "full speed," and while going at 26 knots was made to turn and reverse her course—all by radio direction. Then somebody in the radio office gave another command, and the distant ship turned off her steam, stopped, and, as the Associated Press reported it, "whistled lustily for help."

Among electromechanical control devices in current wartime use, one of the most remarkable is the apparatus designed to direct antiaircraft gunfire. Machines are caused to follow the flight of a moving target, and by doing so they anticipate its movement, compute where it will be at a given time, and then point the gun, determine the fuze-setting and fire the shell in the split second that will insure its bursting at the predicted spot. The predicted spot may be five or six miles up in the air and two miles in advance of the present position of the enemy plane. The time available in which to get the projectile from the gun to the predicted position can be only a few seconds. Complicated calculations must be made, orders given, orders implicitly followed; and all these things must be done instantaneously. Nothing but electricity could move so swiftly and surely. The instruments involved are so intricate, so exacting, so precisely integrated that, as Colonel Henry W. Miller has said, "their use in warfare seems impossible." And yet their use in warfare is routine. During the Battle of Britain antiaircraft fire from ground batteries brought down more than 200 German planes.

Most of this development of automatic gunnery has come since about 1926. During the first world war artillery was hastily improvised to fire upward at moving planes, and a good many hits were scored on the relatively slow and low-flying aircraft of that day. Then in the early 1920's special guns for defense against air attack were designed, but they were aimed by means of sights on the barrel and manually operated. At that time various observations were used to determine the approximate height, speed, and direction of flight of the enemy aircraft; these with other factors influencing its flight were calculated, and the resulting data was telephoned to the gunners. On this information, the sights were set and the guns fired. The scheme was to throw up a curtain of bursting shells, and by a continuous firing, keeping the barrage ahead of the plane, sooner or later a hit should be registered. But the theory didn't work out very well in practice. Calculation of the probabilities showed that hundreds of thousands of rounds would have to be fired to provide a cloud of shell fragments sufficient to assure a destructive hit.

So the ordnance engineers gave up the "cloud method," and

began to concentrate on the problem of making the antiaircraft gun an instrument of precision. As the speed and ceiling of airplanes increased, the ingenuity of inventors and designers was taxed to produce a gun-control system that would be as nearly automatic as possible. What came of these efforts was an electromechanical device known as the "antiaircraft director." By 1929 the chief of the design section of the Watertown Arsenal, Major George M. Barnes,* was able to report as follows in an article which he published in *Army Ordnance*:

For many years attempts have been made to lay guns in azimuth and elevation by electrical methods so that the guns could be trained from a distant point. Devices built for this purpose have been unreliable, costly and inaccurate. About three years ago the Sperry Gyroscope Company working with the Ordnance Department undertook the development of a new mechanism for this purpose. These efforts have been so successful that during the last two years the Ordnance Department has been able to direct guns automatically from a distant point without having any operating personnel at the guns except the loading detail. It has been found that the new electromechanical device will direct guns with greater accuracy than was formerly possible, using skilled gunners. The torque amplifiers are connected to the antiaircraft director through the same data-transmission system, and the guns (are) thus operated direct from the antiaircraft director. This device, which has been called a torque amplifier, is rugged and relatively simple. It has been extensively tested at target practices in which targets towed by bombing planes were used. Occasionally one reads what are considered fantastic stories in newspapers of the possibilities of firing guns controlled only by mechanical robots. As a matter of fact, this has already been successfully accomplished.

If the "firing of guns controlled only by mechanical robots" had already been successfully accomplished by 1929, imagine what may be the state of the art today. In the last dozen years important improvements have been made in the gun-on-the-ground which opposes the gun-on-wings. Today's antiaircraft artillery can fire faster and send its shells higher, and necessarily the robot must work faster.

* He is now Brigadier General Barnes, assistant chief of ordnance, U. S. Army.

THE ANTIAIRCRAFT DIRECTOR

The antiaircraft director is boxshaped, its top somewhat higher than a man's eyes. Its equipment includes two eyepieces through which the operators train telescopic sights on the plane. The mere act of following its movement through the telescopes sets the internal mechanism to computing the path, the instantaneous position, range, and ground speed of the flying target. However, the director is not able to determine the altitude of the plane, and this is done by an auxiliary device known as the stereoscopic height-finder.

The heightfinder is an optical instrument built on the principle of the old-fashioned parlor stereoscope; but it is a large stationary apparatus with a tubular body about the diameter of a stovepipe, about 14 feet long and mounted horizontally. Its eyepieces for viewing the targets receive their light from two outer lenses which are about 12 feet apart. The effect of this arrangement is to make the men at the eyepieces "wider between the eyes." By thus broadening the base of the angle of vision the heightfinder provides a stereoscopic means of measuring altitude by the surveyor's well-known method of triangulation. Two operators track the airplane to keep it centered on the cross-hairs of the heightfinder. The third man, called the observer, controls the operation of the optical system. He puts the image of the plane as seen by one eye on the same level as that which is seen by the other eye, and thus the triangulation is completed. From its automatic determination of the base angles, the heightfinder computes the height of the target and electrically communicates this information to the director, which proceeds to add it to the computations already under way.

The director then figures how long it would take the projectile to reach the present position of the plane; figures how far the plane would have traveled in the interval, and to what point; adds corrections for wind, drift, and variations in the muzzle velocity; and thus, by a series of corrections and integrations, it arrives at a predicted set-forward position of the moving target. It then electrically advises the gun, the fuze and the firing mechanism of this result, and the artillery fire is directed accordingly. The whole process, from the first sighting of the plane through the director's eyepieces to the discharge of the shell, is a matter of a few seconds.

At night, when it would be difficult if not impossible to get a bead on the plane through the telescopes, special locating devices are used. One is the soundlocator, an arrangement of movable horns, designed to determine the position of a plane from the sound of its motors. After the night raider has been spotted by sound, its position is communicated electrically to a powerful searchlight (or series of searchlights) which at once trains its beam in the direction indicated. When the beam is on the plane it can be made to follow the object in the sky, and in so doing the searchlight provides the necessary visual target for the director.

Antiaircraft fire is also controlled by radar, and this device is even more versatile than the searchlight or the soundlocator. Its invisible radio beam is able to penetrate fog and cloud, and to range far beyond the sensitivity of microphone or other listening device. As the radar detects the position of the enemy plane, it determines the distance and direction of the plane, and feeds its instantaneous data into the antiaircraft director. The result of this radio-electromechanical collaboration is the most marvelous approximation to completely automatic gunfire that has yet been attained.

Naval operations add a new problem to the control of artillery fire. At sea the director must keep track not only of the target but of the motion of the ship on which the gun is mounted. How can a gun be accurately aimed from the rocking deck of a destroyer or other warship? The answer is that the gun is fired only at the instant when the deck is horizontal. And that instant is determined by infallible electromechanical devices which are sensitive to the "feel" of gravitation. The French battleship *Jean Bart* was smashed at a distance of 25 miles. Two salvos from one United States battleship did that, and of this feat Rear Admiral Stafford C. Hooper has said: "Radio directed and reported the destruction."

USING MATHEMATICS TO AVOID THE USE OF MATHEMATICS

Industrial plants devoted to the manufacture of antiaircraft directors have found that women operatives are peculiarly apt in the work of machining and assembling these high-precision devices, involving delicate and exact manual movements in close co-ordination. One large plant employed college women, some of them holders of degrees in mathematics, and it seemed highly appropriate that mathematically trained brains should guide the hands which put together these mathematical machines. Mention was made of the fact that nail polish is forbidden adornment. Even mathematicians have a weakness, it seems. The polish is an enamel which may chip or flake off; and such particles, falling in the gears, can put a director out of use. The workers wear head coverings, for a stray hair also is a potential wrecker. And the workroom is dustproof, weathertight, and completely air-conditioned.

The marvel of the automatic director is its unbelievable rapidity of operation. Someone has estimated that a result which the director arrives at in a few seconds would take a competent mathematician, given the same data, two or three hours to compute. This electrical mechanism is, in the keen phrase of Thornton C. Fry, "an example of the use of mathematics to avoid the use of mathematics."

It is also a token of the role of mathematics in modern war.

CHAPTER VI

The Next Decimal Place

Mathematics takes us into the realm of absolute necessity, to which not only the actual world, but every possible world, must conform.

—Bertrand Russell, THE STUDY OF MATHEMATICS

ONE day in 1941, according to a story out of England, a Nazi shell from across the channel hit near Dover and killed several civilians of a crowd gathered to watch a tennis match. Before it reached the ground the projectile passed through a zone of foliage, snapping off the branches of several trees and underbrush. As the story goes, two British mathematicians measured the angle of path indicated by the snapped branches, from this calculated the trajectory of the missile, and thereby worked out the probable position of the gun on the French coast. Then an R.A.F. plane went across, dropped bombs on the indicated spot, and thereafter the gun was silent.

The major contribution of mathematics in this incident was not the service of determining the path of the shell back to its source. That was a fairly routine problem in ballistics. A greater achievement was that represented by the design of an airplane able to rise from the ground with a heavy bomb load, fly a given course with sureness and dispatch, and from miles up lay its deadly parcels on a dot on the map. There is of course an element of luck in every hit, but the performance of the plane and of the bombardier is to be credited to mathematics, no less than to the gasoline which propelled the plane or the high explosive which powered the bomb.

For all these weapons which we have called gifts of physics are equally gifts of mathematics. If mathematics is queen of the sciences, as Gauss declared more than a century ago, perhaps physics may be called king. Archimedes, Newton, Gauss himself, Clerk Maxwell, Einstein and many other creative scientists exemplify in their work the fruitful collaboration of mathematics and physics. Their equations not only guided and tested their physical discoveries but in many instances gave the first clue, the spark which was fanned into flame by experiment. It is true that many important inventions have been stumbled upon, or were first crudely conceived by experimenters ignorant and in some cases contemptuous of mathematical procedures, but rarely has one been brought to full utility without the application of mathematical analysis to its problems and design. This is particularly true of the complicated high-speed machines of today, including those on which we rely for victory in warfare.

The branches of physics which have borne the brunt of the struggle—ballistics, aerodynamics, optics, acoustics and electronics —have derived much of their improved facility and accuracy from men working with paper and pencil to increase the approximation of perfect design to the next decimal place. Their work, in turn, rests on the heritage of observations, theorems, demonstrations and techniques which have come down through the centuries. "If we can now calculate beforehand the parts of the most complex machines," said M. Lévé in his presidential address of several years ago to the French Academy, "it is because long ago the shepherds of Chaldea and Judea observed the stars; because Hipparchus combined their observations with his own and handed them down to us; because Tycho Brahe made better ones; because two thousand years ago a great geometer, Apollonius of Perga, wrote a treatise on conic sections, regarded for many centuries as useless; because the genius of Kepler, utilizing this admirable work and the observations of Tycho Brahe, gave us those sublime laws which themselves have been considered useless by the utilitarian, and finally, because Newton discovered the law of gravitation."

MATHEMATICS FOR USE

The pure mathematician is conventionally portrayed as a cold intellectual who esteems the skillful manipulation of symbols as of more importance, or at least of more interest, than the control of forces and materials. A modern example of the Archimedean disdain for engineering is provided by the Oxford professor who thanked God that the system of quaternions could never be defiled by any utilitarian application. It isn't on record what the gentleman said when, a few years later, quaternions were found to be useful in attacking certain practical problems.

Perhaps there is no product of mathematics, however theoretical, which does not or may not eventually find use. The world of nature, which we try to classify into the physical, the chemical, the biological and the psychical, is so interrelated and interdependent that it is doubtful if any bit of truth or shred of logic can be outside of or unnecessary to the whole. Consider, for example, the history of imaginary numbers—as fine an instance of the theoretical giving birth to the practical as you will find in the storybooks.

Classical algebra held that the square of any number, positive or negative, was always positive. But suppose you had a negative number and wished to determine its square root. Since the square of all positive numbers is positive, and equally so the square of all negative numbers, the inquiry seemed at an impasse, offering no prospect of a number which when squared would give a negative number. But mathematicians are accustomed to idealizing a situation. They deal not only with the actual world but with possible worlds. It is their practice to assume a set of facts, apply logic to the assumed facts, and see where the reasoning leads. Thus it came about one day that a mathematician, annoyed by this gap in his number system, decided to assume that the square root of a negative number was obtainable. If minus one, for example, is a real number, why not the square root of minus one? Of course he couldn't figure out what the square root was, but he put it down $\sqrt{-1}$, adopted a symbol to stand for the imagined quantity, and went on with his equation. Used in this way, it helped to explain certain behavior of real numbers; indeed it filled the gap, and the mathematician was elated. The procedure was described as "elegant" and "beautiful," terms often used by the theorist, but it is not likely that he would call it "useful" or think of it as ever serving any purpose in the workaday world.

Meanwhile the science of electricity was growing up. Engineers were finding certain advantages in using alternating currents instead of the more familiar direct currents; but the accustomed mathematical techniques did not lend themselves to the description and analysis of these rapidly oscillating streams of electricity, and progress was halting. In this dilemma someone tried the square root of minus one, and found that it fitted the mathematical requirements like a key its lock. With it in their equations designers were able to explore the possibilities and limitations of alternating currents, and from these notations were able to develop the machines and networks which serve the world today in the far-ranging electrical industries. The 60 cycles of your incandescent lamp rest securely on the "imaginary" foundations of $\sqrt{-1}$.

The quantities now called "imaginaries" are not the first to have received questionable labels. There was a time, as Warren Weaver has pointed out, "when the concept of number was so naive and simple that a common fraction was not called a number at all. At another moment of mathematical history, even a negative integer was dubbed as 'absurd' and as 'fictitious below zero.' We recognize today that taken alone, apart from its relationships, every number, no matter how 'real,' is but a symbol. Viewed as abstract unassociated symbols, all numbers are imaginary."

Something needs to be said about the practical man's attitude toward mathematics. Edison's poor opinion of paper-and-pencil research is characteristic. Even the great Faraday questioned the prestige accorded to mathematics. On one occasion he said: "I do not perceive that a mathematical mind, simply as such, has any advantage over an equally acute mind not mathematical. . . . It could not of itself discover dynamical electricity nor electromagnetism, nor even magneto-electricity, or even suggest them."

Coming from Faraday, this turned out to be a boomerang. For although his brilliant experiments with electricity and magnetism led him to propose the theory of the electromagnetic field, they were not able to suggest, and his non-mathematical mind was not able to formulate, the full implications of this theory. A few years later James Clerk Maxwell took Faraday's vague idea of lines and tubes of force extending through space, translated the basic assumptions into mathematical terms, and then by a process of pure logic—of projecting the known into the possible—predicted the unknown phenomenon of radio waves.

Maxwell said radio waves must exist—because his equations revealed them. Heinrich Hertz the physicist set up a spark-gap apparatus in his laboratory and found that radio waves do indeed exist; and they were called Hertzian waves. Some years later Guglielmo Marconi took these and the findings of other research scientists, improved their devices, added to them, and invented a practical system of radio communication—sending messages which were called marconigrams.

Thus radio was born of mathematics wedded to physics, and disciplined to useful service by engineering. But basically our debt for radio and all its applications is to mathematics, the primary tool of Maxwell's discovery.

And for many other weapons too the debt is to mathematics. It is a science in which republican Germany led the world, with its incomparable Mathematical Institute at Göttingen. This institute was one of the beneficiaries of the International Education Board, an agency created by John D. Rockefeller, Jr., in 1923, to aid research and learning in post-war Europe. The University of Göttingen had been an important abode of mathematical and physical studies for many decades, but World War I left it impoverished, and its mathematical faculty especially was handicapped by inadequate teaching quarters and library facilities. On recommendation of Dr. Wickliffe Rose the board made an appropriation to the university to build and equip a mathematical institute, at the same time granting other funds to enlarge its adjoining physical institute. Thus fortified, the two sciences flourished at Göttingen after 1926 as never before. The already exceptional faculty was strengthened by the addition of several new luminaries, and in a few years Göttingen was the world's chief center of mathematical studies. From the United States and other countries students went there for advanced work. Germany's technology, as well as its intellectual prestige, was enormously enhanced by the presence of this brilliant group of teachers and researchers.

All is dispersed now. If, in the present state of world affairs, it seems an irony that this German institution was assisted to maturity by American philanthropy, it is an even deeper irony that the institution was destroyed by the blind intolerance of the Nazi regime. The Jews on its faculty were compelled to leave; others, of "Aryan" stock, were unable to abide the chauvinism and despotism, and resigned. By 1939 only one of the original faculty remained active at the institute, and one other was living at Göttingen in retirement. As for the rest, most of them are in the United States today. A recent survey shows that 16 Göttingen mathematicians have come over in the last decade. Most of them are now at work in American universities and research centers. They and other mathematical migrants from Europe proved to be very valuable human assets as the United States moved into the orbit of war and of war's exacting demands.

MATHEMATICS IN WAR

It is the progressive mechanization of war that makes the need for mathematics and mathematicians so insistent. As weapons become more speedy in operation and more forceful in the blows they deliver, standards of precision in their construction and of accuracy in their performance become ever more exacting. A minor departure in aircraft shape which makes no serious difference in a plane moving at 200 miles per hour adds a prohibitive drag when the plane moves at 400 m.p.h. As the velocity and altitude of flight increase, the speed of operation of antiaircraft defense must be increased still more. This means cartridges built to specifications measured in ten thousandths of an inch instead of mere thousandths, shells streamlined for the minimum of air resistance, and time fuzes correct to the four-hundredth part of a second. Many of these devices must be made and assembled in air-conditioned factories, because dust and temperature changes are silent saboteurs of the new instrumentation. Narrow margins of error may be decisive between defeat and victory, and the determination and control of these slight differences lie within the scope of applied mathematics. Old easy-going methods of cut-and-try are not only wasteful of time, labor and materials, all so precious in war, but may miss the goal altogether.

In high-speed aircraft there may come a particular speed at which the wings will vibrate in a violent and self-destructive manner known as "flutter." One of the problems of design is to make sure that the highest speed at which the plane can be flown is less than this critical flutter speed. This question may be investigated by building a specimen plane, or a model on a small scale, and testing it in a wind tunnel. Or the specimen plane may be tried out in the air with a test pilot. But both methods require labor and material, to say nothing of time, and such flight testing is very dangerous. Nor are these experimental procedures possible in the initial stages of designing a plane. By means of applied mathematics one can predict the critical speed at which a wing of a given type, shape and size would develop flutter. Moreover, through the use of the results of mathematical analysis, favorable departures in design can be discovered and their effects explored theoretically while the plane is still in the paper or blueprint stage.

After a design has thus been worked out a model may be built for testing in a wind tunnel, and here again mathematics becomes an indispensable tool. For suppose your model is one-fourth, one-third, or one-half the full size—how are you going to determine from the performance of the model what the performance of the full-size plane will be? In aerodynamics there are many variables, and its physical laws require mathematical formulation to enable the aeronautical engineer to infer the actual flight performance from the wind-tunnel performance of a small-scale model.

Many of the complicated mechanisms, instruments, control devices and auxiliary equipment which are necessary for the proper functioning of the aerial warship are subjects for applied mathematics. This is true, for example, of the gyroscope which operates in the automatic pilot, the compass, turn indicator, and in other devices. The employment of the gyroscope in such equipment can be understood and engineered only by persons familiar with that branch of applied mathematics known as dynamics.

Another important branch of applied mathematics is the theory of elasticity, which embraces our fundamental knowledge of the stretch of materials under load. Those who design artillery, tanks, warships, airplanes and armor plate rely indirectly on the mathematician for formulae which will enable them to predict the behavior of materials from tests made on specimens.

Electrical circuits and electronics are territory for the mathematician. Without his aid the highly complicated devices of military communication, aircraft and ship detection, and gunfire control would be far more limited than at present. Several of the advances in telephone communication were mathematical inventions; the single sideband system of carrier transmission, for example, which doubled the number of long-distance calls that could be handled over a single line, came out of a single trigonometric equation. The design of electric filters and equalizers also was born of mathematics. "Mathematics," declared an authority of the Bell Telephone Laboratories, "has been as essential to the development of nationwide telephony as copper wire or carbon microphones."

One fascinating field of mathematics which finds important application in war is the theory of probability and of mathematical statistics. The applications of probability to artillery fire are classical; but in the present conflict the emphasis on bombing, on submarine hunting, on antiaircraft destruction of airplanes, and on battles in the air, all give rise to a great variety of important problems in which the laws of chance play an important role. Some of these problems are highly complicated and involve so many factors that the actual computation of results requires weeks or months, even when the most powerful modern computing machines are used. In a war of the present type one can trace a very real connection between the success of the superb Russian offensive and the fact that a Stalin prize is given for a paper entitled "On Dispersion, Probability of Hits and Mathematical Expectations of the Number of Hits."

Mathematics, which has contributed so much to the improvement of electrical services and devices, has in turn been served by electrical developments. Vacuum tubes harnessed in oscillating circuits have made possible mathematical machines such as the differential analyzer at the Massachusetts Institute of Technology, which solves problems in dynamics involving as many as eighteen variables. This electronic apparatus can accomplish in hours a solution that required weeks and even months of the old-style mechanical analyzer, and that would require years of human computation, granted that brains and fingers were nimble enough and persevering enough to follow the complicated calculations through to the end.

MATHEMATICS IN THE UNITED STATES

Such resources as the differential analyzer in Cambridge, the renowned faculties of mathematicians at a few universities and institutes, and the current programs of intensified training in applied mathematics are all comparatively recent arrivals on the American scene. When the American Mathematical Society was organized in 1888, it could muster only six members. It was not until after the turn of the century that a few universities began to acquire men of high professional rank in this science, and their tendency was to magnify the theoretical aspects to the neglect of practical applications. Harvard developed an exceptional group for research and teaching, to be followed by a similar development at the University of Chicago, and then about a dozen years ago came the establishment of the Institute for Advanced Study at Princeton. These three centers have become fountainheads of mathematical study, and by the 1930's had attained a position of world leadership in pure mathematics. In addition to the powerful faculties at Harvard, Chicago, and Princeton, a dozen other American universities had departments strong both in teaching and in research; but with rare exceptions the theoretical was exalted. The alternative to "pure mathematics" seemed to be not "applied mathematics" but rather some less desirable discipline which one might call "impure mathematics."

The layman might suppose that if a person knows mathematics, he ought to be able to apply it to any problem subject to mathematical treatment; but the situation isn't so simple. Professor S. R. Williams of Amherst tells of an engineer in a large industrial-research laboratory who confessed his inability to cope with certain problems despite the fact that he had been trained in the calculus, vector analysis, elliptic integrals, complex variables, and modern theories of differential equations. "The trouble, as he saw it, was that the courses were given by mathematical instructors who placed too much emphasis on manipulations and neglected or ignored the applications to practical problems." This engineer appealed for help to four professors of mathematics, three of whom in turn failed to provide the needed solution; but the fourth man, who was able to see the correspondence between a physical situation and its mathematical form, did succeed.

A few years ago the National Research Council was asked to make a survey of scientific, industrial and business research in the United States for the National Resources Planning Board. One of the subjects for consideration was the resources of mathematics for industrial research, and the council turned to Thornton C. Fry, mathematical research director for the Bell Telephone Laboratories. His resulting report on "Industrial Mathematics" was published in 1940 and provided a critical review of the entire field. The author discussed the many uses of and needs for mathematics in industrial research in contrast with the fewness of fully trained industrial mathematicians. "Though the United States holds a position of outstanding leadership in pure mathematics, there is no school which provides an adequate mathematical training for the student who wishes to use the subject in the field of industrial applications rather than to cultivate it as an end in itself," said Dr. Fry. "Both science generally and its industrial applications in particular would be advanced if a group of suitable teachers were brought together in an institution where there was also a strong interest in the basic sciences and in engineering."

Not all have entirely agreed with these statements. Some disagree with the extent to which Fry identifies "applied mathematics" and "industrial mathematics." Others think he was too pessimistic about the state of applied mathematics in this country in 1940. But the timely challenge presented by his article, combined with the developing necessities of the war, are surely resulting in a great change of emphasis. A recent president of the American Mathematical Society, a pure mathematician of great distinction, has argued for a "renaissance of applied mathematics," and has himself become a special consultant to a branch of the War Department. At Brown University there has been established a strong graduate school of applied mathematics. To its special intensive summer session a considerable group of high-grade young mathematicians came for training, and presumably its regular sessions have now been established on a permanent basis. At Massachusetts Institute of Technology such departments as mechanical and electrical engineering, aeronautics, meteorology, and geophysics have long had men of the highest research-engineering type, well versed in advanced mathematics; and such men, together with representatives of the M.I.T. mathematics department itself, now form an inter-departmental committee to sponsor and develop applied mathematics. At New York University a smaller but excellent group is similarly emphasizing applied mathematics.

In addition to these specialized groups, almost every one of the former centers of pure mathematics has begun to give increased attention to the applied fields. Men who were noted as theorists turned their talents to the mathematics of dynamics, elasticity, electrical networks, and other specialties involved in the technology of war. In a number of instances men who were already engaged in teaching pure mathematics enrolled in courses in applied mathematics to get abreast of the latest developments. Significantly also one finds applied mathematicians among the theoretical physicists as well as in specialized departments of mathematics.

Obviously the whole atmosphere of mathematics in America is changing. It is a change that may be counted on to permeate the future of science and industry on this continent. The review made for the National Resources Planning Board in 1940 showed that, despite the enormous magnitude of American industry, it employed only about 150 mathematicians (not including statisticians and actuaries). Of the 150, one-third were in the electrical communications industries alone. Today, when refinement to one additional decimal point may mean the difference between a mediocre and a superior weapon, the demand for industrial mathematicians by the Office of Scientific Research and Development, the Navy Department, the War Department, the National Advisory Committee for Aeronautics, and by the various laboratories and manufacturing plants which are producing the new weapons is in excess of the number that the existing schools can supply. Indeed, the output of several more schools of applied mathematics could easily be used in the war effort, but there are not teachers enough to man them.

One fortunate circumstance is the presence among us of refugee scholars. The Nazi policy of driving independent brains out of Germany has been of inestimable advantage to the democracies, especially to the United States; and in no field are the benefits more marked than in mathematics. The former director of the Mathematical Institute at Göttingen, who left his homeland the year that Hitler came to power, is now head of the department of applied mathematics at New York University, and two of his associate professors are refugees from Göttingen. The school of applied mathematics at Brown also is strongly reinforced by emigré-scholars who were among Germany's most proficient applied mathematicians a few years ago. They include the former director of the Institute of Applied Mechanics at Göttingen, the former director of the Institute of Applied Mathematics at Berlin, and the former director of the Institute of Applied Mathematics at Kiel. Altogether, 131 professional mathematicians had migrated from Axis-dominated countries to the United States by the end of 1942, and many of them are filling important positions of teaching or research.

MATHEMATICS IN THE ARMY AND NAVY

The service of mathematics in war is not limited to assisting or guiding engineers in the design, production and testing of a weapon. It extends to the use of the weapon, the organzation and direction of the fighting resources, the participation in battle. At West Point and Annapolis the courses for the training of cadets and midshipmen are founded on solid years of mathematics; the study of physics, chemistry, and other technological subjects is mathematized, and these subjects are not elective.

In contrast with this tradition of rigorous training in analytical and objective habits of thinking at West Point and Annapolis, most of the American universities and liberal arts colleges have gradually through the years broadened their requirements, made mathematics an elective subject, and in consequence undergraduate interest in it sagged to a new low. Only a handful studied any mathematics in college, and accordingly many of the high schools and preparatory academies reduced their mathematical requirements to a very elementary level. In 1942 a prominent industrial-research director said that even the boy who finished high school with an "A" grade in mathematics has a poor foundation on which to build his future work in science.

These deficiencies in our educational system have been a serious handicap in the present emergency. The wartime army and navy, confronted with the problem of recruiting large numbers of men as future officer material, found ignorance of mathematics one of the most serious bottlenecks. From his experience as chief of the

Naval Bureau of Navigation in 1941, Admiral C. W. Nimitz reported that 4,200 freshmen in twenty-seven leading colleges were examined for admission to the Naval Reserve Officers' Training Corps, and 68 per cent failed to pass the entrance test in arithmetical reasoning. Only 10 per cent had studied elementary trigonometry; only 23 per cent had studied more than a year and a half of any mathematics in high school. When it came to college graduates, of 8,000 who were considered for commissioning as ensigns 3,000 had to be rejected because they were woefully deficient in mathematics.

Army examiners report much the same conditions. Sifting young men for the highly technical and specialized services of the Engineers Corps, the Signal Corps, the Air Force and the Artillery, they found that a large proportion of the recruits were unfamiliar with geometric relations and many were unable to perform simple arithmetical computations. In one Coast Artillery regiment arithmetic was so foreign to the capacities of most of the men that the entire group had to be put through months of instruction. Aviation in particular calls for a firm groundwork of elementary mathematics in its pilots, navigators and bombardiers; they must be proficient in arithmetic and geometry, and also must have some grasp of physics and trigonometry. With an average crew of three men per plane, and aircraft production on the scale of 100,000 a year, the training courses must care for several hundred thousand men per year for the air arm alone; while other mechanized branches of the army are demanding equal or corresponding mathematical training for their personnel.

The high school and college curricula have been made over on a nationwide scale to meet these needs of the army and navy, and mathematics is resuming its historic place in education. Whether this will continue as a post-war policy one can only conjecture. But, at any rate, when the war ends, many hundreds of thousands of young Americans will have been introduced to a scientific tool of great usefulness and to a method of thinking which cannot fail to have its influence on their lives in peace as well as in war.

While the army and navy, through their contractual arrangements with selected colleges, are thus training military and naval recruits, hundreds of other institutions have made shifts in their teaching arrangements. These are designed to provide training for young civilians, to prepare them for service in war industries, laboratories, arsenals, ordnance works, navy yards, and other places where mathematical knowledge is essential to efficient production. At the close of 1942, for example, Brooklyn College in New York had 4,000 students studying mathematics—3,000 in day courses and 1,000 in night courses, with an increasing proportion of young women in the classes. The program here is typical of the intensive acceleration of teaching in scores of institutions, particularly municipal colleges and colleges in large population centers.

The return to mathematics has educational significance. It lies in the fact that the teaching can be harnessed to practical problems. Instead of taking up mathematics as recent college graduates have done—as an enforced exercise in mental gymnastics, a cultural something necessary to fulfill the law and win a college degree—young people of today approach the subject as a tool to be used. Newton invented the calculus because he needed a tool with which to describe the path of a moving body whose velocity was changing at a fixed rate, a very real problem with which he was wrestling at the time. Similarly vector analysis had its origin in the need for a tool with which to attack a particular problem in mechanics. When youth are taught the calculus and vector analysis as tools to be used in making and using guns, aircraft, submarine detectors and warships, they partake of some of the satisfaction of the inventors who devised these powerful techniques. A beautiful thing loses none of its beauty and none of its importance by being found useful; and at the same time it becomes more interesting, more comprehensible, and more acceptable. Therein lies a promise of possible permanence for our mathematical renaissance.

CHAPTER VII

Out of the Crucibles

And as force, when brought against us, can only be repelled by force, the chief support of war must, after money, be now sought in chemistry.

—Hermann Boerhave, ELEMENTA CHEMIAE

THE chemical genius of the first world war was Professor Fritz Haber. His process of nitrogen fixation, which was of such first-rate scientific importance as to win him a Nobel Prize, was crucial to German military power in the great war. Without it the Kaiser's armies could hardly have lasted beyond two years, since it is known that Germany's reserves of saltpeter were woefully meager and the British blockade completely shut her off from access to the world's sources of supply in Chile. But there are 34,500 tons of free atmospheric nitrogen loose above every acre of the Earth's surface, and, thanks to Haber's inventiveness, Germany was able to snatch the element out of the air and combine it into compounds for the manufacture of explosives, fertilizers, and other useful chemicals. It was this highly efficient process of nitrogen fixation, *plus* the wide ramifications of the long-established German chemical trust, whose enormous resources of plant, techniques and personnel were completely mobilized to make munitions, *plus* the introduction of gas as a weapon that gave chemistry foremost place in the war of 1914--'18.

These German developments naturally stimulated counterefforts on the part of the British, French and Americans. In the United States the synthetic nitrogen industry was born of World War I demands and shortages. The shutting off of foreign sources of dyes, pharmaceuticals and other manufactured chemicals forced American interests to develop plants, processes, and personnel; and when the second world war came the United States was a major power in virtually every field of industrial chemistry.

NITROGEN

The Germans were not the first to take nitrogen from the air and combine it in a practical way into a useful compound. Indeed, there is a little-remembered American chapter in the prehistory of industrial nitrogen fixation. In 1900 the American chemists McDougall and Howles demonstrated a process of combining nitrogen with oxygen in the arc of a high-tension electric current. Shortly thereafter the Atmospheric Products Company was formed to utilize electric power generated at Niagara Falls to manufacture nitric acid; but the project was a commercial failure. More successful was an undertaking in Norway. In this process high-voltage currents were used to produce very large arcs—in effect, huge disks of flame having temperatures of 5400° F. and more. Through these fiery spaces air was blown, and the intense heat of the arc provided sufficient energy to unite the refractory nitrogen of the air with the oxygen of the air to form nitric oxide. By 1910 a substantial Norwegian nitrogen industry was operating, energized by the surplus water power of Norway's mountain streams.

Several German chemists had experimented with the arc process, but only in a land of abundant waterfalls or other cheap sources of power could these high-energy methods be regarded as industrially sound—and Germany was not such a land. What was needed was a method of manufacture that would be at least as economical as the importation of nitrate from Chile.

Fritz Haber, born in Breslau in 1868, had been teaching at the Polytechnic Institute of Karlsruhe since 1894, and since 1898 had been professor there. He was a specialist in physical chemistry, the "science of chemical energetics" whose laws connecting physical change with chemical change had recently been formulated by the Yale mathematical physicist Josiah Willard Gibbs (1839-1903). It would be difficult to find a more striking contrast than that pre-sented by these two scientists. Gibbs, physically frail and angular, taciturn, typically New Englandish, mathematical and abstract in thought, performed no laboratory experiments. His papers specify no particular chemical substances for the theoretical reactions with which he dealt, but these symbolic equations indicate the proce-dures by which experiments with any substances whatever can be made to yield the most precise and productive results. Haber was heavy-set, bald, genial and expansive, loquacious and positive in speech; he wrote poetry for relaxation; but his mind was keenly objective, with an admirable respect for experimental facts. He knew the theory of energetics perfectly, and at Karlsruhe pursued the fascinating study of gases and measured their behavior under the control of heat and pressure.

Often he had pondered the problem of nitrogen—this element so important to industry, so essential to agriculture; prodigally loose in the atmosphere of which it constitutes nearly four-fifths of the volume, and yet so unsocial, so chemically inaccessible in its free, unbound state. How could a nitrogen system be set up so that a minimum of physical energy would produce a maximum of chem-ical change? What chemical ruse would most economically trap the inert element into union? The Gibbsian equations were his chart and compass in this search. These equations pointed to the joining of nitrogen to hydrogen as offering a more economical solution of the problem than trying to combine nitrogen with oxygen, as in the electric-arc process.

So Professor Haber began a series of experiments. Hydrogen was rather cheaply available. It could be procured by passing steam over heated coke. Nitrogen of course could be taken from the air. He confined one part of nitrogen by volume with three parts of hydrogen, subjected the mixture to various degrees of heat and pressure, and found that the two gases would conveniently unite at a temperature of about 1112° F. and a pressure 200 times that of the atmosphere. The product was ammonia, NH_3, which could be converted to nitric acid, explosives, fertilizers and other useful com-pounds.

This synthesis of ammonia was achieved by 1908, and the secret was turned over to the Badische Aniline and Soda Works for indus-trial application. Thereafter Carl Bosch, chemist in this plant of the

I. G. Farbenindustrie, had charge of the engineering development of the process. Bosch made important contributions, including the discovery of an inexpensive and effective catalyst, and the method that finally emerged was called by Badische the Haber-Bosch process. The first large-scale installation was a plant at Oppau, completed in 1913, and nitrogen fixation was just getting into operation when the affair at Sarajevo touched off the war. It came earlier than the war lords would have preferred, for one nitrogen plant was not enough to supply wartime needs. Through their secret service, however, the German military authorities learned that 50,000 tons of Chilean nitrate were in warehouses in Antwerp, and a contributing reason for the 1914 invasion of Belgium was to capture these chemical stores. They reinforced the output of the Oppau plant and enabled explosives manufacturers to keep going until the vaster nitrogen works near Merseburg began to pour out their synthetic product early in 1917, and thereafter the Reich had no fear of a nitrogen shortage.

Haber meanwhile had moved to Berlin, where he had been appointed director of the recently erected Kaiser Wilhelm Institute for Physical Chemistry and Electrochemistry in the suburb Dahlem. It was one of the most distinguished posts in German science. Here all his time was free for research, in a laboratory equipped with everything to delight the heart of an investigator. When the war came this institute had been in operation two years. Haber was intensely patriotic. He was German through and through; his family had been important in Breslau for over a century; and the war touched him to the innermost fiber. He dropped all work at the institute and placed himself and his laboratories at the service of the War Ministry, which at once appointed him head of its department of raw materials. He was an indefatigable worker, helping greatly to speed up production of the much-needed explosives, and when the stalemate of trench warfare dashed the German hope of quick victory it was to Haber that the army command turned for advice on the use of gas.

GAS AS A WEAPON

Gas warfare is not a modern invention. It is older than gunpowder. During the prolonged war between Sparta and Athens in the Fifth century B.C., the Spartans soaked wood in a mixture of pitch and sulphur, and the burning of these saturated fagots under the walls of the Greek cities, or thrown into Greek garrisons, released sulphur dioxide and other smothering gases. On another occasion, during their siege of Plataea, the Spartans are said to have ignited a mixture of arsenic, pitch and tar—an early anticipation of Twentieth-century arsenicides. Greek fire, though its original formula is lost, apparently contained pitch, resin, petroleum, saltpeter, sand and quicklime. It burned with explosive violence, giving off clouds of smoke and gases which rendered its victims helpless. In the Fifteenth century, when the Turks overswept the Balkans and besieged Belgrade, the beleaguered Christians burned cloths impregnated with chemicals, and a wind carried the fumes to the enemy. After Belgrade had been saved from the infidels, it was agreed that Christ's followers should never use such a weapon against one another.

Actually the first employment of a gas in World War I was by the French. They fired rifle grenades containing a bromine tear gas as early as August, 1914. In November, when bromine became scarce, the French substituted a chlorine compound. There is no report of any military results gained by the tear-gas attacks, but the use of these lachrymators enabled the Germans to charge a technical violation of the Hague pact.

It was after they were stopped at the Marne that the Germans began to consider gas as a weapon. They were short of explosives for the static warfare that the French and British had developed to counter the mobile tactics that had broken through Belgium and France. So gas was proposed both as a substitute for explosives and as an auxiliary to drive the Allies out of their trenches. There is some doubt as to whether Haber was first to propose the use of gas by the Germans. Professor Walther Nernst of the University of Berlin made some early experiments for the high command, and it is possible that the suggestion of the new weapon actually came from him. However, Haber was the man to whom the job of developing the chemicals and techniques for their projection was committed, and in December, 1914, his Kaiser Wilhelm Institute became headquarters for these preparations. The first casualty of German gas warfare was one of Haber's associates. Otto Sakur. He was experimenting with a compound which had been sent by an industrial chemist to be tested as a war gas, when a few drops of the experimental substance exploded in a test tube in Sakur's hands, killing him instantly. Thereafter more familiar gases were considered, and the final choice fell on chlorine. A plan for releasing it on the ground from metal cylinders was worked out, and by April everything was ready for the first trial in actual combat.

CHLORINE—PHOSGENE—MUSTARD

The day dawned—April 22nd, 1915. The place—Ypres. It was perfect spring weather; mild, clear, with a gentle breeze from the east. Morning waxed to noon, and the shadows lengthened with rarely the rumble of a gun to mar the soft vernal calm. The French and British troops were hoping for an equally quiet night, when suddenly at 5 o'clock the Germans let loose a furious bombardment from heavy howitzers, and high-explosive shells began to drop into villages and towns northeast of Ypres. This was the opening salvo, the prelude, the preparation for—what?

The men in the front trenches saw a strange yellow fog drifting toward them from the German line. Some said it looked like two clouds that crept forward separately, then interlaced and merged, greenish-yellow, hovering over the ground and billowing forward with the spring breeze. Above the yellow mist loomed the blue sky. A few minutes later men were coughing, choking, clutching at their throats, running away, stumbling, terrified. "It was at first impossible for anyone to realize what had actually happened," reported Field Marshal French. "The smoke and fumes hid everything from sight, and hundreds of men were thrown into a comatose or dying condition, and within an hour the whole position had to be abandoned." Twenty thousand were rendered helpless, and 5,000 of them died.

There was a gaping hole in the Allied front; but the Germans acted as though they were surprised by their advantage. With sufficient troops they could have swept to the channel ports—it is conceivable that in one bold stroke they might have won the war that April day. But the attacking forces were slow to follow up; they had not been provided with adequate reserves, and they made only a timid advance. Meanwhile the Allies hastily reestablished their line.

It has been said that the German high command had no confidence in gas warfare; that the military rather resented the innovation, coming as it did from a civilian—worse still from a Jew, and that they deliberately ignored recommendations to exploit it to the full. Haber made no such charges, but it is known that he believed in gas warfare, believed it was more humane than warfare with high explosives, and did his best to insure it a fair trial. Whatever the explanation, the chance was muffed that April evening; and thereafter the golden opportunity was gone. For within a few days the British and French had improvised gas masks out of cotton pads saturated with washing soda and photographer's "hypo"; and these makeshift respirators, tied over mouth and nose with gauze, "ate up" the stifling chlorine.

The German command now took the matter up in deadly earnest. It selected phosgene, a colorless gas which has an insidious delayed action that fools the victim. It concentrated heavy reserves of infantry behind the front, ready to rush forward as soon as the Allied line was broken, and on December 19, 1915, released 88 tons of phosgene and chlorine. But the British Intelligence Service had got wind of these preparations, knew that phosgene was to be used and that the attack was to be made before Ypres. So the Allies were ready. They had provided their soldiers with special masks containing sodium phenolate, which neutralizes phosgene, and the casualties were only 1,069 with 120 deaths. Meanwhile a furious Allied artillery bombardment inflicted heavy damage upon the tens of thousands of German infantrymen massed for the follow-up.

Gas now became a weapon on both sides. Soon the Allies were loosing huge clouds of chlorine against the German lines, then clouds of phosgene; and even the weather took a hand, for the winds were prevailingly from the west. On the average, there was only one day in six when the Germans could successfully launch a gas-cloud attack; on the other five days the wind favored the Allies, and they made effective use of it. Right up to the last year of the war they continued to harass the enemy with gas clouds, and inflicted serious casualties. Meanwhile, in the summer of 1916, the German general staff abandoned cloud tactics, and thereafter made their poison attacks by bombarding the Allies with poison in shells.

These shell fillings were not really gas. Most of them were

liquids, a few were solids, and the effect of the burst was to scatter the chemicals in the form of minute droplets or particles. The most effective proved to be the amber, oily, liquid dichlordiethyl sulphide, known as mustard gas, first introduced to the battlefield by the Germans in July of 1917, with Ypres again the objective. Haber had warned the generals against using mustard gas unless they were confident that they could end the war in a few weeks. "Our enemies have far more raw materials than we have, and unless you can get a quick decision they will have time to manufacture quantities of this gas far beyond anything that we can do."

Mustard is a terror. As a lung irritant phosgene is ten times more poisonous than chlorine, but mustard gas is five times more poisonous than phosgene. And mustard has additional effects. It causes inflammation of the eyes, temporary blindness, sneezing and nausea; and wherever it touches the skin it blisters. Pound for pound, according to Professor James Kendall, mustard "produced nearly eight times as many casualties as the average of all other poison gases used in the World War."

The Germans also fired shells filled with solid substances which were dispersed by the heat and violence of the explosion. Some were poisonous. Some merely induced fits of sneezing and vomiting, but they forced the victim to remove his mask, whereupon the accompanying mustard gas got in its work. In reprisal, the French developed sternite, which combined toxic effects with the sneeze-inducing effect. Even more powerful was the arsenic compound adamsite: named for Professor Roger Adams, of the University of Illinois, who invented it. Adamsite never saw battle service, but tons of it were on the docks awaiting transport to Europe when the armistice came. Another arsenic compound also ready for use was lewisite: named for Professor W. L. Lewis, who first put its molecule together in a laboratory of Catholic University of America. Although its chemical structure is very different, lewisite is like mustard in that it penetrates fabric, blisters and burns the skin, and is a highly toxic lung irritant.

Recent chemical research has developed new gases, including a group of blistering agents known as the nitrogen mustards. They are actually not so severe in their blistering effect as straight mustard gas, but are more insidious because they are without odor. The garlic smell which attaches to mustard gas betrays its presence immediately, but a few shells of nitrogen mustard dropped during a bombardment might escape detection until hours later when blisters, blindness, lung action, and other delayed effects began to manifest themselves.

THE WEAPON OF TERROR

Of all forms of warfare gas seems to the humane sense the most revolting. It is terrifying, perhaps more feared than any other weapon. But this attitude is more emotional than rational, probably grounded in fear of the unknown. Gas warfare is horrible, as all war is, but its record of destructiveness does not match that of explosives and projectiles. Gas is to be deplored not as more deadly than other weapons, but rather because it provides an additional weapon—and the more weapons, the more slaughter. If gas could be substituted for gunfire, with all nations honestly renouncing the use of explosives, there is reason to believe that the mortality rate of war would actually be reduced. An objective study of this matter is reported by Colonel A. M. Prentiss in his *Chemicals in War*. After making a careful analysis of the casualty records of World War I and comparing the effects of the various lethal weapons, Colonel Prentiss arrives at the conclusion that "chemical warfare is the most humane method of warfare yet devised by man."

In the first place, its casualties suffer less at the time of injury than the victims of bayonet, bullet, or shell-inflicted wounds. Many of the gases occasion no initial pain, and there is evidence that the pneumonia caused by chlorine or phosgene is less distressing than the usual wounds inflicted by shell fragments. *The Official Medical History of the War* records that gas casualties, on the average, were confined to hospitals only half as many days as were men injured by gunfire.

The proportion of deaths to the total number of casualties is less for gas than for other weapons. For all nations, in 1914-'18, one out of every four battle-wounded soldiers died; but of those suffering from gas injuries only one out of fourteen died. Records of the American Expeditionary Force strengthen this statistical picture. In the ratio of total deaths to the total number of battle-wounded, the figure for the Americans is the same as that for the other Allies:

out of every four wounded one died. But in the case of American gas casualties only one out of fifty died. The reason is clear. The American forces entered the battle line after gas warfare was established, with gas masks and other countermeasures already developed.

Moreover, the after effects of gas are less permanent than those inflicted by shot and shell. One of the most often deplored horrors of gas is its effect on eyesight, but in 1931 General H. L. Gilchrist found that among veterans of the American Expeditionary Force only 33 cases of blindness could be traced to gas, whereas there were 779 whose blindness was cause by other weapons. Medical records of the A.E.F. show that the incidence of tuberculosis among the soldiers who have been gassed was actually less than the average rate for the entire force. Referring to all injuries, "it must be realized," said General Gilchrist, "that the great majority of gas casualties make a complete recovery."

The use of aircraft to drop gas bombs was not attempted in World War I. Italy first employed the combination against Ethiopia, and Japan has used it repeatedly against China. Perhaps the personnel who are most vulnerable to gas raids are the populations of large cities. Dropped in association with explosives and incendiaries, a persistent gas like mustard can contaminate streets, cellars, subways, and areas around bombed structures for days; slowing if not preventing rescue measures, breeding fear and panic. A German writer, referring to the experience with gas warfare during 1915-'18, called it "the greatest disappointment of the war"; a destroyer of fighting spirit on both sides, most successful when directed toward the disintegration of civilian morale. Both before and during the present war, the threat of gas and hints of the secret chemical horrors held in reserve have been among the weapons of German psychological warfare.

AFTERMATH IN GERMANY

Exact figures of German losses from gas have not been published. It is known that during the war the authorities sought to conceal the extent of gas casualties, camouflaging many of them under other classifications in the official reports. But certain data are on record, and from these and other evidence Colonel Prentiss estimates that during the first world war gas disabled not less than

200,000 German soldiers, of whom 9,000 died. The British gas casualties were 188,706, of whom 8,109 died, and the French approximately 190,000, of whom 8,000 died. On this basis, the death rate among the Germans was slightly higher than that among the Allies. Whatever the actual German losses, they were sufficient to confirm the wisdom of Haber's warning.

From prisoners of war, intercepted letters and other captured documents the Allies learned of the panic caused in enemy ranks by their giving back the Germans as good as they sent. "Not a day passes but the British let off their gas waves at one place or another," wrote a German soldier from the Somme in 1916. Among the captured documents was a special order from Ludendorff dated in 1918, shortly after the French began to bombard the original mustard-gassers with their own medicine. "Our yellow cross (mustard gas) has caused much damage to the enemy, formerly less protected than now," writes Ludendorff. "But as a natural sequence he has developed through it a gas discipline which can certainly be taken as a model. On this account enemy troops have been able to cross, at once and without loss, areas which their artillery had just bombarded with gas." And Ludendorff adds, "We also must train our troops to an excellent standard of gas discipline if we expect to avoid the grave dangers which threaten the fighting forces of our army."

As Germany was collapsing under the weight of the war which had lasted too long for her strategy, Haber received a message from the Swedish Academy of Sciences. It announced the award to him of the Nobel Prize in Chemistry. The citation made no mention of gas warfare. It was his invention of a "technically practical process of procuring ammonia synthetically from its elements" that won him the great recognition.

Some of the gloom that swept over a finally conquered Germany, with public realization of defeat, was lightened by a rumor that began to circulate. The ingenious Professor Haber, it was said, would pay the German war indemnity. He would get the necessary gold from the sea. There is more gold in the sea than has ever been mined—hundreds of thousands of times more; and it was true that Haber had begun an investigation to test methods of extracting it. After a few months he came back with some glistening granules—

gold from the ocean, but he had to report that the cost of processing the water was many times the value of the yield.

He buried himself in his researches at the Kaiser Wilhelm Institute, companioning with a few old friends. His most intimate crony was Richard Willstaetter, professor of chemistry at the University of Munich, Nobel prize winner in 1915. It is reported that when Haber first told Willstaetter of the scheme for gas warfare, the latter protested and argued against it. But no difference ever marred the comradeship of these two. On one occasion, it is said, they chartered a yacht and put to sea in order to discuss a scientific problem without interruption.

In Munich Willstaetter finally found himself uncomfortably near the center of the mounting Nazi furor. Dahlem, the genteel Berlin suburb in which Haber worked, was different; more exclusive, more conservative. But even there the Brown Shirts marched, and Haber was beginning to sense a change that was more than physical change or chemical change: a destructive social change whipped up by this small but ruthless group of political terrorists.

An American scientist recalls a visit to Haber in Dahlem in 1930. They met in the director's residence on the grounds of the institute, and the German drew his visitor outside on a balcony and paced back and forth, talking vehemently as he walked, deeply troubled by the growing intolerance, lawlessness, atrocities, and the timid attitude of the government. Haber was a man of positive character, frank and outspoken. At scientific meetings he was always a dominant figure. Some of his conferees playfully called him "King of Dahlem."

In 1933, after Hitler became German chancellor, the Kaiser Wilhelm Institute observed Easter vacation in its usual way by closing for a fortnight. The day before the end of this recess Director Haber received a telephone call from a subaltern official in the Ministry of Education: "Herr Direktor, the institute will remain closed temporarily."

Professor Haber expressed surprise at the peremptory order, and asked in whose name the order was given, and for what reason.

The order came from Kultusminister Rust, said the voice, and there were certain Jewish members of the staff who must be dispensed with before the institute could resume operations. In particular, the director must immediately dismiss Herbert Freundlich and Michael Polanyi.

These were two of Haber's ablest collaborators, and the director was furious. "If they are dismissed on account of their Jewish race," he answered, "I too shall be among the people who leave the institute."

"But this is not directed against you," protested the official. "You are a former officer of the army, you are a distinguished consultant of the state, you are Geheimer Regierungsrat, your service is indispensable."

"Nevertheless, I also am a Jew. And if the conditions you name are carried out, I shall resign."

The official repeated his protestations, and asked the director to withhold action until he could consult his superiors. A few days later an appointment was made for Haber to meet Dr. Rust, but when he called at the ministry Rust sent a subordinate to see him. A second engagement was made, and again the minister failed to keep the engagement. It is rumored that when Haber's determination was made known to him, Rust retorted with a sneer, "Well, that will be one Jew less." A few days after the formal letter of resignation was received, Rust stated in a radio broadcast that he would crush all attempts to interfere with the racial principles of the Reich, "even though they originate with the most famous professor of chemistry."

Invitations came from Professor Jean Perrin at the University of Paris, Professor F. G. Donnan at the University of London, and Sir William Pope of Cambridge University offering Professor Haber a place in which to carry on his scientific work, and he finally accepted the arrangement at Cambridge. But he made it his first business to find positions for his purged laboratory men, placing some in Switzerland, others in France, England, Belgium. Then he went on to Cambridge, and spent two months there completing a research report that had been rudely interrupted by the collapse of his world at Dahlem. But he was restless and not happy. He had a serious heart ailment which had bothered him for years. Friends recall that Professor Haber used to carry a small vial of nitroglycerine in one vest pocket, a silver spoon in the other, and whenever he felt "it" coming on he would measure himself two drops and swallow the dose. Sometimes on the platform, in the august presence of a learned society, he would stop, administer the fortifying drops, rest a moment, and then resume his discussion. But hearts don't heal in exile or grow younger with anxiety. Haber longed for his old haunts, wanted to see Willstaetter again, and in January went to Switzerland. His son Hermann, who accompanied him, recalls that even during that last illness he was discussing plans for future research. He died in Basle January 29, 1934.

It is worth noting, by way of postscript, that German shells and bombs continue to owe their nitrogen to Fritz Haber's inventiveness—and so too, for that matter, do American and British shells and bombs. For today more than ninety per cent of the world's synthetic nitrogen compounds are fabricated according to Haber. There are improvements, of course. Chemistry has not stood still. But the fundamental creative achievement remains his.

THE NATURE OF EXPLOSIVES

Nitrogen is valuable as an explosives ingredient because of its peculiar chemical habit of joining loosely with oxygen and then franticly breaking loose and rushing away at the least disturbance. Every time a sixteen-inch gun is fired, ninety pounds of nitrogen take part in the propulsion of the shell, and when the shell explodes another thirty pounds assist its fragmentation. When a naval torpedo hits its mark, one hundred pounds of nitrogen locked up in the solid explosive suddenly changes into many times its volume of gas. Nitrogen helps to burst almost all the shells, bombs, grenades and other projectiles used in war.

And yet an explosion can take place without nitrogen, and there are powerful detonants which contain none. For example, a strong nonnitrogenous explosive can be made of oxygen in its liquid form and some other element for which oxygen has great affinity, such as carbon in the form of soot or charcoal. If a bag is first filled with the carbon and then soaked in liquid oxygen until the carbon is saturated, the combination becomes a high explosive. From time to time there have been rumors that Germans or Japanese were dropping lox (liquid oxygen) bombs, but no evidence of such usage has been made public, and the difficulties and hazards render it improbable. Liquid oxygen is inconvenient to handle, because it is extremely cold (296 degrees below zero F.) and is continuously evaporating. On account of this evaporation, the bomb or other container must be open. For the same reason, the mixture is continuously deteriorating, and ceases to be explosive when the oxygen has vaporized. Moreover, the mixture is so quick-tempered that a slight jolt is sufficient to explode it. Such a bomb carried in an airplane would constitute a serious hazard to its carrier.

There are also explosives which contain no oxygen. An example is cuprous acetylide, composed of copper and carbon. This compound is so unstable that a little heat, friction, or a slight shock will cause its molecule to fly apart into solid copper and solid soot. No gas is formed, but the decomposition is accompanied by a sudden release of much heat, and the instantaneous heating of the air causes its rapid expansion and results in a violent explosion. Copper acetylide is too sensitive to be of military use, but is representative of a large class of substances which explode by the breakdown of the molecule. Mercury fulminate and lead azide are also of this nature, though more stable.

Other explosives accomplish their sudden evolution of heat through the opposite chemical reaction. Not the breakdown of a molecule but the uniting of molecules or parts of molecules to form new substances releases the inherent energy. The liquid-oxygen explosive operates on this plan: here the saturated soot or charcoal combines with the oxygen to form gaseous carbon dioxide, and the swift emergence of this gas with heat is the explosion. The reaction is a rapid burning, and explosives which follow this pattern require oxygen as a necessary ingredient. For various reasons the oxygen is more manageable when it is associated with nitrogen, therefore most explosives of this type contain both oxygen and nitrogen.

An example is gunpowder, a product that probably has influenced more history than any other man-made material. It is not a pure substance, but a mechanical mixture of charcoal, saltpeter and sulphur. Charcoal of course is our old stand-by, carbon. Saltpeter introduces us to the use of nitrogen in explosion, for it is a nitrate, a compound containing nitrogen linked to oxygen. The third component, sulphur, is yellow brimstone, easy to catch fire. It is this flammable property of sulphur that accounts for its presence in gunpowder, for charcoal and saltpeter alone will burn but require considerable heat to ignite. Sulphur, however, has a low ignition point; a spark is sufficient to start combustion. And as it burns in gunpowder, the sulphur releases heat which activates the saltpeter to give up its oxygen; the oxygen then combines with the charcoal to generate more heat, producing gases which are further expanded by the high temperature of the reaction. Saltpeter readily releases its oxygen, apparently because the nitrogen holds its chemical bonds so lightly. We may picture the saltpeter as bringing the oxygen into the mixture on a loosely held tether, and letting it go when shaken by heat. As the freed oxygen flies to join the carbon and form carbon-dioxide gas, the nitrogen stampedes for the open. The total effect is the rapid conversion of solid substances of small volume into gaseous substances of large volume.

During the Nineteenth century, chemists discovered that they could make explosives enormously more powerful than gunpowder by putting the oxygen atoms and the combustibles into the same molecule. Instead of a mechanical mixture of sulphur, saltpeter and charcoal they built single compounds, combining in one molecular structure all of the desired properties. It was found that glycerine treated with nitric acid produced a liquid substance composed of hydrogen and carbon (contributed by the glycerine) and nitrogen and oxygen (contributed by the acid). Both hydrogen and carbon are highly flammable in the presence of oxygen; and all that was necessary to explode this new liquid was a little heat, friction, a slight jolt, or almost any minor disturbance. At the slightest stimulation the nitrogen atoms took flight; and, since there was nothing to separate them, the oxygen rushed into explosive union with the hydrogen and the carbon.

This was nitroglycerine, too sensitive to be used in guns. A somewhat similar explosive was made by treating cotton with nitric acid. Like the glycerine of the previous experiment, cotton fiber is a structure of carbon, oxygen and hydrogen. It is known as cellulose. The effect of the treatment was to detach NO_2 from the acid and hook three of these nitro groups into separate places in the cellulose molecule, resulting in trinitrocellulose or guncotton. The cotton did not look very different after treatment. It was still a white fluffy fiber. But it was vastly different chemically, and if heated slightly it would detonate with a loud report.

Many years passed before these two independent discoveries received application. First it was found that guncotton is soluble. When soaked in a mixture of alcohol and ether its fibers disappeared, and the solution took the form of a jelly. On evaporation the jelly became a stiff paste which could be extruded like spaghetti, sliced, or chopped into pieces of any size; and on further evaporation the pieces became hard. This was smokeless powder. Various improvements have been made through the years, but the basic formula remains, and today nitrocellulose smokeless powder is the principal propellant used by the U. S. Army and Navy. The German and French ordnance authorities have also generally favored this type, whereas the British give their preference to cordite.

Cordite originated from Alfred Nobel's idea of combining guncotton with nitroglycerine to make the paste. He found that the explosive fiber would dissolve in the explosive liquid in the presence of acetone, and when diluted with a mineral jelly the resulting colloid could be squirted through holes into cords of any diameter. While still plastic the cords were cut into rods of the desired length. This cordite was the smokeless powder with which the British fought the South African War. It is widely used in the present war to charge the cartridges, both of rifles and of artillery. The size of cordite varies according to its purpose. In a rifle cartridge the charge consists of about fifty rods each of the thickness of a darning needle, whereas in the cartridge of a big naval or coast-defense gun the rods resemble large sticks of candy and may exceed an inch in diameter.

PICRIC ACID AND TNT

The South African War not only introduced cordite to the battlefield but demonstrated the shell-bursting qualities of high explosives. Heretofore various gunpowders had been used as shell fillings, but they were too slow in action and were unsatisfactory for other reasons. Nitroglycerine and guncotton were too sensitive; the impact of the propellant against the shell was likely to set them off and burst the shell before it left the gun barrel. What was needed was a stable compound that would endure the tremendous blow of the gun's discharge, that would travel undisturbed through whatever range the shell was fired and detonate only at the dictation of the fuze, but at high speed and with violent fragmentation of the shell casing. Lyddite was the British answer to this need, and it was used with devastating effect upon the Boers.

Lyddite proved to be only a fancy name for picric acid, a well-known yellow compound used industrially as a dye for fabrics. Its base was carbolic acid or phenol, derived from coal tar, which under appropriate treatment with nitric acid took up three nitro groups and became trinitrophenol. When the Russo-Japanese War came the Japanese used shimose to fill the shells they fired at the Russians, and meanwhile the French war office had adopted melenite as its high explosive—but both were picric acid. With the call to arms in 1914 all countries enlarged their operations for manufacturing picric acid. American production of phenol multiplied nearly twentyfold between 1914 and 1918. By 1917 we were turning out 3,500 tons of picric acid annually, and by 1918 this had increased to 70,000 tons.

Joffre stopped the invader at the Marne with picric acid, but the Germans fought back with t.n.t. For while they were applying Fritz Haber's method of fixing nitrogen, they were also developing a large-scale industrial process to produce this new explosive. Not the phenol of picric acid, but toluol, a compound of hydrogen and carbon derived from coal tar, was the base material. When the toluol was properly treated with nitric acid it took unto itself three nitro groups—just as the glycerine, the cellulose, and the phenol did—and the result was trinitrotoluene.

Of all the high explosives practicable for military use, t.n.t. is perhaps the simplest to manufacture and the safest to handle. A rifle bullet can be fired through a bomb of t.n.t. without disturbing it, and yet a kick from the booster charge in the primer shocks it into immediate and powerful explosion. It melts at a lower temperature than picric acid, pours easily, and can be stored without danger of deterioration. Moreover, t.n.t. does not react chemically with steel, as picric acid does; therefore tin-plating of the inside of the shell is not necessary. The coal-tar operations of the I. G. Farbenindustrie yielded German ammunition plants ample quantities of toluol for t.n.t. manufacture; but the industries of the Allies, particularly of England, were better geared to the production of phenol. Nevertheless, all resources available were turned as soon as could be managed to the production of toluol. In the United States its extraction from coal tar increased nearly tenfold in the four years of war and stood at 14,100,000 gallons in 1918. In the present war, t.n.t. is the supreme explosive on both sides of the conflict. The annual production of toluol in the United States had reached 25,000,000 gallons by 1940. The editors of *Chemical and Metallurgical Engineering* estimated in November, 1940, that an American armed force of 2,000,000 men in the field would require an annual production of 65,000,000 gallons to supply ammunition needs. The War Production Board's program for 1943 calls for 300,000,000 gallons.

Despite the industrial speed-up, the Allies in World War I never got their toluol production up to the level of requirements, so they resorted to the expedient of mixing their limited supplies of t.n.t. with ammonium nitrate. It was a fortunate expedient, for this mixture, known as amatol, is more powerful than straight t.n.t. Ammonium nitrate has a surplus of oxygen beyond its own explosive needs, while t.n.t. has a surplus of carbon. It is because of the extra carbon that the burst of a t.n.t. shell gives off clouds of black smoke. Amatol detonates with no smoke, because the surplus oxygen of the ammonium nitrate combines with the extra carbon of the t.n.t. to complete combustion. An even more powerful explosive is made by adding powdered aluminum to amatol. This metal has a high affinity for oxygen, it burns with the release of white heat, and the explosion of the ammonium nitrate plus the explosion of the t.n.t. under the acceleration of the aluminum combustion carries tremendous explosive force.

The gases produced by the explosion of black powder occupy nearly 500 times as much space as the original explosive; those generated by t.n.t., 1,100 times the original volume; while mercury fulminate expands 1,400 times. These figures do not give a true comparison of the strength of the three explosives, however. Mercury fulminate, because of its high density, gives virtually the same amount of gas per pound as black gunpowder; but t.n.t. gives more than twice as much per pound as either black powder or the fulminate. This is one reason that t.n.t. is more practical than either black powder or mercury fulminate for use as a bursting charge in shells.

Each explosive material has its characteristic velocity of detonation. An explosion moves through black powder at the rate of 500 to 2,000 feet per second, the precise speed depending on the degree of granulation of the powder. Mercury fulminate explodes at about 2.4 miles per second, t.n.t. at nearly 4 miles per second. It is also possible to measure the heat of an explosion, the amount of energy released, the strength of the explosion, and the sensitiveness of the explosive. Each of these factors may have a bearing on whether a particular mixture or compound is to serve as propellant, detonant, or high explosive.

PROPELLANTS, DETONANTS, HIGH EXPLOSIVES

Because it burns slowly, gunpowder gives the projectile time to move out of the cartridge and through the barrel; whereas t.n.t., mercury fulminate, or any explosive which reacts with high velocity would burst the gun. The smokeless powders which have superseded gunpowder are all relatively slow. Indeed they are built to specified velocities of explosion determined by the dilutant used in manufacture and by the size of the powder grains or rods. In the present war the principal propellants are nitrocellulose smokeless powder and cordite, with minor use of ammon powder (a mixture of ammonium nitrate and charcoal).

Mercury fulminate, because it detonates instantaneously—releasing all its energy in one stupendous push, is used as an initiator to start detonation in the more stable explosives. A pinch of it is in the cartridge cap or primer, and when the trigger is pulled the firing pin, plunging into this sensitive substance, causes the struck molecules to fly apart, communicating the shock to their neighbors; and the rushing explosion creates an instantaneous pressure of nearly 200 tons to the square inch. It is the shock of this tremendous kick and the sudden release of heat that set off the smokeless powder. Similarly, in high-explosive shell or bomb, mercury fulminate provides a priming charge that will unfailingly explode at the moment of impact or of timing, and kick the t.n.t. into explosion. Usually, however, there is an intermediate charge of some other material—the booster it is called—which the primary detonation strikes first. The larger charge of booster then explodes and communicates its heavier shock to the main charge of t.n.t., thereby insuring complete detonation. In the present war mercury fulminate, lead azide and nitromannite are used as initiators or primary detonants. As intermediate detonants or boosters, the present favorites are tetryl, picric acid, tetra-nitro-aniline, and hexyl.

T.n.t. represents the third type of military explosive—a detonating chemical that is both powerful and stable, sensitive to the shock of the initiator or booster charge, but not too sensitive to endure the ordinary shocks of handling, firing, and collision. The compounds possessed of these properties are the true high explosives, and are used as the main charge for filling shells, bombs, torpedoes and mines. After t.n.t., the principal high explosives now in use are amatol, Explosive D (picric acid mixed with ammonium picrate), t.n.a. (tri-nitro-anisol) and penthrite. The last named, most important of the newer explosives, is economically made in large quantities from acetaldehyde and formaldehyde, materials which are readily available in the United States.

American production of explosives had reached an all-time high by 1943. The Du Pont output per day was greater then than its total for the entire four years of the American Civil War.

Despite their complicated names and alphabetical nicknames, most of the military explosives are simply various groupings of carbon, hydrogen, nitrogen and oxygen atoms. For the hydrogen-carbon part of the explosive molecule we formerly depended on coal. So complete was the dependence in 1918 that many city coal-gas plants were stripped of their toluol to supply the t.n.t. manufacturers. Today we have a richer, more abundant, purer source in petroleum. This mineral which supplies gasoline for our aircraft and other motorized weapons not only supplies toluol for our shells and bombs but acetone for our cordite, alcohol and ether for our smokeless powder, and butylene and butadiene for our synthetic rubber. The extraction or synthesis of these products from petroleum is an achievement of the last few years. Petroleum chemistry not only has provided powerful new technological resources for war but has opened vistas of unimaginable richness and variety for the postwar world.

SUPERFUELS AND SUPERLUBRICANTS

Crude petroleum is a mixture, a vast hodgepodge of hundreds of thousands of substances. Most of them are composed of just two elements, hydrogen and carbon. But nature has combined the two in so many proportions and arrangements that these hydrocarbon molecules are of bewildering diversity in size, shape, weight and in other properties. Some are so light that they drift off as gas. Others are so heavy that they settle out of the viscous soup as solids. And between these extremes are thousands of liquids. If ever there was a mess of heterogeneous substances, this is it. Without Willard Gibbs's equations to guide the application of the forces of heat, pressure, and surface phenomena, it is difficult to see how the results could be other than a dubious gamble. As it is, physical chemistry gives direction to processes for which an earlier technology could only trust to luck.

America's first advantage lies in its endowment of raw material. We have within the United States nearly half of the world's known petroleum deposits. And there are additional stores in the near-by fields of Mexico, Venezuela, and other Central and South American lands. Having so much of nature's wealth to start with, we have in times past dipped into these resources with prodigal recklessness; taking the parts of the mineral that were desired at the moment, allowing the rest to escape, or even deliberately throwing it away as so much waste.

There is no waste today. The gases, liquids, solids; every fraction of the crude petroleum, every molecule or fragment of a molecule— all are useful in these ingenious processes. It would be possible to convert the whole mess, from the lightest gas to the heaviest solid constituent, into gasoline. The processes necessary for 100 per cent conversion are known and can be readily applied. But the demands upon petroleum are so many-sided that an all-out conversion would be uneconomic and wasteful. Millions of barrels of fuel oils are needed for our battleships, transports and cargo carriers. Thousands of barrels of lubricating oils are needed to smooth the way of our engines, pistons, wheels, and wheels within wheels.

There is a giant octopus-like molecule, a huge hydrocarbon chain with many side chains swinging out like tentacles, which has the rare faculty of wrapping itself around sharp-edged oil molecules and promoting their flow under freezing conditions. A single molecule of this paraflow contains thousands of atoms. It is being used as a dilutant for antifreeze lubricants, for use in aircraft in the subzero altitudes. But extreme heat also affects lubricants adversely, causing them to thin out unduly; and a remedy for this has been found in another synthetic hydrocarbon known as paratone. It is used, for example, in the oil-recoil system of modern artillery, a peculiarly hot spot. Paratone also circulates in the oil-pressure system of the hydraulic-power mechanisms used to turn the gun turrets of bombing planes. Both of these synthetic lubricants are being made to order, processed from petroleum fractions.

Separation of the complicated petroleum mélange begins with distillation. This obvious process was introduced in the Nineteenth century when kerosene was the most valuable part of rock oil. In those days it was a problem to get rid of the useless gasoline. With the rise of the motorcar and other machines making use of the internal-combustion engine, the amount of gasoline that could be separated finally reached its maximum. The boiling points of the various petroleum components had been determined, and before the beginning of World War I it was clear that little more could be gained from improving the process of fractional distillation.

It occurred to William M. Burton, a chemist with the Standard Oil Company of Indiana, that additional gasoline might be made from the heavy oils. The natural gasolines were molecules of various sizes, but they averaged about eight carbon atoms to the molecule. This fairly typical eight-carbon structure was called octane. Other gasoline molecules had seven carbon atoms, heptane; others six, hexane; and the lightest had five, pentane. Dr. Burton knew that among the kerosenes and heavier oils were many structures of sixteen, eighteen, twenty, thirty, and larger numbers of carbon atoms. The idea struck him that if heat and pressure were applied many of these big molecules would crack up, with the likelihood that some of the pieces would be within the size range of gasoline. Thus, if a molecule containing sixteen carbon atoms broke exactly in half, there would be two fragments containing eight carbon atoms each; and if they carried along or picked up the necessary accompaniment of hydrogen they might serve as two molecules of gasoline. And so with other heavy molecules. It was too much to expect all to break evenly into gasoline patterns, but the probabilities were that some would.

This was the underlying idea of the cracking process, introduced in 1913. By 1919 it had come into considerable use. The war had given impetus to the motor industry, gasoline engines were being built with higher compression ratios to get more power out of fuel, and it was a gratifying but unexplained fact that the gasolines derived by cracking were better fuels than most of the natural gasolines. Cracking seemed to put more power into the fuel. In particular, it reduced the annoying knock in the engine.

A young mechanical engineer was deep at work on a related problem in a Dayton, Ohio, laboratory at this time. Thomas Midgley, Jr., had set out to find why engines knock, and by accident, intuition or hunch discovered that the addition of a little iodine to the gasoline eliminated the knock. He installed a heavy quartz window in the side of the combustion chamber and watched what happened inside when the engine was operating. Under favorable conditions the explosion started at the spark and spread like a prairie fire. It traveled at the rate of about 90 feet a second. But when the motor knocked there was no such steady spread of the fire. Additional explosions popped at interior spots within the chamber, and these premature detonations were responsible for the injurious "ping-ping-ping."

Iodine was costly and objectionable on other grounds, so Midgley, whose laboratory meanwhile had come under the wing of the General Motors Corporation, began the search for a substitute. He tried everything that had chemical properties which suggested it as a possible anti-knock agent. After making fifteen thousand experiments, the quest ended in 1922 when he dropped a dash of tetraethyl lead into gasoline, turned this mixture into a badly knocking motor, and heard it quiet down into a steady purr. Tetraethyl lead is produced by treating ordinary lead with an alcohol; its ingredients are plentiful, easy to process; and as an anti-knock agent it is vastly superior to iodine.

THE OCTANE SCALE

Thus the technologists had hit upon two ways to improve fuel quality: first, by cracking; and second, by the addition of tetraethyl lead. But there was no standard, no systematic way of rating gasoline. In 1926 Graham Edgar, a chemist who had recently left the University of Virginia to conduct research for the Ethyl Gasoline Corporation, undertook to devise a scientific scale. He began by trying to separate from commercial gasoline its various fractions so that he could test each one. This was a truly arduous project, for many of the mixed liquids have the same or nearly the same boiling point, and in other physical properties are quite similar. But Dr. Edgar succeeded in obtaining pure concentrates of many of the more voluminous components of gasoline—at a cost of hundreds of dollars the gallon—and then proceeded to test each in a high-compression engine. All the criteria of performance were taken into consideration, and each fuel was tried under completely standardized conditions.

The gasoline that gave the best performance on all counts, including absence of knocking, was an iso-octane; one of the forms of the eight-carbon molecule. Dr. Edgar decided to take the word octane as the designation of his measuring unit, so he called the performance of this best fuel 100 octane. The gasoline fraction that gave the worst performance, causing the most knocking, was the straight-chain molecule of seven carbon atoms known as heptane; he called its performance 0 octane. And then he proceeded to rate blends of fuels in terms of this scale. A mixture of 75 per cent of the iso-octane with 25 per cent of the heptane gave a blend which was 75 octane. A half-and-half blend was 50 octane.

The chemists could now mix proportions of iso-octane and heptane to form a blend which would duplicate the engine performance of any commercial gasoline. It was found, for example, that pentane—the gasoline molecule containing five carbon atoms in a straight chain—performed with the same fuel efficiency as a blend containing 61 per cent of iso-octane; so it was rated 61 octane. When a few drops of tetraethyl lead were added to a gallon of pentane, the fuel then performed as though it were a blend containing 75 per cent of iso-octane; therefore it was rated 75 octane. And so with the various blends, and the addition of tetraethyl lead to them—each combination found a precise place on the octane scale.

The scale was announced in 1927, and it placed the subject at last on a scientific basis. This result was important not only to the chemical engineer designing fuels but to the automotive and aeronautical engineer designing engines. In the years immediately following, the chief burden was on the chemists to produce gasolines adapted to the capacity of the then best engine design. But today the chemists are ahead. They have discovered how to produce gasolines better than 100 octane: gasolines so powerful that engines capable of making maximum use of their calories do not exist. Actually the challenge today is up to the engineers to design a motor to fit this superfuel.

MAN-MADE GASOLINE

The octane which Dr. Edgar called 100 was not the molecular structure that chemists recognize as normal octane. This normal octane has eight atoms of carbon linked together in a straight chain, thus:

Carbon Structure of Normal Octane

A complete map of the octane molecule would show a hydrogen atom at each end of the chain and also one attached above and below each carbon atom; but for the purpose of our discussion the hydrogen fringe may be ignored. The point is that under pressure and heat the normal straight chain gets mangled. A carbon atom from the chain may be squashed out on one side, or two or three may, or they may be pushed into positions on the other side. So long as they hang together in some fashion as a bundle of eight, they are octane. But to distinguish them from the normal chain structures these deformed molecules are called isomers (or "like structures"), and in the case of octane are known as iso-octanes.

The particular iso-octane which turned out to be tops in Dr. Edgar's tests is one in which two of the eight carbon atoms are piled on one side of the chain and a third is shifted to a position on the other side, in this arrangement:

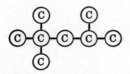

Carbon Structure of Iso-octane

Here is the original 100-octane gasoline, the standard, the "royal cubit" by which all other motor fuels are qualitatively measured. Even the poorest gasoline has a few molecules of it, but to distill them is impossible on any commercially profitable basis. Nor is it necessary. For chemistry has found a way to build up smaller fragments of petroleum into this iso-octane pattern.

Among the fragments that interest the chemist for this purpose are certain gaseous molecules that are cracked out of the heavier parts of petroleum. One of these gases is known as iso-butylene, a four-carbon structure hooked together like this:

Carbon Structure of Iso-butylene

Except for that double bond joining the central atom with its neighbor on the right, this looks like half of the iso-octane molecule. If you take two of them and lay the second on its side, the similarity to two halves of iso-octane becomes apparent at a glance:

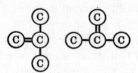

The Two Iso-butylene Molecules in Position

Chemists have a process known as polymerization by which small molecules of the same architecture are joined together to form large molecules, or polymers. By this process the union of the two iso-butylene molecules has been accomplished on an industrial scale, producing this structure:

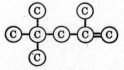

Polymer Resulting from the Merger

It is the same arrangement of atoms that is found in iso-octane except for one detail: that double bond connecting the right-end atom with its neighbor. Though this seems slight on the map, the difference is tremendously influential chemically. It indicates an "unsaturated" molecule, and such molecules behave differently from saturated ones. This abnormality may be corrected by resorting to another chemical stratagem, a process known as hydrogenation. By this process a single atom of hydrogen is added to the new molecule, the hydrogen absorbs one link of the double bond, and thus the molecule becomes saturated. By these successive steps of synthesis, first polymerization, then hydrogenation, it is fashioned into the exact pattern of iso-octane, thus:

Synthetic Molecule of Iso-octane (100-octane Gasoline)

But hydrogenation requires extensive investment in plant, the process is expensive to operate, and when iso-octane began to come out of the hydrogenation stills in 1934 the cost was around $1 a gallon. It could be regarded commercially as a rather precious blending agent, mainly for use in fuel and engine research. Then, in 1938, came a new process—alkylation! In one swift step the cost of iso-octane was sliced to a small fraction of its former figure.

Alkylation was independently discovered in the research laboratories of four of the great petroleum companies at about the same time. It is a method of combining alkyls, the chemist's name for the branching type of molecule like iso-butylene; and, in particular, it is a method of combining alkyls of *different* degrees of saturation.

Prior to this discovery chemists found it impossible to combine an unsaturated hydrocarbon with a saturated one. In the polymerization process first described, the two molecules of iso-butylene are *exactly alike*, therefore they will unite chemically. But even so their union leaves that unsaturated bond which can be satisfied only by the extra step of hydrogenation.

In alkylation this final step is not necessary. One molecule of iso-butylene is united directly to one molecule of iso-butane. Both are gases, derived of course from petroleum; and although iso-butane is saturated and the iso-butylene as we have seen in the diagrams is unsaturated, the two readily combine because of the presence in this alkylation process of a third agency, a catalyst. No one knows just how a catalyst works. It takes no part in the chemical reaction, but in some way promotes the reaction. The suggestion has been made that a catalyst is a molecular parson who presides at the marriage of molecules. A better analogue perhaps is the mediator who brings antagonistic or unsocial individuals together and persuades them to join in a single harmonious team. There are scores of substances which are serving in various processes of synthetic chemistry as molecular mediators. Some are metals, some are salts, powders, crystals, liquids; but in this particular process of alkylation the catalyst is sulphuric acid, the familiar H_2SO_4 of elementary chemistry. Without it the two gases are indifferent toward one another. But with H_2SO_4 present in the mixture, the unsaturated molecule of iso-butylene is drawn near to the saturated molecule of iso-butane, somehow one link of the double bond of the iso-butylene shifts around to hook onto the iso-butane, and the result is an authentic molecule of iso-octane.

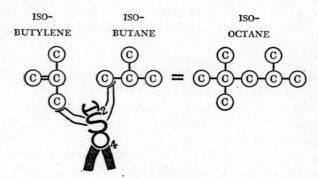

The Process of Alkylation is Catalyzed by Sulphuric Acid

Scores of plants in the United States are turning out this gasoline today. Our military and naval requirements have standardized engine designs on compression ratios and other specifications to make full use of it as aircraft fuel. But there is no necessity to use the synthetic stuff pure. The quantity of 100-octane gasoline can be greatly increased and the cost can be lowered if the fuel which is thus produced by alkylation is used as a blending agent to improve the octane number of other gasolines obtained in enormously larger quantities by the cracking processes. And today's cracking processes are light-years ahead of the methods in use even five years ago.

Instead of merely turning on the heat and pressure to do what they will with the heavy residues, and trusting that the results will yield a good ratio of gasoline, the modern petroleum chemist is able to give direction and velocity to the cracking. He is able to increase the percentage of isomers formed. This is highly important, for it is these deformed molecules rather than the straight-chain structures that provide the best fuel. Moreover, the chemist is able to increase the proportion of isomers which are high in octane number. Cracking is still a mass reaction, but today the statistical balance can be weighted to produce a higher proportion of the desired structures. The factor that made this possible is the catalyst.

Three types of cracking catalysts are in use. In one process the catalyst is a refractory material laid in a fixed bed through which the vaporized oils pass. In another process the catalyst is in granulated form: beadlike pellets of porous material which mingle with the hot mixture. The third process has a pulverized catalyst—it is almost as fine as talcum powder—and flows along with the hot vapors in a continuous cycle. The gases and gasolines whose formation is promoted by its presence are drawn off; and the powder, cleansed and reclaimed, is returned to the system to be used again and again in endless sequence.

This third process is called fluid catalytic cracking, because the powder in suspension in the petroleum vapors acts as a fluid—it actually flows. In the great Bayway plant of the Standard Oil Company of New Jersey the powder moves through parts of the unit at the rate of hundreds of tons every hour, night and day. Gasoline with an octane number above 80 pours out. In order to have 100-octane fuel, built to the specifications of military aviation, it is necessary to blend only a small proportion of iso-octane (obtained by alkylation) with this gasoline (obtained by catalytic cracking) and add a few cubic centimeters of tetraethyl lead.

War is responsible for these rapid developments. When the first synthetic iso-octane was attained in the early 1930's, the only motors capable of making full use of the then top-grade fuel were a few radial engines developed for aircraft. The demands of the growing aviation industry were exacting, but they were then small in volume, insufficient to warrant iso-octane production on a commercial scale, and the gasoline industry was necessarily geared to the demands of the automobile industry. It was not until 1934 that the first sale of a substantial quantity of iso-octane was made: the U. S. Army Air Corps purchased 1,000 gallons for testing engines at Wright Field. With the disillusionment of the Munich Conference and the hasty efforts of the democracies to set their arms in order, the results of this chemical pioneering became recognized as of high strategic military value. As the demands for airplanes increased, the demands for fuels correspondingly increased—and 100-octane leaped into demand. By the beginning of 1943 sixteen petroleum companies were making 100-octane gasoline in the United States, and the price was down to 15 cents a gallon.

What this fuel means to the air warrior may be suggested by comparing the performance record of a plane which was powered by 87-octane gasoline (1939's best aviation fuel) with that of the same plane when served by 100-octane. The aircraft climbed to 26,000 feet in 19.5 minutes with 87-octane, in 12.2 minutes with 100-octane; its speed increased from 236 miles per hour to 260, and its ceiling rose from 32,800 feet to 36,700. This test was made before the bombs fell on Pearl Harbor: there are more spectacular contrasts in performance now. Because of the higher power packed in present-day fuel, engines are made smaller and of lighter weight; heavier cargoes are carried; a fighter plane can be equipped with thicker armor, a bomber loaded with more bombs. One gentleman with a pencil has computed that a bombing expedition of 1,000 planes from London to Berlin can carry nearly five million more pounds of bombs per trip as a result of substituting 100-octane fuel for 87-octane.

In terms of postwar application, these findings of chemical research mean that tomorrow's automobile can go forty to fifty miles on a gallon of gasoline.

CHAPTER VIII

The New Materials

Chemistry creates its object.

—Marcellin Berthelot

WHAT tomorrow's world will be depends on how far off tomorrow lies—that is, on the duration of the war. Every month that the emergency continues is pushing scientific research to new heights of chemical creativeness and new lengths of industrial application. At the same time it is expanding industry to new dimensions of large-scale low-cost production. The war is crowding decades of technological development into a few years. Most of the physical aspects of human living will feel the impact of these changes— some of them revolutionary, some perhaps only superficial, but all carrying possibilities of a safer, happier, richer and more humane world. Commodities that were luxuries in the prewar world will be easily within reach of the whole populace, and other products that were necessities will be better adapted to their purposes, more convenient, more manageable, more economical and serviceable.

Tomorrow's automobile, for example, will be so cheap that our highways will have to provide traffic accommodation for perhaps 50,000,000 cars, instead of the prewar 25,000,000—which poses a problem of thinking also about the postwar road. The postwar car need weigh only half as much as the prewar car. At the same time it can be more spacious, more comfortable, more powerful. Significant gains in the saving of weight and the conservation of power will be provided through redesigning the engine, equipping it with a supercharger and building it to use fuel of 100-octane and higher. The modern airplane engine demonstrates some of the possibilities. It weighs less than one-fifth as much per horsepower as the 1942-model automobile engine, and it develops twice as much power per cubic inch of displacement. Nor are the gains in engine economy and efficiency confined to the high-powered machines. An American designer recently built an aircraft engine of 100 horsepower, weighing only 100 pounds. Can you imagine the postwar automobile not profiting from this sort of ingenuity? The private car on the highway will have to compete with the private plane in the sky, and the postwar citizen will benefit from this competition—whether he rides on the highway or in the sky, or both.

The principal wartime developments, other than new fuels, which influence the design, production and cost of tomorrow's automobile are synthetic rubbers, new plastics, light metals, new alloys and new methods of welding, molding, and combining metals, plastics, plywood and other materials. Also the fact that when industry resumes production of automobiles it can start at scratch must be placed very near the top of the list. Designers will not be bound by the traditions and limitations of old machine tools. The methods born of the speed-up of war production, plus the new materials and new uses of materials developed under the pressure of its needs and shortages, will be available to the automobile engineer to use as he wills. At least we may hope that the engineer, rather than the stylist, will be top man when the industry resumes. Lessons learned in the design, production and use of the army jeep, with its powerful traction, no less than those acquired in the design, production and use of the tank, airplane and submarine chaser, will be available to automotive engineers and manufacturers —and to all engineers and manufacturers.

The new materials are for the most part chemical contributions. Even the plywood—such as is used to make the highly efficient Mosquito bombing planes, gliders, and other aircraft—owes a debt to the chemist. For it would not be possible to produce these workable, adaptable, and durable sections of wood to current standards of quality without the plastics and other synthetic materials used as binders. The new metals too are right out of the chemists' crucibles. The rate at which they are pouring forth carries its implications of what tomorrow will be—not only the automobile of tomorrow, but tomorrow's railway train, tomorrow's aircraft, tomorrow's ocean liner, even tomorrow's house equipment and garden tools.

METALS AND ALLOYS

Most spectacular is magnesium. The metal weighs a third less than aluminum and possesses exceptional strength, toughness and durability, especially when alloyed with aluminum, beryllium, and certain other metals. It is "new," of course, only in the sense that it is just coming into large-scale industrial use. The photographer has snapped his night pictures in the brilliant flash of burning magnesium for decades, and during 1914-'18 the powdered metal was employed in shell flares and incendiary bombs. At that time magnesium sold for $5 a pound and the annual production of the U. S. was only 87,000 pounds; the price today is 22½ cents and our production is scheduled to reach an annual 600,000,000 pounds. The contrast of those two sets of figures epitomizes the present importance of magnesium, though its American industrial usage is largely a growth of the last five years. An average of half a ton goes into the construction of every combat plane, several tons into the big bombers, and with each improvement in aircraft design it seems that more magnesium is used.

An important factor in extending its versatility is the recently invented method of welding the metal in an atmosphere of helium. At high temperatures, such as are developed by the electric arc and other welding torches, magnesium bursts into flame; but helium gas is inert, and will not support combustion. By performing the operation within an "envelope" of helium, two sections of magnesium can be smoothly joined by the electric arc with no risk of fire. The helium not only forbids combustion, but its property of conducting heat cools the metal; and it also operates as a cleansing agent. This welding process has made magnesium a practicable material for primary constructions, in aircraft frames and wings, in addition to its more usual use in engines, wheels and accessories.

As spectacular as the metal are the ways by which magnesium is extracted from its sources. In Texas, on the shore of the Gulf of Mexico near the mouth of the Brazos, are huge plants which suck up water from the sea, separate the magnesium compounds from the salty solution, and treat these ocean "ores" to produce pure molten magnesium. Eight hundred tons of water yield one ton of the metal. It is estimated that every cubic mile of sea contains 5,700,000 tons of magnesium, so there is no danger of exhausting the raw material supply. Magnesium is also present in many rocks and in the brine of lakes and wells. A new ferro-silicon process for recovering the metal from the common dolomite limestones was recently imported from Canada, and is being applied in "war baby" plants in Michigan, Ohio, Connecticut and other regions. By 1942 the American magnesium industry equaled in volume the output of the prewar (1939) aluminum industry.

Meanwhile aluminum too has moved ahead. In 1943 the United States was producing about eight times as much aluminum as its output in 1938, or 75 to 85 per cent more than the whole world produced in 1938. The price was down to 15 cents a pound, and it may go lower when projected plants come into production. One of the wartime achievements has been the utilization of low-grade bauxite of the South and Southwest, in place of the purer ores imported from South America. The chief bottleneck has been electric power. Enormous quantities of energy are required to reduce aluminum from its reddish ore, and many huge hydroelectric developments have been spurred to completion by the demand for aluminum and yet more aluminum.

Aluminum's largest "consumer" is the aircraft industry. During 1914-'18 the U. S. military airplanes were about 80 per cent wood by weight, 10 per cent steel, with the rest fabrics and miscellaneous materials of which aluminum was but a tiny fraction. By 1940 aircraft weight averaged almost 80 per cent aluminum. Planes weighing seventy-five tons are already in use, one-hundred-tonners are in the laboratories, and engineers foresee postwar skyships of at least double the latter weight. Without aluminum these giants would hardly be feasible. Aluminum also occupies an important place in the construction of ocean ships, railway cars, automobiles and smaller mechanisms; and in the new industrial age this historically first of the light metals will play a predominating role. At 10 cents a pound aluminum should compete in many fields with 2-cent steel.

But steel is not passé; far from it. Metallurgists are producing alloy steels of extraordinary strength which can be used in thinner sections than aluminum or magnesium alloys; and in the war shortage of critical materials these new steels have served many emergency needs in airplanes and elsewhere. It is now possible to give steel almost any desired property—strength, hardness, resilience, ductility, toughness, a stainless skin, a resistance to heat. These man-made steels are in effect synthetic materials, like blends of high-octane gasoline. They are formed by mixing varying quantities of other elements with molten iron, and treating the product with various electrical or chemical hardening processes. The formulas are so precise that they give metallurgy some of the exactitude of physical chemistry.

In the construction of ships, guns, tanks, railway locomotives and other rolling stock, bridges, derricks, machine tools, and a thousand other implements of industry and war, steel remains the master metal. Iron, its principal ingredient, is being dug from the rich Lake Superior region in such quantities that industry must anticipate the early exhaustion of Mesaba's high-grade open-pit ores. At the present rate of withdrawal this region, which normally supplies 85 per cent of our iron, may be exhausted early in 1950. Already industry is turning to lower-grade ores and smaller deposits of the high-grade. New steel plants have been built in Texas, Utah and California to make use of the near-by iron mines.

POWDER METALLURGY

Another advance which has soared with a rapidity almost bewildering, even to those familiar with its application, is powder metallurgy. This process was invented a number of years ago as a means of working platinum, tungsten, and other refractory metals whose melting point is so high that industry had no furnaces hot enough to melt them for casting or forging. It was found that if the metal was reduced to a fine powder, the powder could be pressed into molds and, under tremendous hydraulic pressure, with or without the added influence of heat, could be made to solidify into the shape of the mold.

Today the technique is being used in a multitude of ways, not only to handle the refractory metals but the more fusible ones, including iron, copper, chromium, nickel, aluminum and magnesium. Very remarkable properties can be imparted to a metal through the powder process. It is possible to produce bearing surfaces that are perfectly hard and yet porous and self-lubricating. Mixtures of dust-fine powders of two or more metals are pressed under many tons to the square inch to form "diffusion alloys" which possess unique qualities, some peculiarly advantageous in the manufacture of electrical equipment, for example. Since there is no scrap from the process and the molding can be made to proceed at a fast rate, great economies of material and of time are derived. This procedure has speeded up war production in a number of critical specialties.

Although it was used at first only for the manufacture of small parts, technical considerations no longer limit powder metallurgy to minor pieces. In 1942 one of the metal-working shops was producing bearings of 18-inch diameter from powder pressings, and larger ones have since been made. The last crop of prewar automobiles manufactured by General Motors, Ford, and Chrysler contained a number of small parts made by powder metallurgy, though it is said that their weight altogether did not exceed two pounds in each car. In the postwar car it is likely this proportion will be much greater, utilizing refinements and skills born of the intensive war-industry use of this technique.

THE MANY-VALUED PLASTICS

Originally plastics were used as substitutes for more costly natural materials. The first celluloid was offered as artificial ivory for the manufacture of billiard balls and piano keys; and there were also artificial ambers and other imitations. Today the plastics, of more than a hundred varieties, are basic materials for thousands of uses in the war. And they have been accepted not merely as substitutes for something else that would be preferred if it were not scarce, but as the designer's first choice in many strategic places in weapons.

The demand was so great, and they have been of such critical value to the war effort, that in 1942 several types of plastics were carried in Group I, the War Production Board's list of the scarcest and most valued critical materials. "Metal is strong, wood light, and glass transparent, but plastics can be all three," said a General Electric engineer.

Highly dramatic among the new uses of plastics is the employment of certain types for machine bearings in naval ships, steel mills, and other spots demanding tough service. Plastics are taking the place of metals here because they generate less friction, lend themselves better to lubrication, endure harder punishment, and last longer. This stuff out of a test-tube actually outperforms and outlasts certain metals on heavy duty.

Transparent plastics, which can be molded in thick sections to any curve and shaped to any configuration, form the airplane noses, turrets, blisters, and other constructions in which a high degree of visibility is desired. Plexiglass, lucite, lumarith, plastacede, and other tough, durable, lightweight, crackproof, and shatter-proof transparencies are used. Plastics can be made to pass ultra-violet sunlight or to filter it out, as desired. Other plastics, more opaque, are serving in place of metal tubing to pipe gasoline, oil, acid, oxygen, water. They do the job without rusting, corrosion, scaling, or other deterioration; and water can freeze in plastic pipes without bursting them. Imagine the postwar applications of these two wartime developments—windows of transparent plastics, and corrosion-resistant freezeproof plumbing.

Every combat plane has hundreds of plastic parts; every tank has its scores of appliances, knobs and fittings made of plastic; and in the battleship the uses run into the thousand. In radio sets and other instruments the peculiar electrical properties of plastics make them vital to rugged and unfailing performance under battle conditions. Plastics are in the fuzes of antiaircraft shells, in the detonators of torpedoes, and in the helmets which protect the skull from shell fragments. Tests show that a plastic helmet will withstand a one-pound hammer dropped from a height of 15 feet. For battle duty a metal cover fits over the plastic and increases the protective power so that the helmet becomes capable of withstanding the impact of the one-pound weight dropped from a height of 50 feet.

Plastic lenses serve in gunsights and gas masks and there are reports of scratch-resistant plastics which in time of peace may provide lenses for spectacles, field glasses and other optical pieces.

SYNTHETIC FIBERS

Plastics are not only molded into buttons, knobs, disks, lenses, and other small designs—cast into plates, sections, strips and films, and extruded as rods and tubes, but some are spun into filaments as fine as silk or as crinkly as wool. Nylon is a plastic of this fiber-forming type, and so is vinyon—both synthetics whose counterparts do not exist in nature.

Rayon, called "artificial silk" in the days when the man-made material looked up to nature's product, is not a synthetic in the literal meaning of the word. It is made of cellulose, and cellulose is a natural product, the structural stuff of wood or cotton. Rayon is simply regenerated cellulose. It is nature's product which has been purified, reduced to a pulp, and then squirted into filament form. By chemical and physical treatments it has been possible to impart various properties to rayon, and tough durable fabrics of this material are serving in the tires of heavy bombers, in parachutes, and in many other military rough spots; offering a remarkable contrast to the weak and capricious "artificial silk" of a few decades ago.

Cellulose is also the base material for the manufacture of acetate yarns, such as celanese and acele; but here the chemists do not merely regenerate the cellulose molecule. They break it up into parts, and then by a process of chemical selection they take what parts they want, add other elements, and so build an entirely new structure—cellulose acetate—which is extruded through fine holes to make the yarn.

Nylon yarn is still more remote from the ordinary sources of natural textiles. It has no kinship with rayon, nor does it have a counterpart in nature. It is derived from molecules found in coal, water, and air—molecules which the chemist can with certain manipulations turn to the manufacture of beneficent drugs, and with still other procedures to the manufacture of powerful explosives. As the war of 1914-'18 destroyed Germany's world monopoly of chemicals, so the present war has destroyed Japan's world monopoly of silk. The work that silk has done in previous wars is now being done, at least in part, by nylon yarn. Early in 1942 every pound that could be produced was earmarked for military uses, and facilities were enlarged to increase the output. Window screens of nylon monofilament are already out of the laboratory, but will not be generally available until after the war. Army and navy doctors are using nylon for surgical sutures.

Another rival of the natural textiles is glass. New types of glass are being produced which can be spun into fine filaments of unusual tensile strength. The fabrics woven of these glass yarns have a high resistance to damage from water, fire, acids, alkalis, mildew, and other destructive agents. Industry is using glass fabrics as filter cloths for both liquid and gas, in handling high temperatures and corrosive substances. They are also an excellent substitute for silk and rubber, as an insulating material for wrapping telephone wires. Another development is a foamy glass. This bubbly mass will sustain many times its weight, and is providing material for life preservers, corrosion-resistant floats, and refrigerator insulation.

Glass is a silicon compound, a material of the inorganic world. The plastics are carbon compounds, a fact which rates them as materials of organic chemistry. In 1933 Dr. William J. Hale predicted that by 1950 chemists will succeed in incorporating partly oxidized silicon into a carbon plastic to make a new material which will combine the advantages of the organic and the inorganic. He forecasts exceptional properties for the predicted plastic: tremendous strength, high rigidity, unusual resistance to weathering and oxidation, lighter weight than any plastics now used as engineering materials; and, as a final clincher, lower cost. Early in 1943 news came that a collaboration between the Corning Glass Works and the Dow Chemical Company had produced a silicon plastic for which valuable military uses were found.

THE HIGH AND MIGHTY POLYMERS

At the bottom of all this seeming magic, a sort of scientific legerdemain, stands a familiar concept: the idea of building up complex structures out of simple ones. A mason creates a chimney by attaching one brick to another in a certain sequence. Or he may combine bricks with stone blocks to produce a different kind of chimney, or a wall, or a bridge, or a tunnel, or a house. Whatever the end product may be, it is more than the collection of bricks and stones that go into it. The pattern of its togetherness is what determines whether a given collection of bricks and stones will make a chimney to conduct smoke or a bridge to conduct traffic. As the Chinese adage puts it, "A cart and a horse are three: the cart, the horse, and the two together." The rule holds for chemistry, as well as for transportation and architecture.

The science of molecular masonry, of putting molecular bricks and stones together to form a molecular chimney in one instance, or a molecular bridge in another, is chemical synthesis. The alkylation process, by which two molecules of gas are joined to form one molecule of iso-octane gasoline, is an example. But the plastics are more complex creations. Their molecules are many times the size and weight of even the largest gasoline molecule; therefore a large number of molecular bricks must go into their construction. Recent chemical research shows that the molecules of the fibers, plastics, and rubbers are all long chains. Each is a structure of 2,000 atoms or more.

Carbon compounds which have molecules of this general order of size are called high polymers. Polymers are the giant molecules which result from a synthesis in which all the bricks are alike, and the larger the molecule the higher is its polymerization. Included among the high polymers are many natural organic substances, such as starch, cellulose and rubber. Also many synthetic ones— for example, the fibers vinyon and nylon; the plastics bakelite, styron, and the rest; and the rubberlike ameripol, buna, butyl, koroseal, neoprene, thiokol, and others.

Now the interesting thing that recent research has brought to light is the role of crystallization in determining the properties of a high polymer. The fibers, it is found, are crystalline structures— both the natural ones, cotton and silk, as well as the synthetics. The rubbers are at the opposite extreme, noncrystalline. Their molecules also are long chains, but the mutual attraction among them is not high, as in crystals, so they easily stretch; this is true of natural rubber as well as of the various synthetic rubbers. Between the two extremes are the plastics, substances less crystalline than the fibers but more active in their mutual affinities than the rubbers; and this is true of both the natural resins such as amber and the synthetic ones of the familiar trade names.

This growing knowledge of the molecular peculiarities of the various materials is giving the chemists ever-increasing control over their creations. It is becoming possible to plan a material, as an architect plans a building, and then select the particular molecular bricks or building blocks which will combine to make such a building. The old idea of imitating nature has given way to a new chemical wisdom, one that studies the structures and mechanisms which condition the physical properties of a substance. It was this approach, for example, that won the first real success in the long search for synthetic rubber.

SYNTHETIC RUBBER

Natural rubber is principally a chain molecule made of hundreds of units of C_5H_8 joined. This unit of 5 carbon atoms linked with 8 of hydrogen is called isoprene, and has been known since about the time of the American Civil War. Scores, perhaps hundreds, of chemists have tried to join units of isoprene. Although they have made an isoprene polymer, none of them in all the decades has succeeded in producing a product identical with natural rubber. At last it occurred to one of these researchers that the properties of rubber, rather than rubber itself, might make a more practicable laboratory goal. Perhaps something other than C_5H_8 would produce a rubberlike material. This hunch prepared this scientist's mind to receive a fertilizing clue.

The clue came in a paper which Professor Julius A. Nieuwland presented in 1925 at a symposium of the American Chemical Society. The professor was an enthusiast on the subject of acetylene. Its curious chemical behavior, the results he could get by combining or treating acetylene with other substances, simply fascinated him; and all his spare time at Notre Dame University, Indiana, went into studies of the smelly gas. One of his hearers at the American Chemical Society meeting was Elmer K. Bolton of the Du Pont laboratories; and a certain compound of acetylene mentioned by Professor Nieuwland made Dr. Bolton sit up. He recognized at once, from the description, that here was something which might have rubberlike qualities. He consulted Nieuwland, made arrangements for collaboration, and assigned a crew of industrial chemists to the practical problem. What came out of that quest was neoprene.

Neoprene, a long-chain synthetic molecule, is built of units containing four carbon atoms, five hydrogen atoms and one atom of chlorine, an element which is completely foreign to rubber. The new compound was attained in 1930, was first publicly announced in 1931, and several thousand pounds were produced in 1932. When war came it was classified as one of the most critical of the synthetic materials.

Thiokol was compounded in 1930; koroseal, another chlorine compound, in 1933. And in 1935 came news from Germany of the synthesis of the buna rubbers, whose basic raw material is butadiene, a gas composed of four atoms of carbon and six of hydrogen. One type of buna has styrene as its co-polymer to join with the butadiene, and because of the styrene this is known as buna-S. The major part of the United States synthetic-rubber program is concentrated on the production of buna-S. Another type of buna is known as buna-N, the N referring to the nitrogen compound which serves as co-polymer in its manufacture. Butyl rubber, still another synthetic which occupies a place in the American program, is made of isobutylene plus small amounts of other unsaturated hydrocarbons, including isoprene, the unit of natural rubber. Thus chemistry has learned how to use nature's own brick in assisting one of its synthetic processes; but it is still unable to make rubber out of isoprene. Perhaps we shall overtake that problem some day, and make actual rubber in a laboratory just as today we make actual camphor, thiamin, riboflavin, adrenalin, and other substances which a few years ago could be had only by processing vegetable and animal extracts.

Among the dislocations of world industry wrought by the war, rubber promises to occupy a conspicuous place. If the recommendations made in 1942 by the President's Rubber Committee are realized, the United States will come out of the war with a synthetic industry capable of producing twice as much man-made rubber a year as the nation imported of natural rubber in prewar years. In other words, we shall be able to supply double our prewar rubber needs without importing a particle of the tropical product.

Meanwhile, research will not have stood idle. At the beginning of

1943 it was true, as stated by the U. S. Rubber Company, that "natural rubber is superior to synthetic in most performance characteristics, synthetics are superior to natural rubber in resistance to most influences that cause deterioration." But give the chemists time. A similar comparison applied to silk and rayon half a century ago. Half-centuries are being condensed into a few years in the present era of research, and we may confidently look to the laboratories to add new values to our synthetics, to improve their performance in the rubberlike properties, to increase their superiority in those advantages which the synthetics possess over natural rubber, perhaps building into the man-made molecules entirely new and revolutionary characteristics. Certainly we shall have installed and established a huge industry, geared to use by-products of the agricultural, petroleum, and other basic chemical industries; and we may look to low costs in step with large-scale operations. It is conceivable that by 1950 natural rubber will be no more essential to our economy than the nitrate of Chile is today.

CHAPTER IX

War Medicine and War Surgery

To preserve a man alive in the midst of chances and
hostilities is as great a miracle as to create him.

—Jeremy Taylor

MECHANIZED warfare has a terrifying reputation as a killer, but its
actual death rate does not bear out this reputation. It does range
over a wider territory and engage more of the civilian population
than the former less mobile methods of waging war, but in proportion to numbers involved its deaths are fewer. Colonel Robert
Sears of the United States Army Ordnance Department has compiled this sequence of representative battles:

"At Cannae in 216 B.C., 60 per cent of the Roman army were
killed by Hannibal's Carthaginians in one day of fighting with
swords and spears. At Waterloo in 1815, after muzzle-loading firearms and black powder had come into existence, the English lost 22
per cent of their army, killed on the battlefield in one day. At
Gettysburg in 1863, when breech-loading rifles began to make their
appearance, 8½ per cent of the Union army were killed in three
days' fighting, or less than 3 per cent per day. At the Meuse-
Argonne in the World War (1918), after the development of
smokeless powder, magazine rifles, and automatic weapons, the

American army lost 2½ per cent in battle casualties in 47 days, or 0.05 per cent a day."

It seems indisputable, as Colonel Sears says, that "this trend is due to scientific development of armaments and protective measures." But the protective measures are not only guns, armor, trenches, and other devices for repelling the enemy and shielding the soldier from his missiles. They include also the resources of medicine and surgery. If there had been a corps of stretcher bearers to follow up the carnage at Cannae in 216 B.C., to pick up the wounded and carry them to nurses and doctors possessed of the knowledge, equipment and skills of modern medical science, the chances are that a large proportion of the victims of sword and spear would not have died.

DEATH ON THE MICROBE FRONT

Guns and other instruments of violence are secondary in lethal effect to the epidemics and other infections which through the ages have accompanied armies. The Crimean War, occurring in the pre-Pasteur, pre-Lister period nearly a century ago, can be discussed with some confidence because unusually accurate records were kept. They show that 300 out of every 1,000 British soldiers in the Crimea perished per year—230 of them from disease. The French fatality record is higher, 411 out of each 1,000; and 341 of these French soldier deaths resulted from disease. Perhaps nothing is more eloquent of the contrast between then and now than the record of mortality following operations. In the Crimea amputations were performed on 5,972 French soldiers who were wounded in an arm, forearm, thigh, or leg, and 4,023 died—more than 67 per cent. Of those who had an amputation of the thigh, 92 per cent died. And of those who suffered from broken hip joint, every man died.

The losses of the United States Army in the Mexican War of 1846-'48 were seven times greater from disease than from battle casualties. During the American Civil War (1861-'65) disease killed 224,586 Union soldiers, the guns 110,070. During American participation in World War I (1917-'19) the competition became more nearly balanced, but even then disease with its 58,119 deaths had the edge on explosives and gas with 55,976.

Dr. John S. Lockwood, of the surgical staff of the University of Pennsylvania Medical School, has analyzed the U. S. Army records of 1917-'19 to see what difference might have been made if the sulfonamide drugs had been available. He found that three-fourths of the 58,119 American soldiers who died of disease were stricken with pneumonia, either primary pneumonia or secondary pneumonia following influenza, bronchitis, or other respiratory disease. Today, with sulfadiazine or sulfathiazole treatment, the death rate from pneumonia is less than one-third the rate at which American soldiers died in World War I. When he came to examine the statistics of the 55,976 who succumbed to injuries, the surgeon found that more than a third of them died in hospitals where presumably the best available treatment was given. Many thousands were victims of wounds infected with microbes which we can combat today with the sulfonamides. From all the data, making full allowance for first-aid improvisations, delays in getting the wounded to the surgeon, and other handicaps of battlefront medicine, Dr. Lockwood estimates that "the risk of death for men in the army service during the present war is less than half what it was during the last war—assuming similar conditions of warfare."

Of course, we cannot assume precisely similar conditions. No two wars have ever presented completely parallel circumstances. The development of the aircraft and tank has introduced factors which are without precedent. The wide spread of the present conflict, with battlefields in tropics and arctic—and in the stratosphere, creates problems in biological as well as mechanical engineering. Fortunately, the military doctor has powerful resources. Not only the sulfonamides, but even more potent microbe-fighters are available. There are toxoids against tetanus, vaccines against yellow fever and other contagions, plasma for transfusions, and surgical units so compact that they can be transported to the front line when necessary. Ambulance planes get a wounded man from the battlefield to the operating table often in a matter of minutes, whereas the motor ambulances of 1918 required hours and sometimes days.

SOME RECORDS FROM THE SURGICAL FRONT

Wounds of the abdomen have usually killed. In past wars more than half of the men wounded in this way, and on whom the surgeons were able to operate, died. In the present war, almost all published reports show a recovery rate higher than 50 per cent. Thus a medical officer of the British navy, reporting to the Royal College of Surgeons the results of abdominal operations on 600 wounded men rescued from Dunkirk and other early British engagements and air raids, stated that "the percentage of recoveries for injuries to stomach, small intestine, rectum, and spleen was actually higher than that in 1914-'18, and for large bowel injuries it was the same as it was then." In stomach wounds the recovery rate was 60 per cent, comparing with less than 37 per cent in 1914-'18.

Two years and more after Dunkirk came the battles in the Solomon Islands, and the records of the U. S. services there show a recovery rate of 95 per cent from abdominal wounds. When all hospitalized cases, including every kind of wound, are in the reckoning, the percentage of fatalities following treatment falls to an even lower figure—1.5 per cent for the wounded of Guadalcanal.

One U. S. Navy hospital ship operating in combat zones during 1942 had only 7 deaths among 4,000 wounded men: 0.18 per cent. These wounded were gathered from several months of fighting in the Pacific area, and included about every type of battle injury: wounds from machine guns, rifles, shell fragments, and bomb-bursts; severe burns and bone fractures; head wounds, chest wounds, belly wounds; arm and leg injuries, and a smattering of the unusual, such as injuries from immersion blast and shark bites. The surgeons reporting the experience remarked on the unusual number of multiple-injury cases, in which fractured bones, burns, and metal fragments were found all in one patient. Of course, these 4,000 were those who survived the first-aid and other early treatment on fighting ships or battlefield stations, and therefore represent a certain selection; but even so the death rate of 0.18 is perhaps an all-time low for so large and representative a series of war wounded. The results confirm the record made by the medical men at Pearl Harbor, and suggest that their high percentage of success was no mere stroke of chance.

PREPAREDNESS AT PEARL HARBOR

Pearl Harbor presents a story unique in the annals of the present war. Here was no battle array of opposing forces, no balancing of an alert defense against a daring offensive, but a treacherous surprise raid which was conceived as a massacre of unsuspecting victims. It would be difficult to give the medical corps a more severe test. The fact that the doctors were ready, that they had preparations adequate to the vast emergency, is one of the bright spots of that somber and dreadful morning of falling bombs, exploding ships, burning docks, and dying men. Hundreds, perhaps thousands, did not die simply because modern medicine was competent to save them, and was there, equipped, alert, prepared to do the impossible.

It is a striking coincidence that on the Friday evening preceding the Sunday morning of the attack, some 300 medical men of Hawaii, including most of the army and navy surgeons stationed at Pearl Harbor, gathered to hear a lecture on "Treatment of Wounds, Civil and Military" by Dr. John J. Moorhead of New York. This distinguished professor of surgery in the New York Postgraduate Medical School has had a wide experience with wounds of violence, both as an army medical officer in the first world war and as chief surgeon of the New York subway system; and he had arrived in Hawaii just two days before, in response to an invitation from the Honolulu Medical Society to give a series of ten lectures. On that Friday night Dr. Moorhead reviewed the principles and procedures of modern traumatic surgery. He emphasized the preliminary necessity of cleansing the wound thoroughly with soap and water; the importance of drastic debridement or cutting away of all crushed and dead tissue; the remarkable outwitting of certain bacteria to be obtained by packing the wound with crystals of sulfanilamide or sulfathiazole; the value of leaving the wound wide open for the first three days, meanwhile dosing the patient at four-hour intervals with a sulfonamide drug to guard against infection and with a sedative to suppress pain. There were questions and answers. Many of the minutiae of operational technique and post-operative treatment of victims of gunshot, explosive bombs, incendiaries and other instruments of violence were rehearsed by the professor, little dreaming that within thirty-six hours he and his audience would be called upon to put these methods to a large-scale test. Sunday morning he was beginning a lecture on "Burns" when the summons came from the army, and thereafter Moorhead spent a stretch of eleven hours in the operating room. The surgeons in one big army hospital by common consent placed the New York professor in charge, as if to say, "Here, you have been telling us how to do this thing, now—" Four extra operating rooms were hastily improvised and put into commission besides the regular three, and at times there were as many as twelve surgical teams operating simultaneously. Similar scenes were being enacted at other hospitals of Honolulu and vicinity.

"The results were better than I had ever seen during nineteen months in France in 1917-1918," said Dr. Moorhead when he returned to New York a month later. "The death rate following operations was only 3.8 per cent; no deaths at all resulted from gas gangrene; purulent discharge was almost absent. I attribute the results to five main factors: first, early receipt of the wounded, within the golden period of six hours; second, preliminary shock treatment by transfusion with whole blood, plasma, or other fluids; third, adequate debridement with no primary suturing; fourth, use of sulfonamide drugs in the wound and by the mouth; fifth, adequate aftercare." The fact that most of the victims were not wearing puttees saved them from the contamination of dirty fabrics driven into the wound. It was also fortunate from this point of view that the attack came early Sunday morning, when the men were clean and not war-worn. The mild climate was favorable, and the fact that there were few flies seemed important to the surgeon.

One detail of this story focuses on a little black box which Dr. Moorhead brought from his New York surgery. In outer appearance, it resembled a portable radio set. Within the box were vacuum-tube amplifiers and a recording dial; but instead of picking up radio waves this set was able to pick up electromagnetic variations caused by the presence of metal. There was a wand-like rod attached to the apparatus through a flexible wire. By slowly passing this rod over the surface of the body, or into a wound, it could be made to serve as an antenna to detect the presence and position of hidden bullets, imbedded fragments of shell, splinters of steel, and the like—working on the same principle as the "outdoor carpet sweepers" used in North Africa to spot the presence of buried ground mines. The locator had been developed at the surgeon's suggestion by Sam Berman, an electrical engineer of the New York transit system, and had already been used in civilian practice. Dr. Moorhead intended to demonstrate it in one of his lectures, but the apparatus got its first Hawaiian demonstration in critical emergency use that Sunday afternoon when it revealed a machine-gun bullet lodged in the spinal canal of a severely stricken soldier. "Despite the use of x-rays, I would have failed had it not been for the aid afforded by the locator," said Moorhead. Other surgeons too used this instrument. Twenty-one imbedded metal fragments were removed from wounds without a single failure. The locator was left in Honolulu and continues in service there. Meanwhile, a number of sets have been produced for the army and navy. The performance of this sensitive wand of electromagnetism is part of the medical miracle of Pearl Harbor.

Shortly after the attack, the Committee on Medical Research in Washington sent Drs. I. S. Ravdin and Perrin H. Long to Honolulu to survey the medical results. Their detailed observations went to the surgeons general of the army and navy in a confidential report. But it is no secret that the two observers were enthusiastic over the way that operations and treatments had turned out. "It is quite possible," they declare, "that we shall look back on the experiences gained from the casualties which occurred during the raid on Pearl Harbor as opening a new era of surgical therapy."

THE COMMITTEE ON MEDICAL RESEARCH

Many of today's medical advances can be traced to beginnings in 1914-'18. The casualties pouring back from the Marne, the Somme, Verdun, the Meuse-Argonne, and other battlefields converted France into a vast pathological laboratory. For the first time trained physiologists were able to make large-scale studies of traumatic shock in human bodies, and out of these studies came recognition of the imperative importance of blood transfusion for the wounded. Overworked but daring doctors, confronted with thousands of head injuries, developed the modern techniques of brain surgery. Dr. Winnett Orr introduced his plaster-cast system of immobilizing wounds in 1917 as a young medical officer of the A.E.F., though it was not until the Spanish Civil War that the method won public attention. X-ray apparatus was ponderous and photographically slow, but it demonstrated its usefulness. Though there were units called mobile in 1918, they were elephantine compared with the compact x-ray installations which now travel by airplane. Today also there are new anesthetics to facilitate field surgery: pentothal, administered swiftly to the bloodstream by hypodermic needle, has won high praise. An early report from the New Guinea battlefield rated blood plasma, sulfanilamide and pentothal as "the three most important agencies for the treatment of battle wounds that science has discovered since the last war." Pentothal is of the same chemical family as veronal, the familiar sleeping compound whose formula was discovered a few years before the first world war. And sulfanilamide was actually on the chemists' shelves all during 1914-'18. It was first synthesized in 1908, and immediately proved useful in the manufacture of dyes, but not until the 1930's were its germ-fighting properties recognized and demonstrated.

Science is exploring many strange trails in the quest for new drugs, immunizing agents, healing remedies, and for new uses of the old ones. Work of this kind has been going on for years. It is carried on independently in universities, medical schools, hospitals, pharmaceutical laboratories, and other research centers. But today, in place of the scattered efforts of individual investigators, we have in the United States a closely co-ordinated program under the national Committee on Medical Research. During 1942 a total of $3,430,480 was allocated by this committee in contracts with various universities, drug manufacturers, and other institutions for research on particular problems in medicine. By 1943, more than 300 laboratory investigations in 85 institutions were under way. The committee, which is headed by Dr. A. N. Richards of the University of Pennsylvania Medical School, is a department of the all-inclusive Office of Scientific Research and Development. While other agencies of OSRD are exploring physics, chemistry and related specialties for improvements in weapons to use against hostile man, this Committee on Medical Research is prospecting biophysics, biochemistry, pharmacology, physiology, pathology, psychiatry, and various biological fields in the search for weapons against disease and death.

To illustrate the sort of work sponsored by the committee, three research undertakings which have received its support will be reviewed. One, having to do with the separation of blood plasma into fractions for transfusion and other uses, is already in production; its products have been moving to the battlefronts since 1942. Another, concerned with the extraction of a fungus product which has amazing power to neutralize bacteria, is just emerging from the stage of testing and pioneering into full-scale clinical use. The third, a search for more effective drugs against malaria, is still in the exploratory stage.

BLOOD PLASMA

During the first world war tens of thousands of lives were saved by injecting the blood from a donor into a severely wounded man whose blood was of compatible type. In the years following the war it was realized that whole blood was not necessary for many of these transfusions. What the wounded man needed was a liquid which would restore volume to his circulation, provide sufficient fluid for the heart to pump on; and it was found that the plasma, or straw-colored liquid which remains after the red cells and leucocytes have been removed, was admirably suited for these transfusions. Moreover, with a plasma transfusion the blood did not have to be typed. The main differences which distinguish the blood types from one another are in the cells, and plasma transfusions were therefore more convenient and time-saving. Then a few years ago it was demonstrated that plasma could be evaporated to a brownish powdery residue, that this dry plasma would keep indefinitely and that, when dissolved in sterile distilled water, it was ready and safe for use in transfusion.

The first dry plasma was obtained by direct evaporation of liquid plasma, but the results were not uniformly successful, and in 1935-'36 a different method was introduced. In this process the liquid part of blood is first frozen and then subjected to the suction of a vacuum. The frozen mass is kept at a temperature of about 4° below zero Fahrenheit, while the suction of the vacuum leads through a closed tube which is kept around 94° below zero. The effect of the temperature difference is to cause the water to "boil" out of the frozen mass. Its temperature of $-4°$ is so much hotter than the $-94°$ that there is a thousandfold difference in vapor pressure between the two regions, and in consequence water particles literally fly from the frozen mass to the colder region of lower pressure where they condense into ice. The effect is to dry the plasma to a spongy mass of powder, which instantly redissolves when water is added to prepare it for a transfusion. The quick freezing has no ill effect on the biological properties of the substance, and nearly all plasma for the Red Cross is now dried by this process.

As World War II began its carnage, the three degrees of blood material were available—whole blood, liquid plasma and dry plasma. It was not long, however, before dry plasma became almost standard for wartime surgical use. Neat little containers were devised to hold a can of the brownish powder, a bottle of distilled water and a coil of tubing; and these units by the thousands were shipped by the American Red Cross for use in Britain and France and stored in convenient centers as reserves for our army and navy.

Interest in plasma took a sudden rise in the spring of 1940 with the German invasion of Holland, Belgium and France. Authorities of the Red Cross and the National Research Council foresaw an accelerated demand from Europe, perhaps a call for 300,000 transfusion units. Although this is a relatively small amount compared with the present rate of Red Cross collections, it was far beyond the dimensions of any blood-donor program which had been proposed up to that time. In the face of this emergency, medical men thought of the possibility of using the plasma of animal blood.

An important center of study in this field is the laboratory of physical chemistry at the Harvard Medical School, where for twenty years Dr. Edwin J. Cohn and a group have been exploring the proteins of blood. So medical representatives of the Red Cross and the National Research Council went to Dr. Cohn with this extremely difficult but important task. They asked that he find out if it would be safe and beneficial to put the plasma of a cow or horse into the veins of a man.

Cohn and his group took over this job in the summer of 1940, and they are still at work on it, with a considerable harvest of experimental results. But the most profitable outcome of their study is not the answer to the question whether or not the plasma of animals can supply a useful substitute for blood in transfusions. That problem is still in the testing stage, and tests with thousands of human subjects must be completed, and the compatibility of the animal material with the human system must be thoroughly established before it can be accepted for clinical use. A more immediate practical result of the Harvard research is the new knowledge that has been gained of human plasma through the application to it of the processes developed in the study of animal blood. As Dr. Walter B. Cannon remarked, after reviewing the progress of the investigation, "it may well be that the by-products of this study will turn out to be of more value to medicine and surgery than the success of the original quest."

First among these by-products is the technique for separating plasma into its constituents. Indeed, this separation was fundamental to the basic problem. For plasma is not one substance but a mixture, and Dr. Cohn recognized that before he could make any controlled tests of animal plasma he would have to sort it out into its components and test each fraction separately. Blood carries in solution all the products which the living body releases into its circulation, and most significant among the plasma constituents are its proteins. These are what give character and individuality to plasma. Their molecules are huge structures of thousands of atoms, but most can be classified under four headings: the albumins, the antibodies, the clotting factors, and a heterogeneous group whose members are less known. The Harvard chemists found a method of precipitating the groups one by one. They applied this method to the plasma of human blood, and thus obtained concentrates of human albumin, concentrates of human antibodies, concentrates of human clotting factors; each of which appears to be of value in medicine.

The albumins, for example, which in the course of the process are separated from the mixture as a white crystalline powder, constitute 60 per cent of the total plasma proteins. Tests show that they are responsible for 80 per cent of the osmotic effect of blood. This osmotic effect is the property which causes circulating blood to draw water out of cells and tissues, a highly important function in time of wound shock when the fluid content of the circulation leaks out of the capillary walls and a quick restoration of volume is necessary. Because of this superior water-gaining property, transfusions made with concentrates of albumin have proved to be very effective in the treatment of shock. A given quantity of albumin will pull more water into the circulation than an equal quantity of total-plasma proteins. Moreover, a transfusion unit of albumin concentrate is more compact than a unit of whole plasma. It is sufficiently stable to be bottled as a 25 per cent solution, it weighs less than a unit of whole plasma, and nine times as many albumin units can be carried in the same space in a plane or ship.

When Drs. Ravdin and Long flew to Pearl Harbor after the Japanese raid, they carried units of this human-albumin concentrate, and the material demonstrated its value in use there on wounded sailors and soldiers. By 1942 the desirability of human albumin for tailoring a transfusion to the emergency needs of a wound-shocked body was so well established that the navy ordered large quantities. By 1943 seven commercial pharmaceutical houses had built special processing plants to concentrate albumin from blood collected by the Red Cross. These plants were strategically placed in the east, middle west, and Pacific coast, and in the summer of 1943 an eighth plant was erected in the southwest to care for blood donated from that area.

Meanwhile the Harvard chemists were exploring other separated components of plasma. The antibodies proved to be highly interesting. These are the protective agents which the body builds and releases into the circulation when it is invaded by an infection. In a large blood bank, such as that accumulated by the American Red Cross, the blood of each donor contributes certain antibodies. One person may have had measles and mumps, another typhoid, another typhus or spotted fever; and so with other infections. The blood bank contains among its mixture the antibodies resulting from these numerous experiences with microbes. The Harvard chemists found a way to concentrate the proteins containing the antibodies. They then went on to select from this mass the antibodies of virus diseases, with the result that little ampoules of the concentrates were prepared for test use, to see if injections with them would protect against the viruses. Very favorable results have been obtained from the concentrated antibodies of measles. They are effective both in prevention and modification of this contagious disease, and in the summer of 1943 plans were under way to concentrate measles antibodies from parts of the blood collected by the Red Cross.

There are many other antibodies, most of them found in concentrations too small to be of practical use in medicine. However, a closely related fraction of the plasma contains the factors which agglutinize noncompatible red blood cells, and these have been concentrated and prepared for convenient use in typing the blood of a patient when his need calls for a transfusion of whole blood. They are known as iso-agglutinins.

Still another group of plasma components which have been

separated in highly concentrated form are the clotting factors, prothrombin and fibrinogen. By certain well-known treatments the prothrombin is converted to thrombin, which appears on precipitation as another white powder. The fibrinogen also is like fine snow. When solutions of these two substances come together they react to form a clot, and the Harvard investigators have found it possible to make clots with widely varying properties from solutions of thrombin and fibrinogen. The clots can be produced as membranes, filaments, jointures, or plugs. Plastic tubes and disks of fibrinogen have also been prepared. In which state these products of human blood may prove to be of most value remains to be determined by surgical research. The use of the clotting factors in the treatment of hemorrhage and burns is being investigated.

Each of the concentrates—fibrinogen, prothrombin, iso-agglutinins, antibodies, and albumin—is a dry white powder which readily dissolves in water. Each serves a different function in the blood stream, and each would appear to have a different use in medicine and surgery. Investigations in progress promise to yield still other parts of the plasma, concentrated and stable, in forms which may prove of value not only to our armed forces, for whose welfare these medical researches were undertaken, but also for the civilian population.

ANIMAL, VEGETABLE, MINERAL

Blood is of the animal kingdom. Bacteria, which poison blood and destroy cells and tissues, are of the vegetable kingdom. And sulfanilamide is a coal-tar derivative of the mineral kingdom. Until very recently man's most powerful known ally against the virulent little parasitic plants was this mineral compound of sulphur. It has been made into tablets for dosing by the mouth, into a solution for injection into the circulation, into a powder for dusting on wounds; and more recently various sprays containing sulfanilamide, and ointments, films, and other plastic membranes compounded of sulfanilamide mixed with soothing oils and analgesics have been fabricated as dressings for wounds and burns. Reports of the value of these treatments have come from many battlefronts, base hospitals, and casualty stations, as they have been coming too from civilian hospitals. Destructive infections have been cleared up; periods of illness and wound healing have been mercifully reduced; lives have been saved. Undoubtedly the discovery of the bacteriostatic properties of this synthetic chemical is one of the great achievements of modern medicine.

And yet, sulfanilamide is not an infallible remedy. There have been tragic disappointments. There are some serious germ infestations against which it seems to be powerless, or nearly so.

For example, the massive invasion of the blood stream known as staphylococcal septicemia suffers only a moderate setback from even the most powerful dosing with sulfonamide drugs. Before sulfanilamide came into use the death rate from this blood poisoning was 85 to 90 per cent; under sulfonamide treatment it has been reduced to an average of 65 to 70 per cent, but that is still cruelly high. There is also a rare type of pneumonia caused by staphylococcal infection of the lungs against which the sulfa drugs are only feeble protection, though they are usually victorious in combating the pneumococci and streptococci of ordinary pneumonia.

Gas-gangrene bacilli yield grudgingly to sulfanilamide and only in a limited degree: a severe infection, even though heavily treated, is often fatal. Staphylococcal infection of burns is also a stubborn problem, for the microbes multiply with overwhelming rapidity among the dead and dying cells of the seared flesh, and they seem to be able to develop a tolerance for the drug. After the first day or two sulfanilamide doesn't seem to have much effect. The British have produced a new drug, proflavin, for which many advantages are reported. It is said to be more potent than the sulfonamides against the staphylococci. But since proflavin is toxic in the blood stream, and therefore can be used only on the outside of wounds, some surgeons won't risk it. A more recent British introduction is propamidine, another synthetic compound which also is applied only externally.

If that were all that could be said of the present medical front against sulfonamide-resistant bacteria, there wouldn't be much point in bringing up the subject. But there are exciting new developments, powerful reinforcements already on the scene; and this time the defense comes, not from the mineral kingdom, but from the vegetable.

PENICILLIN

There is a tiny fungus, a greenish-blue scum similar in appearance to common bread mold. This fungus produces a substance, a fragile, unknown chemical compound, which is by far the most potent known agent against bacteria. Tests show that a dilution of 1 part in 100 million is sufficient to prevent the growth of the highly infectious blood-destroying Staphylococcus aureus. The mold is known botanically as Penicillium notatum, and its mysterious germ-fighting extract has accordingly been named penicillin.

A recent case in a New England hospital will illustrate its power. The wife of a university official lay at the point of death, her blood the prey of a spreading infection of Staphylococcus aureus. Sulfonamide compounds had been used from the first appearance of symptoms, but with little effect; the invasion was racing through her system and would be fatal when the multiplication of bacteria reached the critical stage. The attending physician had heard of penicillin. Though not yet on the market it has been produced in a few laboratories for experimental and clinical testing, and as a last resort the doctor appealed for a dosage for his dying patient. The penicillin was rushed to him by airplane, injected into the poisoned blood stream, and thereafter the golden germs simply fell away as though mowed down by an invisible reaper. It seemed miraculous, but there are scores of equally moving rescues in the case histories of penicillin.

The discovery of this remarkable weapon against disease dates back to 1929. It was purely accidental. Dr. Alexander Fleming, in St. Mary's Hospital, London, was growing colonies of bacteria on glass plates for certain bacteriological researches. One morning he noticed that a spot of mold had germinated on one of the plates. Such contaminations are not unusual, but for some reason, instead of discarding the impurity and starting afresh, Dr. Fleming decided to allow it to remain. He continued to culture the plate, and soon an interesting drama unfolded beneath his eyes. The area occupied by the bacteria was decreasing; that occupied by the mold was increasing; and presently the bacteria had vanished.

Dr. Fleming now took up this fungus for study on its own account. He recognized it as of the penicillium genus and, by deliberately introducing a particle into culture mediums where bacteria were growing, he found that quite a number of species wouldn't grow in its presence. There were other species which did not seem to be bothered. As he pursued his experiments the scientist noticed that the bacteria which were able to live with the penicillium were of the group known as gram-negative, so called because they give a negative reaction to a certain staining test named after its inventor—the gram-test. Those which were unable to endure the mold and died in its presence were gram-positive bacteria. In his laboratory, whenever he wanted to get rid of a growth of gram-positive bacteria, Fleming would implant a little penicillium, and after that the microbes disappeared.*

There are beneficial bacteria among the gram-positive group, but it also includes some of the most predatory microbes known to human pathology. For example, the causative agents of such horrible afflictions as septicemia, osteomyelitis, gas gangrene, tetanus, anthrax, and plague are gram-positive. The streptococci, staphylococci, and pneumococci are all of this grouping. So the medical scientists began to speculate. Since the mold destroyed gram-positive organisms on a culture plate, could it be used to destroy gram-positive disease germs in the living body?

This question was the starting point of a medical research which has multiplied into many studies in both Great Britain and the United States. Fundamental to the whole program were the separation and concentration of the active substance, an achievement which was first accomplished by British investigators. The British also were first to report the treatment of human disease with penicillin. A team of biochemists and bacteriologists at Oxford has been especially active, and has reported many cures. In the United States studies have been made at the College of Physicians and Surgeons in New York, the Mayo Clinic, the National Institute of Health, the Evans Memorial Hospital of Boston, and by almost all the large pharmaceutical houses. Since 1941 the development of penicillin in quantities sufficient for clinical use has been a major interest of the Committee on Medical Research, and its support of the work in several centers undoubtedly has had much to do with

* Fleming later discovered that there are a few gram-negative bacteria which are vulnerable to the mold.

the progress recently made. At the same time, independent groups have contributed important findings which are part of our advance.

Recent clinical tests leave no doubt of the medical and surgical value of penicillin. It has cured acute cases of blood infection, bone infection, eye infection; has conquered severe infestations of gonorrhea, has cleared bacteria from massive burns and other wounds; and often it has done these jobs after the sulfonamides had failed, and with no adverse reactions in the patient. A surgeon has reported, for example, that whereas the death rate of staphylococcal blood poisoning before sulfanilamide was 85 to 90 per cent, and since sulfanilamide 65 to 70 per cent, "even our limited use of penicillin has brought it down to 36 per cent." And, he added, "with further knowledge of this new material, we think it can be reduced to 20 per cent." Virtually every complication of staphylococcal infection except one seems to yield. Endocarditis, a bacterial infestation of the delicate lining of the heart, is resistant even to penicillin.

The principal factor limiting the use of the new germ-fighter has been production. Enormous quantities of the mold have to be grown to obtain even meager supplies. Also the product is somewhat unstable, sensitive to changes in temperature, and therefore it has to be kept under refrigeration. Until we know its chemical formula and are able to synthesize it, we are wholly dependent on the fungus to produce penicillin by natural vegetative processes.

Penicillium notatum is cultivated in bottles or vats, and grows on the surface of a liquid from which it draws nutriment. As the velvety mat spreads and thickens, it releases by-products which descend and dissolve in the medium; and by processing this liquid the substance is extracted. On evaporation the residue appears as a reddish-brown powder, and this is penicillin as the doctor gets it. The powder dissolves readily in water, and is administered by injection into the blood stream, though it may also be laid on a wound by spray or other means. Penicillin has been used to treat wounded soldiers hospitalized home from the battlefronts, and about all of the present production is going into military and naval use.

In the summer of 1943 production operations were still in the pilot-plant stage, although considerable progress has been made in increasing the yield. In 1941 it was necessary to process 100 liters (about 26½ gallons) of the liquid to get 1 gram (a thirtieth of an ounce) of the extract, and this extract was only about 25 per cent "pure" penicillin. By 1943 the strains of fungi had been so selected and cultivated for high yield, and the methods of processing so improved, that 100 liters were producing 10 grams, and the 10 grams were 88 per cent penicillin. The processors are confident that in time they will be able to concentrate their extract to a purity close to 100 per cent.

Meanwhile, the number of concerns engaged in production has been stepped up. Even with no gain in percentage of yield, substantial increases in output may be expected from the multiplication of producing units. An interesting development is the turning of a group of Pennsylvania mushroom growers to the new industry. They are familiar with the ways of fungi and now cultivate penicillium for the drug market instead of mushrooms for the food market.

AGAINST MALARIA

Many bacterial infections have recently been put on the defensive, as the story of penicillin and the sulfonamides suggests, but unfortunately the world's most prevalent epidemic disease is not of this class. The agent of malaria is not a bacterium at all, but a little animal, Plasmodium malariae. For some reason the little animals seem to be tougher parasites than the bacteria. Quinine has been in commercial production for over a century, and tons of it have been consumed. About a dozen years ago two synthetic chemicals, atabrine and plasmochin, also came into use as anti-malarial drugs. But none of the three is a real remedy. "Not one will cure with certainty," said Dr. Paul F. Russell of the U. S. Army Medical Corps; "not one is a true prophylactic drug, and not one is of much value in the control of community malaria."

The organism of malaria is able to hide out in tissues during a barrage of quinine, temporarily disappearing from the blood stream and giving a show of defeat, only to come back and strike its victim with renewed chills and fevers after the drug has ceased firing. Throughout the world 300,000,000 people are ill of malaria, with an annual death rate of at least 3,000,000. Those who develop a tolerance which enables them to carry on some sort of existence despite the infestation remain carriers of the disease, requiring only the visit of a mosquito to transmit it to new victims.

Quinine, atabrine, and plasmochin are helpful allies in the present stage of our therapy, for until a better drug is found or fabricated they remain our most important aids in the treatment of malaria. Quinine can interrupt the acute attack, and, as Dr. L. W. Hackett has said, "that alone, for the lives and suffering it has saved, will always entitle it to a medal of honor." Indeed, quinine became more precious than gold after the Japanese shut off imports from the sources of supply in the Far East, and for a while such reserves as could be accumulated were hoarded in U. S. Treasury vaults. For general use in malaria treatment many physicians regard quinine more highly than either atabrine or plasmochin. These synthetic compounds have unfavorable aftereffects on many patients, and it is generally recognized that they will have to be improved before they can be accepted as complete substitutes for the natural product. In fact, plasmochin is used only in combination with quinine, for alone it is not sufficient.

Meanwhile the shortage of quinine, the fact that quinine is only about 50 per cent effective against malaria, and the importance which malaria occupies as Disease Hazard No. 1 in the war zones constitute an emergency combination of first rank. Shortly after the war began, the search for new and better anti-malarial drugs assumed a special interest in several laboratories. With the organization of the Committee on Medical Research in 1941, the search became another of its major interests, and funds were provided to support the work on a wide front.

Several important leads have been opened up by these studies. Two promising substances were found by Dr. Lyndon F. Small at the National Institute of Health, and are being further explored. Dr. Small, an authority on the chemistry of the alkaloids, the family of which quinine is a member, has outlined a whole group of possible compounds for investigation. Under the leadership of a committee of the National Research Council twenty laboratories have been enlisted to pursue these and other possibilities. Several large chemical manufacturing companies opened their shelves of new, rare, and unexploited compounds, and permitted representatives of the Committee on Medical Research to prospect these stocks for possible useful drugs. Thousands of substances have been tested, and thousands more will be.

An army that possessed a specific against malaria would have a strategic advantage, particularly in operations in Africa, Italy, the

Balkans, southern Russia, Asia, the South Pacific. In these areas malaria lurks as an ever-present menace, "no longer an exotic disease, but a difficult military problem." In the Philippines, at the fall of Bataan, 85 per cent of the defending troops were ill of acute malaria. Early in 1943 it was reported that more than half of the American troops stationed in some of the islands of the southwest Pacific had contracted malaria.

"We have vaccines against typhoid, paratyphoid, tetanus, and yellow fever, the protective value of which is well established," said Dr. Thomas T. Mackie of the U. S. Army Medical School. Also "we have vaccines for plague, cholera, and typhus, the efficacy of which remains to be established. We have no method of immunizing against dysenteries, malaria, and a host of other conditions to which these men inevitably will be exposed during the course of their military duties."

The spread of malaria can be prevented by destroying the malaria-transmitting mosquito. A program of mosquito control was introduced in military camps of the United States in 1941, using sprays of pyrethrum extract and other methods of insect eradication. Nearly $2,000,000 was spent on this program, apparently well spent, for the incidence of malaria in 1941-'43 averaged less than half that in corresponding camps in 1917-'19. Pyrethrum mixtures are now packaged in the form of "health bombs," which are one pound cans equipped with a spray outlet. These have been used in the foxholes of the South Pacific, in pup tents in the tropics, in airplane cabins on the ground, and in other mosquito-infested places. The "bomb" may be turned off and on as needed, and three seconds of its spray will effectively fumigate one pup tent or equivalent space.

Insect control is being applied also as a means of typhus prevention, and powerful louse-killing chemicals recently developed in American laboratories are now in standard use in the army. Sprinkled on the underclothes, these powders destroy lice and eggs and repel further invasions.

DYSENTERY AND BACTERIOPHAGE

In some battle areas bacillary dysentery is a close second to malaria. The disease is an acute diarrhea caused by a bacterial infection of the digestive tract, and like typhoid fever is most prevalent in regions of primitive sanitation. In 1940 when sulfaguanidine, a new derivative of sulfanilamide, was found to be poorly absorbed from the digestive tract, medical men hailed it as of possible use against this infection. The fact that it was poorly absorbed suggested that it would stay in the tract and perhaps inhibit the bacilli. Its use for this purpose has been successful in many cases, but of only minor value in others, for apparently certain virulent strains learn to accustom themselves to the chemical and finally resist it. More recently two new derivatives of sulfathiazole have won some success against the dysentery bacillus.

Interesting reports of the current use of bacteriophage have come from a few European sources. This curious germ-killing substance is a natural product found in bacteria-infested sewage, and acts as a virus which preys on the disease germs themselves. In Alexandria, Egypt, bacteriophage has been used to combat bacillary dysentery since 1928; and an English medical officer of the municipal laboratory there reports to the *British Medical Journal* that under this treatment the dysentery death rate dropped from above 20 per cent to less than 7 per cent. This officer also states that the British, in capturing supplies left by Rommel's fleeing Afrika Korps, found bottles of dysentery bacteriophage prepared by the Germans for use by their medical corps. Several papers published in German medical journals of 1940 and 1941 report the use of bacteriophage against dysentery, both in occupied Poland and in occupied France. Some of these accounts assert that preliminary dosing with the phage had a prophylactic effect, protecting the soldiers against infection.

Work on dysentery bacteriophage has been carried on in a few research centers in the United States. Recently the Overly Biochemical Foundation in New York succeeded in reducing the usually liquid preparation to a dried stable powder. Several medical groups are now working with this dried bacteriophage, testing it for use on human cases of the disease.

WAR MULTIPLIES PEACETIME ILLS

One has only to name the diseases which disable the armed forces to realize that war service, for the physician and surgeon, simply means a change in the base of his practice; not a change in its problems, methods, ideals, or purposes. For the medical man, both researcher and practitioner, war intensifies the fight which is his lifetime's daily routine. And that is the fight for more knowledge of the human body, for more light on the mechanism of disease, for more understanding and greater skill in making use of the natural laws which govern life and ward off death. Except for a few isolated perversions, such as the Japanese efforts at spreading epidemics among the Chinese by sowing communities with microbes, the medical weapons are all primarily defensive, preventive, protective, and increasingly effective.

The same contagions, infections, deficiencies, organic and functional infirmities have to be cared for in wartime as in peacetime; but under the stress of war their incidence is multiplied, their virulence or extremity accentuated by the added privations, exposures and anxieties. Even in time of peace the physician is called on to care for gunshot wounds and other injuries inflicted by explosives, but war provides him with richer clinical material. Certainly no doctor in time of peace ever had the problem which confronted a London surgeon called upon to treat an air-raid victim. X-ray examination showed that an unexploded aircraft shell was imbedded in the tissues of his thigh, and when the bomb squad was called its experts recognized the hidden object as an armor-piercing projectile designed to explode on contact. It was a nerve-racking experience for the operating unit, though the patient was blissfully ignorant of what ailed him. The surgeon cut and probed with discretion, and finally drew out the package of high explosive in what a medical colleague described as "the most delicate and dangerous operation of his career.

It is interesting to note that the man who was thus wounded was a civilian. Such is the phenomenon of total war. Even the quantitative differences between military medicine and civil medicine fade out of the picture when, as in the 1940 aerial attacks on London, the killed and wounded civilians outnumbered the killed and wounded troops.

A doctor in one of the large New York clinics reports that during 1940, with the growing fury of the war in Europe, there was a noticeable increase in the number of hyperthyroid patients coming for treatment. In 1932-1935 there was a similar increase, apparently a reflection of the strain imposed on the population by the recurring shocks of the economic depression. However, nervous tension alone is not sufficient to produce hyperthyroid disease. There must be either some constitutional or acquired weakness in the thyroid gland or in its control, or some deficiency in nutrition, or both, to set the stage for emotional excitement to play its role. Cerebral hemorrhage and nephritis attained their highest death rates in the year of American entrance into World War I, and after 1917 receded to lower levels. Inasmuch as both diseases are related to high blood pressure, and high blood pressure is affected by emotional excitement, it is no wonder that this sudden wartime rise took place.

On the same basis, mental disorders may increase, but again the extent of the upset is determined by other circumstances, both anatomical and emotional. Psychiatry has criteria by which it is possible to identify a large percentage of the emotional misfits and potential psychotics in advance, and at least screen them into forms of service where the risk of mental collapse is not at its maximum. It has been stated publicly by psychiatrists that the army and navy are not making full use of these resources. Warnings are already coming from medical men, preparing the home front for the mental cripples who are also part of the havoc of war. Pearl Harbor had its casualties for whom there was no help in sulfanilamide or blood plasma; men whose minds toppled under the shock of that awful experience.

The vitamins, not a one of which was available in pure form in 1914-'18, now share medical importance with drugs and vaccines, since science has traced certain nervous, mental, and other functional disorders to a deficiency of one or more of these food factors. Diets are prescribed according to the service to be expected of the individual, and men assigned to special duties requiring high endurance and closely co-ordinated performance receive concentrates of fortifying food factors. The new methods of processing foods, by dehydration, concentration and other techniques, have their medical as well as their industrial and economic aspects.

The remoteness of battlefields from the home base has increased the problems of the medical corps; for the unaccustomed climates and other environmental changes to which the soldier is subjected by war have their repercussions in his biology.

Consider, for example, the physiological problems imposed by the tank—problems of living for hours in the cramped space; problems of enduring desert heat or arctic cold according to the latitude of the battlefield; problems of gas fumes projected by explosives and motors; problems of lighting, of seeing, hearing, and keeping a cool head and a steady hand in the midst of the din of fighting. Tank designs, constructional details, and interior arrangements and fittings have been considerably revised in the course of the war as a result of searching laboratory studies of the human body under experimental tank conditions ranging from those of a Sahara sandstorm with temperature up to 150° Fahrenheit to those of an Alaskan winter with temperature 70° below zero.

Even more extreme in their demands on the organism are the changes to which an aircraft pilot is introduced in swift succession in the course of his aeronautical operations. Flying subjects man to radically new environmental conditions, as alien to his system as a new synthetic chemical. The possible effects are so critical in their influence on his flight performance, indeed on the very maintenance of consciousness, that a whole new branch of science has developed out of his needs: aeromedicine.

CHAPTER X

Aeromedicine

The fields of air are open to knowledge, and only
ignorance and idleness need crawl upon the ground.

—Samuel Johnson, THE PRINCE OF ABISSINIA

THE human body is adapted to life on the surface of the Earth,
down at the bottom of our ocean of air, while the modern aircraft
is designed to navigate the cold, thin upper atmosphere. On these
two facts and their interrelations hang most of the problems of
aviation medicine.

Primarily they are problems arising from the rapid changes to
which earth-conditioned man is subjected by flight: changes in
atmospheric pressure, changes in atmospheric temperature, and
changes in the rate and direction of motion. There are combat
planes which can cruise at more than 400 miles an hour, climb
a mile a minute, and operate at altitudes of 40,000 feet and above.
Battle tactics place a premium on speed, fast climbing, high ceiling,
and rapid maneuverability; but when the changes to which the
machine subjects the flyer become greater than his body can
compensate for, even with artificial aids, then it is clear that
aviation has its boundaries in human biology.

A growing recognition of this has brought about closer collaboration between the aeronautical engineers who design planes and the medical men who are responsible for the maintenance of the flyer at the highest pitch of efficiency. "In the last few years, the aerophysician has taken on the additional duties of assisting the engineers and designers," said Brigadier General David N. W. Grant, Air Surgeon of the U. S. Army Air Forces. "The awakening of the engineering and medical profession to the great benefits to be derived from co-operative research has brought about a new era of aviation in the United States Army."

Aircraft design has been modified to make the machine more conformable to the human element. Changes have been introduced to remove hazards, to conserve nervous and muscular energy, reduce strain and discomfort; and in other ways to cut down fatigue, step up efficiency, and increase the ratio of safety. Such details as the location of gunsights, the interior arrangements of turrets and blisters, the design of safety belts and other protective devices, including a modern equivalent of the medieval coat of mail, are all results of collaboration between engineers and physicians. The highly efficient oxygen masks, oxygen supply systems, and oxygen flasks with which modern aircraft are equipped also represent joint efforts of medical men and technologists. Still further integration remains to be accomplished, for the airplane today is capable of flight performances beyond the endurance of the airman; but much has been done, and studies are continually in progress in the laboratories.

Aeromedicine, in both army and navy, has two fundamental responsibilities: first, to select from among the candidates for the air services those who are constitutionally fitted for the exacting demands of flight; and second, to provide all known aids to reduce the physiological hazards of these demands and assist the flyer to achieve the highest level of adjustment. It is therefore not concerned primarily with the sick. Its interest is rather with the well. Its first concern is to identify among a group of healthy persons the ones who inherently are best fitted to fly. There are anatomical and physiological tests to determine the state of health of the individual, the soundness of his heart, lungs, nerves, eyes, and other organs. There are psychological tests to appraise his intelligence, his psychomotor co-ordination, his emotional reactivity to the risks and excitements of flying. There are performance tests to determine how well he can withstand the rigors and privations of the upper heights and the inertial violences imposed by acceleration. After the best human material has been selected, aeromedicine seeks to safeguard these precious resources in every way, to insure that the margin of safety will not be overloaded by the demands of flight.

Many ingenious devices have been used to assist these tests. One of the most interesting is the altitude chamber. These air-tight compartments, some of them built of reinforced concrete, others of steel, are able to reproduce atmospheric conditions of the stratosphere. Powerful pumps and refrigeration apparatus provide the combination of pressure and temperature found at every altitude up to more than eight miles, and are able to "climb" at the rate of a mile a minute. More than forty altitude chambers are now in service in various parts of the United States. They are used for the selection and training of airmen for the army and navy, and to indoctrinate them in the problems of aviation physiology and the use of oxygen equipment, cold-resistant clothing, and other appliances of flight.

In addition, a comprehensive program of research is centered in these devices. Much of our modern knowledge of the physiology of flight was gained through studies of animals and human volunteers in altitude chambers. These compartments for simulating atmospheric conditions have been extremely useful in investigating the three main problems of high-altitude flying. These are altitude sickness, decompression sickness, and the physiological effects of extreme cold.

ALTITUDE SICKNESS

Oxygen deficiency poses this fundamental problem of aviation physiology. It derives from the phenomenon of atmospheric pressure, which in turn is a consequence of the weight of air.

The total weight of the atmosphere is five thousand million million tons. Distributed over the surface of the Earth, this weight amounts to a pressure of about fourteen pounds to the square inch. Our bodies are attuned to this surface pressure. Our lungs are built to receive and utilize the amount of oxygen which it delivers to them. All the factors in respiration are regulated to operate in step with this load. It is inevitable, therefore, that when a man rises from his accustomed level at the bottom of the ocean of air, his body's internal mechanisms are affected.

The air is a mixture. About 78 per cent of it is nitrogen, about 21 per cent oxygen, with small amounts of other gases to make up the remainder. This proportion of oxygen to nitrogen remains the same from the ground up to an altitude of about twelve miles; but as its pressure decreases, the air expands, thins out, has less substance, and therefore provides less breathing material. At sea level a cubic yard of air is so dense that its 21 per cent oxygen weighs nearly half a pound; at 38,000 feet, where atmospheric pressure is a fifth as great, a cubic yard of air is still 21 per cent oxygen, but it is so diffuse that the oxygen weighs only about a tenth of a pound. Thus, a pair of lungs breathing air at 38,000 feet would have to inhale five cubic yards to get as much oxygen as it obtains from one cubic yard at ground level. There are other factors also that determine the intake of oxygen by the blood, but this problem of air density is obvious and fundamental. The lower pressure of the high altitudes not only allows the air to distribute its mass over larger volume, but it pushes this thinner air into the lungs with less force.

The relationship between the living body and the inanimate atmosphere may be so sensitively balanced that even the slighest change in altitude is reflected in the behavior of the human system. Dr. Yandell Henderson has suggested that skyscrapers may exert a slight climatic effect on the tenants of upper stories. As the elevator swishes up in the Empire State Building, the operator's and passengers' pulses may accelerate, and other internal adjustments may occur, though in most persons the differences are too slight for measurement. Studies made in balloons and airplanes, and more recently in altitude chambers, show that for the first mile of ascent only minor differences are detectable in the body's behavior. With continuing rise the changes become appreciable, and as high altitudes are reached changes of different orders of complication manifest themselves. Three levels of behavior have been observed, marking different stages in the body's response to this anoxia, for it is oxygen want that causes altitude sickness. The thresholds vary from

individual to individual, and in general are lower for middle age
than for youth.

THREE STAGES OF OXYGEN STARVATION

First is the *reaction threshold* (6,000 to 10,000 feet), the altitude
at which the body's effort to compensate for the thinness of the
air begins to be noticeable. The heart beats more rapidly, increasing
the velocity of the circulation. At the same time the spleen discharges its stored red cells into the blood stream, thus increasing
the number of oxygen carriers. Normally a number of the capillary
vessels are closed, but now the tiny muscles controlling many of
them relax; and this opening of additional vessels exposes more
tissue to the circulating blood and its cargoes of oxygen. While
reactions of this kind are operating to extract the maximum of
oxygen from the thinner air and to get it into the circulation, other
mechanisms are economizing the use of oxygen, seeking to conserve
it for indispensable functions. In most persons these adaptations
become difficult at 10,000 feet. As the aviator rises above that altitude, the body finally is unable to compensate for the scarcity of
oxygen in every breath. Reinforcing the blood with more red cells
and pumping the stream more rapidly are insufficient to meet the
minimum oxygen requirements, and then a stage is reached at
which the deficiency disturbs the functioning of the body.

This *disturbance threshold* (10,000 to 16,500 feet) marks the level
at which various functions begin to deteriorate. The muscles are
slow to react; eyesight becomes fuzzy; hearing is not so acute;
taste, smell, and other senses are dulled; and the mental faculties
of will power, attentiveness, judgment and insight weaken. The
symptoms are similar to those of alcohol intoxication, and involve
strange shifts of mood. Some men become gloomy and morose,
some have crying spells; others are exuberant, expansive, joyful;
many are reckless.

The British tell of a pilot who encountered five German planes.
Instead of instantly fighting or fleeing, the "happy" fellow waved
blithely to his adversaries, while his astonished observer protested
vehemently and warned him to get down to business. The pilot of
another R.A.F. plane on a mission to Germany noticed that excellent
weather prevailed over the North Sea; in his anoxic condition it

seemed perfectly reasonable to travel where weather conditions were right, so he changed his course—and was thunderstruck later, when he descended to a lower altitude, to realize that he had disobeyed orders and wasted his fuel idly cruising. An American pilot, sent on a flight with orders to stay below 10,000 feet, nevertheless climbed higher, and in the upper altitudes the thin air robbed him of his judgment. He became obsessed with the idea of landing. Sighting a municipal airfield, he signaled it that he was out of fuel and would have to come down. He was so woozy from oxygen want that he made a crash landing, wrecking his plane and the environs, but escaped personal injury—and was deeply chagrined when it was pointed out that his tank had plenty of gasoline. Another American pilot was flying in formation with a squadron above 16,000 feet. He disdained the use of oxygen equipment as "sissy business," and it did not seem strange on looking out to see the nearest plane 100 yards away, a moment later 10 yards away, then 50 yards. The other pilots were frantic trying to keep out of his wobbling zigzag course, but the pilot says he felt no anxiety at the time—"it seemed perfectly reasonable."

During the disturbance stage of anoxia, the body's compensatory mechanisms of respiration and circulation are trying to make up for the oxygen want. Sometimes they succeed in restoring the functions to near normal. But if the ascent continues, deterioration of faculties also continues; until eventually the situation becomes critical, threatening complete collapse.

This *critical threshold*, like that of the other stages, is not a sharp line but varies with the individual, and is represented as a zone ranging from 16,500 to 26,000 feet. At this level of oxygen want, vision becomes dark, the roar of the aircraft engine seems faint and far away, the heart pounds, muscles refuse to move; yet the failing consciousness may bring no sense of peril. Some bodies simply fall into deep sleep; some go into convulsions.

The classic story of anoxia at the critical stage is the account of the flight of three French aeronauts, Gaston Tissandier, H. T. Sivel, and J. C. Croce-Spinelli, in the balloon *Zenith* in 1875. From the record which Tissandier kept during flight we have the first detailed account of how it feels to ascend above 26,000 feet. "I had taken care to keep absolutely still, without suspecting that I had already perhaps lost the use of my limbs," wrote Tissandier. "At about 7,500 meters (24,600 feet) the condition of torpor which overcomes one is extraordinary. Body and mind become feebler little by little, gradually and insensibly. There is no suffering. On the contrary one feels an inner joy. There is no thought of the dangerous position; one rises and is glad to be rising. I soon felt myself so weak that I could not even turn my head to look at my companions. I wished to take hold of the oxygen tube, but found I could not move my arms. My mind was still clear, however, and I watched the aneroid barometer with my eyes fixed on the needle, which soon pointed to 290 millimeters and then to 280. I wished to call out that we were now at 8,000 meters (26,200 feet), but my tongue was paralyzed. All at once I shut my eyes, fell down powerless, and lost all further memory."

The self-registering barometer showed that the balloon continued to rise after Tissandier's collapse, and attained 27,960 feet. When it reached ground both Sivel and Croce-Spinelli were dead, but Tissandier was sitting up. He had revived from his stupor when the descending balloon brought him to an adequate oxygen level. And that is what generally happens to victims of anoxia. After the critical threshold is reached, some human bodies quickly succumb, but others are able to adapt themselves even to the extreme deprivation. Though the mind goes blank, the living mechanism does not disintegrate; and the body needs only to have its oxygen supply restored to resume functioning.

ANOXIA ON THE DAWN PATROL

Tissandier's flight in the lighter-than-air ship was at least not complicated by the danger of going into a spin and crashing to the ground, a risk which confronts every anoxic pilot in an airplane. An experience of this more modern kind, illustrating most of the typical reactions at the disturbance level and the critical level, was the lot of a lieutenant of the U. S. Army Air Forces who was sent on the Dawn Patrol one morning at 2:55 o'clock. Let me say at the beginning that this man was a competent pilot; he had been "officer of the day" the day before this experience, and everything that happened to him was a consequence of oxygen want. The object of his flight was to get automatic readings of the state of the weather at various altitudes up to 16,000 feet. For some reason the pilot misinterpreted his altimeter on the way up, and as a result he read only one foot for every two feet of actual ascent. The plane reached 22,588 feet, as was recorded by the sealed baragraph on the wing, but the pilot believed that he never got higher than 12,500 feet. Indeed, he was keenly vexed and mortified at his "inability" to accomplish the assigned altitude. On the way up he had a series of adventures which he began to notice when he was near 16,000 feet, though at the time he thought his altitude was only 8,000.

At that height his head began to swim; he felt confused and weak; eyesight was affected. He leveled off and circled, hoping that a few moments' relaxation would enable him to get his mental bearings. He looked at the altimeter again. "Only 8,000 feet? It can't be oxygen. I never need a whiff before 12,000." He called the ground by radio, and found that he couldn't talk straight, couldn't even recall what he wanted to say; so he dismissed the problem and started to climb again. While preoccupied with this routine, he dropped the microphone. That was bad business, he thought: "will need the 'phone later, might need it any minute in an emergency." So he leveled off and began a search for the instrument, groping about in the darkness of the cockpit, scratching the floor, fumbling in a semi-somnolence. It never occurred to him to switch on the cockpit light, and after several minutes of helpless search, during which the plane had dropped to "7,000" feet, he gave up. "Time to climb," so he pulled into a steep ascent, and at "10,000" feet (actually about 20,000 as the sealed baragraph later showed), the plane went into a spin. It dropped 4,000 feet before the pilot was able to pull out, and resume his climb; and this sequence— the fall into a spin, the recovery, and the resumed climb—was re-enacted several times in the next hour.

"The astonishing thing is that falling off into spins in the dark, did not worry him at all," says Major Charles L. Leedham who reviewed the lieutenant's experience in diagnostic detail in the *Journal of Aviation Medicine*, to which I am indebted for the story. The dangerous spins only served to harden the determination to reach the 16,000-foot objective; and Major Leedham points out that such a reaction, in this seasoned pilot, shows how profoundly his judgment had been warped by oxygen want.

The airman was fighting mad now, and crying, tears streaming down his cheeks. He could see only the nose of his plane and the instrument board in front of him, but he felt no sense of anxiety, only chagrin. Every now and then he would catch himself in a momentary blackout. "But that's nothing, I'm just tired." And he pulled the ship into a steeper climb. Suddenly he woke up to find himself plunging earthward in a full-throttle power dive. In that spell of unconsciousness he had fallen an actual 8,000 feet before, as he says, the roar of the motor and propeller aroused him, though it was more probably the increased oxygen of the lower altitude. He let the plane drop another 2,000 feet before he leveled off, only to remember that he had not yet accomplished his mission. But his fuel supply was exhausted now, so he turned on the emergency tank, and pulled the plane upward for a renewed ascent. He had climbed about 3,000 feet when his reoxygenated brain remembered that the emergency tank carried only fifteen minutes' supply of gasoline. He looked at the time: nearly 6 o'clock. He had been in the air three hours, on a flight that ordinarily took an hour and a half. Lights glowed in the distance, his clearer sight and brain recognized them as a town about 90 miles east of his take-off. He made for it, and landed successfully in the darkness of the winter morning, without signaling for border lights or landing lights; a bit of foolhardiness which showed that his judgment still suffered from the hours of deficient oxygen. As he straightened up to climb out of the plane, there in his lap lay the lost microphone.

OXYGEN FOR ANOXIA

One consequence of oxygen want is an increase in alkalinity of the blood. To counteract this change, ammonium chloride has been administered, and favorable results are reported. It shifts blood equilibrium toward the acid side and reduces the danger of convulsion, as has been demonstrated by tests in the altitude chamber and in airplane flights, and also in the treatment of persons suffering from mountain sickness.

Certain hormones of the adrenal glands also affect the ability of the human system to adjust to oxygen want. Evidence of this was first observed toward the end of World War I when two French flight surgeons were studying groups of overworked pilots, and noticed a progressive relationship between the nervous condition known as flight fatigue and adrenal insufficiency. In 1938 H. G. Armstrong and J. W. Heim published the results of experiments made with rabbits in the altitude chamber at Wright Field. They found that after the animals had been subjected four hours daily to the atmospheric equivalent of 18,000 feet, their adrenal glands grew to enormous size and eventually the cortex or glandular sheath began to degenerate. It has been noticed that pilots suffering from flyers' fatigue sometimes develop symptoms similar to those shown in the early stages of Addison's disease, a disorder of atrophied adrenal glands. Other investigators have explored this problem too; and the fact is established that anoxia makes exceptional demands upon the adrenals, that the substance required is secreted by the cortex of these glands, that under the stimulus of intensified demand the glands grow to abnormal size and finally deteriorate, and that the extra secretions needed may be supplied by injections of adrenocortical extract.

But the prime remedy for anoxia is oxygen. Drugs and other indirect agencies can be regarded as only supplementary to oxygen supplied directly through a mouthpiece, mask, sealed cabin or other inclosure. For what the body needs above all else is oxygen, and particularly *the body's brain needs oxygen.* "The limiting factor in high-altitude flight is the oxygen requirement of the nerve cells in the cerebral cortex," says Dr. D. W. Bronk. "Without a certain supply of oxygen the cells can neither perform their functions nor maintain their resting state. For the cells of the brain this demand is especially great, due presumably to a highly unstable structure that is revealed by their sensitive response to environmental stimuli."

By recently developed electrical methods and experiments at the University of Pennsylvania Medical School, Dr. Bronk and his associates, Dr. Brink and Dr. Davis, were able to measure the utilization of oxygen in the brains of animals. They discovered that the oxygen tension, or pressure, around the nerve cells of the brain may be as low as one-tenth that in the arterial blood. Since the oxygen moves from places of high pressure to those of low, this gives an index to the avidity with which brain tissue takes up oxygen from the blood. Although venous blood, which has given up most of its oxygen and is streaming back toward the lungs for new supplies, has less than half the oxygen pressure of the richly laden arterial blood, it has four times as much as the brain cells. It is no wonder, therefore, that in anoxia mental faculties are affected—the judgment, the emotions, the acuity of sense organs, and ultimately consciousness itself.

Nor is it strange that the best medicine for anoxia is oxygen. Tissandier revived when his balloon descended to the lower, denser atmosphere. The pilot on the Dawn Patrol revived when his falling plane brought him to richer concentrations of oxygen. It has happened again and again that victims of anoxia recover as soon as they are supplied with enough oxygen to provide the blood stream with its normal cargo. A commercial plane carrying six company employees to Alaska climbed to 21,000 feet to get over bad weather. The co-pilot bethought him to see how the passengers were faring, and on stepping into the cabin found that all six had "gone to sleep." The plane was brought down to 12,000 feet, whereupon the passengers revived. None of them suffered any ill effects, but thereafter this pilot, who had been proud of the fact that he had a high ceiling, became a consistent advocate of the use of oxygen for himself and passengers even at low altitudes.

OXYGEN EQUIPMENT

Army and navy regulations require flyers to wear oxygen masks at 10,000 feet and above. For service in which a plane is likely to be called on suddenly for high climbs and maneuvers at various levels, it is important that masks be adjusted and oxygen be available from the ground up. Tests made in altitude chambers show that if undiluted oxygen is used, and the mask does not leak, a suitably conditioned person can ascend to 40,000 feet without serious anoxia symptoms. Above that altitude the pressure of the atmosphere is not sufficient to push even 100 per cent oxygen into the lungs fast enough to meet the body's requirements. Therefore, around 40,000 feet marks the upper limit for flight with the aid of an oxygen mask. A flyer breathing pure oxygen at that level is getting about as much into his lungs as he would get breathing the air at 10,000 feet. For sustained flight at higher altitudes it is necessary to have a sealed pressure cabin or a sealed pressure outfit, with its private atmosphere maintained at the optimum density. Such aids

enabled an airplane to be flown to 56,000 feet in 1938, a stratosphere balloon to 72,000 feet in 1935. But a sealed cabin is too
prodigal of weight and too vulnerable to the enemy's bullets to be
of general use in the aeronautics of war.

In combat planes, chief dependence continues to be placed on
oxygen masks. A recent development is the "demand mask," an
improved type with automatic valves which admit oxygen only
during the periods of inhalation, when the lungs demand it. An
airplane's oxygen supply is stored in steel tanks, and is piped to the
cockpit and various stations within the plane. When a flyer has
to move around in the plane, he disconnects from the supply line,
hooks a walk-around flask into his belt, and plugs the tubing of his
mask into it. The flask has enough oxygen to keep a man breathing
safely six to twelve minutes, the time depending on the altitude.
If he jumps from heights of two miles or more the aviator carries a
bail-out flask. In 1943 Lieut. Col. W. R. Lovelace, 2nd, of the
Aeromedical Laboratory at Wright Field, perfected a bail-out flask
of improved design which he tested on himself in a parachute jump
from 40,200 feet. It took him 23 minutes, 51 seconds to drop the
7.61 miles, and there was never an instant when he did not have
ample oxygen through his mask from the flask sewn into his clothing. It carries compressed oxygen to support twelve minutes of
breathing. This is ample for even the highest jumps, since it is
usual practice to fall freely for several seconds before opening the
'chute. And of course below 10,000 feet the oxygen flask is not
needed.

The ability to endure oxygen want varies considerably from
individual to individual. Some persons have so narrow a margin of
adjustment that they keel over at altitudes of one or two miles. A
brief session in the altitude chamber will usually identify this easy-
to-faint type. Even the aviator whose altitude tolerance is high
meets conditions which may operate to narrow his margin. Tests
with animals show that the rate of climb bears a relationship to the
critical threshold—the faster the plane ascends, the lower the
threshold at which symptoms become critical.

It is true, however, that adjustment may be cultivated. Persons
who go from near sea level to live on mountain heights usually
suffer from altitude sickness; some of them for weeks, some for

months, a few for years; but eventually most of them develop a tolerance. There have been instances of aviators resorting to this device to lift their tolerance. An American pilot went to a mountain settlement in Bolivia situated above 13,000 feet, and adjacent to an airfield. After an acclimatization period of two months, during which he exercised heavily almost every day and put himself in superb physical condition, the pilot went up in his plane to see how high and how long he could fly without resort to the oxygen mask. He flew habitually at altitudes from 20,000 to 22,000 feet, and on one occasion went to 24,000 feet and flew for 2 hours, all without any oxygen other than that of the upper air. His flight at 24,000 feet was made on instruments, which takes considerable mental co-ordination, and therefore made extra demands upon his brain. This pilot was 24 years old, an upstanding fellow of 6 feet 2 inches and 188 pounds, in the very prime of his flying career.

In 1937 a group of Germans interested in aviation medicine climbed the Nanga Parbat peak in the Himalayas and established a camp on the mountain side. They lived there for a number of weeks. One of the men died, but those who returned found that they had acquired a certain systemic adjustment. They were tested in an altitude chamber at weekly or monthly intervals, and the critical threshold of almost every member of the party showed a higher level than it had been before their mountain experience. Their altitude adaptation lasted several months. In 1939, a few weeks before the outbreak of war, the German scientists Ruff and Strughold published a *Compendium of Aviation Medicine* in which they briefly refer to the Nanga Parbat expedition as a demonstration of altitude adaptation, and add: "Special attention should be paid to the possibility of achieving adaptation to altitude by high flights and tests in the negative pressure chamber. It should certainly be possible to adapt people in that way."

BUBBLES OF NITROGEN

An aviator rising from the ground is like a deep-sea diver rising from the ocean bottom. If the diver has been working at a depth of 100 feet, his body has accustomed itself to a pressure of about 55 pounds to the square inch. This water pressure is approximately four times the pressure of the air at sea level. Therefore, in rising to the surface, the diver's body must readjust its functioning from an adaptation to the weight of the water to an adaptation to that of the air. Many years ago it was found that if he rose quickly, excruciating pains occurred. The victim would bend over and double up in screaming agony, and because of this the divers called their disease "the bends."

The atmospheric pressure at 34,000 feet is one-fourth that at sea level. An aviator rising to that height is subjected to a reduction of pressure corresponding to the relative change which a diver experiences in rising to the ocean surface from a depth of 100 feet. The fast-climbing aviator may suffer the same torturing pains that the diver knows. And they are caused by the same circumstance: the tendency of gas to come out of solution in the blood and tissues and form bubbles in the blood vessels and the joints.

The bubbling in the soda-water bottle after the cap is removed is a familiar demonstration of this effect, for almost any liquid will absorb gas under pressure and release it when the pressure is reduced. Robert Boyle, "the sceptical chymist" of Seventeenth-century England, was the first to report on this phenomenon. In 1662 he placed a vessel containing freshly drawn blood in a sealed glass chamber, pumped the chamber of its air, and saw bubbles forming on the surface of the blood. The bubbles were probably nitrogen. The nitrogen of the air is absorbed from the lungs in the act of breathing; it is taken in along with the atmospheric oxygen. But because it is chemically inert the nitrogen performs no function and is simply held in solution in the blood, the spinal fluid, and tissues. A deep-sea diver on the 100-foot bottom, breathing through his air hose, gets his air under a pressure of four atmospheres. The aviator, on the ground awaiting orders for a flight, is getting his air at the normal pressure of one atmosphere. But when these two men rise—the diver to the surface of the sea, the aviator to 34,000 feet—the pressure on their bodies and on every organ, blood vessel, cell and fluid is relaxed to one-fourth, and the dissolved nitrogen simply bubbles out just as it did in Boyle's decompression chamber. These bubbles may form obstructions or embolisms in the capillaries and other small vessels, and for this reason Dr. Armstrong and Dr. Heim called the condition aeroembolism. It is also known as decompression sickness. It is rarely manifest until the pressure is reduced by one-half or more, which means that it may make its appearance in a mild form at about 18,000 feet. With increasing altitude it becomes more pronounced, and claims more victims, especially if the plane climbs rapidly. In operations at great heights it may seriously cripple a crew, unless effective countermeasures are taken in advance of the flight.

Fortunately, there are countermeasures which have been thoroughly tested and proved, largely as a result of experiments carried out with animals and human beings in altitude chambers. One established method of conditioning requires the flyer to breathe an atmosphere of pure oxygen for a period prior to his taking off. In such an atmosphere the nitrogen gradually diffuses out of tissues and fluids, and is exhaled by the lungs. Consequently, when the aviator begins his flight, there is little left to provide bubbles. Tests have been made on men who were previously susceptible to decompression; when they had been preoxygenated in this way for five hours, no sign of the disease showed up, even at 40,000 feet. Lieut. Commander A. R. Behnke of the U. S. Naval Air Corps reports the case of a man studied in the altitude chamber who developed a severe case of bends between 25,000 and 28,000 feet when he had no preoxygenation. In a later test, he was given 45 minutes in pure oxygen prior to the "flight," and 30,000 feet was reached before bends began to show up. With 90 minutes of preoxygenation, his ceiling was raised to 34,000 feet; with three hours, to 37,000 feet; and after the full five hours in oxygen, he was able to go to 40,000 feet and stay there two hours with no distress or symptoms.

Another method of conditioning uses a mixture of gases. Instead of feeding the lungs 100 per cent oxygen in advance of flight, this system gives it an hour or more in an artificial atmosphere made of oxygen diluted with helium. Helium weighs less than a third as much as nitrogen; it is even more inert chemically; it is only a third as soluble in tissue fat. Calculation shows that if the body were saturated with helium to the same extent that it is normally saturated with nitrogen, only 90 minutes of preoxygenation would be required to accomplish full elimination of the dissolved helium.

Fundamental to all systems of conditioning, however, is the pre-selection of candidates for air service. No one knows just why, but some men are constitutionally more adjustable to this problem of bubbling nitrogen, just as some are better able to endure oxygen deficiency, than others. It has been found that a person previously injured in the knee, elbow, or other joint is likely to develop "bends" at these places. High tolerance goes with youth more often than with age, and tests in the altitude chamber indicate that at least 50 per cent of the men between 18 and 24 years can stand altitudes of around 35,000 feet for four hours at a stretch without developing symptoms.

BELOW-ZERO EFFECTS

Another complicating circumstance of high flight is the biting, numbing, depressing cold. At 20,000 feet the outside temperature is 25° below zero Fahrenheit, at 35,000 feet it is around 70° below; and if there is an opening in cockpit, cabin, or other compartment, the interior of the plane soon acquires a temperature not far from that of the exterior. In single-motored planes the pilot derives some heating from the engine directly in front of him. But the larger aircraft which carry the cockpit centered between the engines, and especially the long-range bombers which have gunners and bombardiers distributed among turrets, blisters, and other positions, present a more difficult problem. The cold gets in through the horizontal gun aperture, through the bomb-bay opening, and by metallic conduction. In these unheated sections the airman's efficiency may be "frozen" to a very small percentage of his normal ability.

Tests have shown that simply changing from a room at comfortable temperature to another at around 30° F. almost doubles the body's oxygen consumption. By putting on additional clothes this need for extra oxygen is cut down. Flight suits, however, are a nuisance; bulky and awkward, they impede the aviator's movements. The thickness of clothing that will give comfort at 15,000 feet is not sufficient to protect against several hours' exposure at 30,000 to 36,000 feet. Moreover, not only clothes but gloves and shoes must be designed in accordance with correct physiological principles; for it has been found that if hands and feet are slightly warmer than the rest of the body, excessive sweating occurs all over the body as a reflex cooling reaction.

Fingers are the parts most commonly subject to frostbite. In order to use his sextant, or some other instrument requiring manual manipulation, the flyer will take off his heavy flying gloves. A few seconds' exposure at 20 or more degrees below zero can cause suffering, and a few minutes' exposure leaves the man with an authentic frostbite. Since the flight surgeons began to prescribe thin, light, flexible gloves to be worn within thick outer ones, this problem has become of far less frequent occurrence than it used to be. A wing commander of the Royal Canadian Air Force reports that recruits from Australia, New Zealand, and the southern United States were prone to have frostbitten ears, hands, and feet, largely "because of a lack of respect for cold, sunny Canadian winter days." But this respect is usually gained with a few weeks' experience.

Electrically-heated suits, gloves and shoes have been developed and are in use in many of the air services. This type of equipment requires electric power to provide its heat, and therefore makes some drain on the plane's power system. Also, if the power supply fails or its wire connection is severed, the airman may freeze to death, for the fabric is relatively light and alone is no match for below-zero cold.

An even more serious menace is the risk of freezing the oxygen supply, a danger which arises from the fact that there is water vapor in the aviator's exhalations. The U. S. army and navy require that the oxygen mask and accessory supply valves used in their services must endure an hour's exposure to 40° below zero in the face of a 10-mile-per-hour wind at 37,500 feet altitude without freezing. These specifications are being met today, but as recently as 1941 every mask then commercially available was unable to withstand 10 minutes of such conditions without freezing solid.

THE PHYSIOLOGY OF ACCELERATION

Anoxia, decompression, and cold are all effects of altitude, but there is a fourth major problem of aviation medicine and it owes no indebtedness to the heights. It can develop anywhere: on the ground in landing, in the catapult of a ship at the moment of launching, or in the air. The engineers call it acceleration, by which they mean any change in the rate or direction of motion.

Speed itself is not an issue, except as it may affect acceleration. The Earth's inhabitants are already traveling faster than anyone can expect ever to move in an aircraft: 72,000 miles an hour is our rate of revolution round the Sun, and astronomers say there are even swifter revolutions of the stars and the Milky Way in which our solar system is swept along. The cosmic motion is so constant that we are never aware of it; the orbit we travel is so vast of radius that we feel no centrifugal effect.

But in an airplane turning sharply or pulling out of a power dive, centrifugal acceleration can become serious. If the plane is going 300 miles an hour and turning in a curve of 2,700 feet radius, the acceleration is 2.2 times gravity; whereas the same plane moving at the same speed, but in a curve with a radius of only 850 feet, generates an acceleration 7 times gravity. This means that if the pilot's gravity (i.e., his normal weight on the ground) is 180 pounds, centrifugal force will multiply it up to 396 pounds when his plane is turning the long curve, and to 1,260 pounds when the curve of shorter radius is taken. Most 180-pound bodies can endure the 2.2 times gravity acceleration without discomfort, but the 7 times gravity imposed by the sharper turn loads the body and its every organ, tissue, and cell with a massive strain. The blood becomes as heavy as molten iron. The heart can no longer pump against the tremendous one-way surge from the head, and the blood tends to accumulate in the abdominal vessels. At the same time the brain and other organs of the head are drained. As the retinal tissue of the eye loses its blood, vision becomes dim and gray, succeeded by a complete "blacking out" if circulation is not immediately restored. The brain deprived of its normal supply of oxygen-bringing blood becomes unable to function. Tests show that a young adult sitting in the upright position can usually endure 7 times gravity for 2 seconds; but if the acceleration continues 5 seconds, consciousness is failing; and in 7 seconds its collapse is complete.

This draining of blood toward the feet is the form in which the air warrior usually experiences centrifugal acceleration. It occurs whenever the plane is banking for a sharp turn; also in dive bombing at the instant when the pilot pulls out of the downward plunge to level off and climb; and in all other turning movements in which the pilot's feet travel along the outer edge of the plane's curving path. In turns in which the pilot's head is pointed outward, as in the outside loop, blood surges in the opposite direction, flooding brain and eyes. The effect is painful—some pilots report a "redding out" of vision—and the aftereffects of mental confusion, headache and tendency to stagger may last from five minutes to five hours. There are only occasional maneuvers which impose centrifugal acceleration in the foot-to-head direction, and because of its more serious consequences pilots are cautioned to avoid tactics which involve this effect.

The response of the human body to centrifugal acceleration is studied in the laboratory by means of centrifuges. German flight surgeons have published details of a centrifuge of 8¼ feet radius which was being used in research at the Air Ministry's Institute in Berlin prior to 1939. At 2.2 revolutions per second an acceleration corresponding to 47 times gravity was generated by this machine. In the United States Dr. Armstrong and Dr. Heim have pursued numerous studies with a centrifuge of 20 feet radius. These investigations, together with observations made on men during maneuvers in actual flight, demonstrate that the capacity to withstand the effects of centrifugal force varies from one person to another. It has been reported that the German authorities made early use of the centrifuge to determine which airmen had a high natural tolerance to centrifugal acceleration. In this way those who were "fit to dive-bomb" were selected and set apart for special indoctrination and training.

Dr. John F. Fulton of the Yale Medical School recently completed a review of the literature of aviation medicine as published in all languages, and reports that "the Germans began publishing papers on the effects of high acceleration in aircraft five years before the flight surgeons of the United Nations had given any general consideration to the problem—and everyone must realize what the dive bomber has meant to the Axis war effort."

After a pilot has been picked for dive-bombing service, there are various measures that can be taken to fortify his tolerance, or even to raise it. Oxygen supply is of the utmost importance, for a body suffering from mild anoxia can withstand less centrifugal acceleration than when it is normally oxygenated. The Germans place emphasis on "the full belly." It is reasoned that when the stomach is full the visceral blood vessels are already distended; therefore the surging of blood from the head toward the feet under centrifugal acceleration meets a barrier which somewhat neutralizes the effect. The

German flight surgeons' prescription of "beefsteaks for the Stuka pilots" is said to have heightened the popularity of this branch of the Luftwaffe. Another German claim holds that the administration of carbon dioxide, which has the effect of increasing the circulation in the brain, raises the level of tolerance to centrifugal acceleration. Pituitrin, adrenalin, and other drugs which enhance the muscular tone of the small blood vessels have been mentioned as beneficial, but details are not available. Pneumatic belts and pneumatic trousers, designed to constrict the abdomen, legs and feet, are discussed in the literature of aeromedicine, together with tight-fitting water suits.

The posture of the pilot is important. The effect of the seated position is to place head and feet at opposite poles of the direction of centrifugal acceleration. Some authorities advise a crouching position, with the legs drawn up against the abdomen. Tests have been made with automatic seats which change the pilot's angle of posture at the moment of leveling off from the power dive. The nearer his position approximates that of lying prone on the floor, the less disturbing is the effect of acceleration. In a prone position the force operates transversely, from back to chest, or from chest to back; and transverse accelerations up to 12 times gravity have been endured with no serious disturbance of vision, and up to 17 times gravity without producing unconsciousness. Gunners frequently operate from the prone position, but a pilot in that posture is unable to see or maneuver. With redesign of the arrangement of cockpit and controls this handicap may be overcome.

ACCELERATION OF CATAPULT, CRASH LANDING, AND PARACHUTE

There is also a linear kind of acceleration. It comes whenever motion in a straight line is either speeded up or slowed down. In launching from a ship's deck, the catapult suddenly increases the velocity of the plane from zero to 91 miles per hour over a distance of only 100 feet. This means an acceleration of 3½ times gravity, which is well within the limit that can be endured without serious discomfort. Linear acceleration resulting from a sudden decrease in velocity, such as occurs in landing, is a more frequent cause of injury. If a plane touches the ground while it is moving 65 miles an hour and comes to a stop within 35 feet, the linear acceleration is 9 times gravity. If a body is properly braced and cushioned it can stand the jolt without serious consequence. But if the same plane, at the same speed, comes to a stop within 12 feet, the linear acceleration mounts to 26 times gravity. This sudden stoppage of motion produces almost certain disaster, although there have been occasional remarkable escapes. A glider accident, in which it was possible to compute from the torn belt the degree of acceleration of the crash landing, generated a shock force of 26 times gravity; and yet the occupant walked out of the wreckage without the slightest injury. Accidental results such as this, and tests made in the laboratory, demonstrate that injuries from linear acceleration can be prevented or greatly reduced by proper design of seats and safety belts, by the use of crash helmets, by elimination of sharp and pointed structures from the interior of cockpit and cabin, and by proper placement of cushions.

As a paratrooper jumps, his body is moving with the velocity of the aircraft, which may be 200 or more miles per hour. If his parachute opens immediately, the effect is to put a brake on this speed, and the shock can be terrific. Chutes have been torn, human bodies have been seriously mauled, by the sudden jerk of the opening "umbrella." The rule is that the jumper wait three seconds before pulling the cord which releases the parachute. In three seconds air resistance will have slowed the falling body to its terminal velocity of not more than 135 miles per hour. Even then, as the 'chute opens, the retardation may be 5 or 6 times gravity, for the velocity of fall in the open 'chute is only about 12 or 14 miles per hour. When Lieut. Col. Lovelace made the jump from 40,200 feet in June, 1943, to test the service of the new bail-out oxygen flask as previously mentioned, the retarding effect of the opening parachute was so great that he experienced a temporary blackout from the force of the acceleration. It also stripped his right hand of two layers of gloves and his left hand of all three layers. As a result, the left hand suffered a painful frostbite.

THE PSYCHOLOGICAL TOLL

Beyond the physical shocks are the even more insidious mental strains of flight which impose their psychological toll. The continuous tension is tiring. Although the lure of flying and the daily excitement of it may crowd out conscious anxiety, the well-conditioned pilot is always aware of his responsibility. "It isn't necessarily fear, certainly not obvious fear," said Colonel L. E. Griffis, "but rather an appreciation of the fact that you're on the spot, and it's all up to you." There is the hazard of so many things that can get out of order, so many dials and gadgets and switches requiring attention, so many contingencies depending on the pilot's alertness, skill and nerve. A mechanical advance, such as the invention of the device to free wings of ice, not only improved the operation of aircraft but had a favorable psychological effect on pilots.

The airman who has been well selected through the screening and other tests, who has been thoroughly trained and soundly indoctrinated, becomes a superb unity of swiftly co-ordinating nerves and muscles. In flight he seems to act instinctively, by a sort of intuitive and infallible autonomy. And yet after prolonged strain the most competent pilot may go stale. He will return from a mission nervous, on edge, querulous, cursing the darkness of the landing field, wondering what ails him; perhaps complaining of a stiff back, a lame leg, a sudden rash, or some other psychosomatic condition. He is dog-tired and goes to bed, but his sleep is a panorama of anxious dreams, nightmares of flying disasters, blackouts, crackups, collisions, falling, falling. He wakes up worn and wan, his zest for flying gone, completely unfit for duty.

Flyer's fatigue is the psychiatrist's name for this neurosis. Physical fatigue may be part of the picture, but the breakdown has its origin in the prolonged suppression of normal fear reactions which arise in flight operations. A stable personality is able to master these reactions over a period of time, but in even the most hard-boiled and seemingly fearless flyers the ability to suppress the conflict between fear and courage, between danger and duty, eventually gives way under the unrelieved stress. Then acute anxiety reactions, hysteria, and other mental symptoms appear. Frequently some personal anxiety, such as the receipt of bad news from home, the collapse of a romance, or even the failure to get a long-expected letter, is the precipitating agency. These worries steal attention that ought to be concentrated on the instrument panel.

Early recognition and prevention are the preferred tactics for handling this neurosis. Rest camps, comfortable homelike quarters in pleasant surroundings, have been provided away from the active fronts; and standards have been developed to afford periods of relaxation after periods of active duty. In general, the pilots of fighter planes get a week to ten days' vacation after 95 to 100 hours of flight; those of bombers get the same after 130 to 150 hours. In some theaters of war it has not been possible to observe these standards to the letter. Certain of the 1942-'43 battle areas of the southwest Pacific, for example, were 1,000 miles from the nearest suitable rest camps, and the problem of transporting the fatigued flyers had its difficulties. Good food properly served, social intercourse, a variety of sports, absence of restrictions, freedom to do as they please—these appear to be the best medicine for flyer's fatigue. "By early and adequate treatment," said Major John M. Murray of the U. S. Army Air Surgeon's office, "most of these casualties are returned to full flying status, and practically all of the remainder salvaged for some important work."

Psychology, psychiatry, and associated studies occupy an important place in the curricula of the Army School of Aviation Medicine at Randolph Field, San Antonio, and the Navy School at Pensacola. Indeed, said an army surgeon, "we spend more time on psychoneurology in the School of Aviation Medicine than on any other subject." But the entire range of medical specialties associated with flying is covered in intensive courses; particularly problems of anoxia, decompression sickness, and those arising from acceleration, below-zero temperatures, night blindness, hearing, and the care of oneself in the event of forced landing in jungles, deserts, ice fields, the sea, and other remote and inhospitable refuges. The courses of training leading to the preparation of officers for service as flight surgeons are open only to graduates of approved medical schools. Recruits for this service are carefully picked for personality qualifications also, since the flight surgeon must live close to the men of his unit and must occupy the role of family physician to the group; and that calls for qualities not found in the typical specialist. In addition, the school at Randolph Field established in 1942 a course of training for aviation physiologists, the purpose of which is to supply men to take over the teaching and indoctrination of flying recruits at the various altitude chambers and other centers of instruction for personnel. The men admitted to this course are for the most part research biologists, picked from the staffs of various universities.

FLYING AMBULANCES AND THE FUTURE OF MEDICINE

Aviation medicine as a specialty is not concerned primarily with the sick. But the flight surgeons are of course charged with the medical care of pilots, flyers and other aviation personnel when they fall ill or are wounded. Also, the medical departments of the air services are responsible for the operation of the ambulance planes which bring out of the battle areas sick and injured men of all branches of the fighting forces. The swiftness with which casualties have been delivered to base hospitals far behind the lines, even to centers in the United States, undoubtedly has had an important influence in reducing the mortality rate. In the North Africa operations, for example, patients were transported by plane from Tunisia to the principal base hospital in two to four hours, whereas the same journey by land would require six days. In New Guinea, where motor roads over the Stanley Mountains simply do not exist, land transport over that formidable barrier is a matter of 19 days; but the boys who were suffering from malaria, dysentery, wounds and other disorders were flown out in a matter of hours. The big cargo planes that carry supplies to the combat zones are fitted with installations which readily convert them into flying ambulances for the return trip. One soldier who had a severe wound in his right lung was served by the plane's oxygen supply system all the way across the Atlantic from Africa, and reached a hospital in the homeland where there were surgical facilities adequate to the operation which he needed. Another casualty of Tunisia had a bullet enter one side, perforate bowels and bladder, and come out on the other side; he was moved in twenty minutes by plane to a field hospital where a resection could be made; and he recovered, thanks to the prompt and skillful surgery. But were it not for the flying ambulance, the surgery couldn't have served him.

This practice, born of war, is almost certainly going to effect post-war medicine. Central clinics with completely equipped surgical units and hospitals will be able to serve areas within a radius of hundreds of miles, brought within a few minutes' or hours' reach by ambulance planes.

In other ways, too, aeromedicine is making its impact on the future. Commonly the family physician or specialist examines a patient who he thinks is ill or is getting ill. The criterion of well-being is absence of disease. Preventive medicine doesn't wait for symptoms to appear; it seeks to find out weaknesses or danger spots in advance, and takes measures to avoid the stresses, exposures, or other risks which may precipitate illness. The criterion here is absence of disease-producing conditions. Aeromedicine goes a step farther. It seeks to determine in the healthy individual how much better he is constitutionally than the greatest demand which his occupation normally will require of him. It is as though health were to be appraised in terms of special demanding tests that measure the supreme effort of which the person is capable. This idea, and the techniques born of it, will almost inevitably modify the medical practice of the future.

CHAPTER XI

The War of Ideas

As he thinketh in his heart, so is he.

—Proverbs xxiii, 7

THIS business of total war is a vast psychological experiment. Physics, mathematics and chemistry may provide the weapons, biology may provide the medical and surgical services, but without the spiritual quality of morale an army would be little better than a jittery mob. Indeed, war can be described as a mass experiment in psychiatry, testing who is better able to endure the inner conflict of the soul.

For there is always a conflict, either hidden or open, between fear and courage. It is present, no matter how brave the soldier or how right his cause, or how powerful the guns with which he is armed. Napoleon thought that God is always on the side of the heaviest artillery, but we have abundant evidence that physical superiority alone does not automatically win wars. Britain's weapons were few in June of 1940 when Winston Churchill announced to the world: "We shall defend our island whatever the cost may be; we shall fight on beaches, landing grounds, in fields, in streets, and on the hills; we shall never surrender; and even if, which I do not for the moment believe, this island or a part of it were subjugated and starving, then our empire beyond the sea, armed and guarded by the British fleet, will carry on the struggle until in God's good time the New World, with all its power and might, sets forth to the liberation and rescue of the Old."

This was magnificent, but was it war?

Yes, the battle for public opinion was the only war that Britain was able to wage at the time. As events have shown, this objective facing of the facts, this attitude of integrity supported by a fighting spirit which did not belittle the odds and yet completely defied what seemed at that time certain fate at the hands of a malign and triumphant foe, was the perfect strategy of psychological warfare. It consolidated Britain's opinion in a nationwide will to resist; it focused the opinion of neutral countries on the idea of the British island as the last outpost against the European aggressor; and it implied the identity of interest of beleaguered Britain, the empire beyond the seas, and the United States in the liberation and rescue of captive Europe.

A few weeks later Hitler countered with mockery. "The people of England are very curious and ask, 'Why in the world don't you come?'" he jeered in a Sportpalatz speech which was beamed to all nations. "We are coming," he shrieked. "When we are ready, we will come. All of England's allies will not help her then— neither Haile Selassie, nor King Zog, nor King Haakon, nor even Queen Wilhelmina. . . . In the east we stand on the river Bug, in the north we stand at North Cape and Narvik, in the south on the Spanish frontier."

Despite its coarse note of ridicule, this blast was part of that technique which Mr. Edmond Taylor has described as "the strategy of terror." The dictator was reminding Britain of what had happened to Ethiopia, Albania, Norway and the Netherlands, and of the fact that he now possessed a continent. Under the terror technique this ought to soften public opinion, undermine resistance, suggest the advisability of being "reasonable" and "avoiding needless shedding of blood." Contrarily, however, mention of the refugee monarchs could conjure up memories of Axis perfidy, faithlessness, mania for domination, brutalities practiced on helpless minorities, and thereby stiffen the will to resist. Thus the strategy of terror can backfire and actually strengthen the morale of the intended victim.

One may argue that Britain's survival is a stroke of luck, that Hitler could have occupied Britain in June of 1940 if he had made the attempt. He had the heavier artillery, more aircraft, more munitions of every kind, more soldiers. Various speculations have been published as to why he did not push on in those critical days of Allied military collapse and emulate William the Conqueror. But all surmises are guesses, and perhaps Hitler himself cannot honestly say what was the precise combination of circumstances that delayed the attack. Whatever the explanation, Britain fought back over the radio waves in the voice of her Prime Minister, in the voices of writers such as Priestley and Walpole, of army and navy experts, and of lesser personalities. Somehow the dominating idea got across. Somehow it was dinned into the consciousness of the listening world that Britain had not gone down, that Britain was not going down without fighting, that invasion would be resisted to the last doorstep.

In July, after the armistice with the Vichy regime had been signed, Hitler addressed his Reichstag in a speech offering the British government a negotiated peace. "I consider myself in a position to make this appeal," he said, "since I am not the vanquished, begging favors, but the victor speaking in the name of reason. I can see no reason why this war must go on. I am grieved to think of the sacrifices it will claim."

American correspondents and other neutrals then in Berlin have told of the astonishment which burst from German officials a few hours later when they heard a BBC broadcast rejecting "the Fuehrer's outstretched hand." They had supposed his peace offer would be seriously considered by the British Cabinet, by the House of Commons, or at least by some responsible minister or government official; but here was a routine broadcast saying it was unthinkable to negotiate a peace with Germany.

"I remember the incident very well," said a former executive of the British Broadcasting Corporation now in the United States, "for I was the one who wrote that broadcast. There was no necessity of consulting any Cabinet member, or of waiting for the Prime Minister to make an official statement. In those weeks and months after Dunkirk we had just one message, 'We are not beaten, and will

never negotiate'—everybody knew it, and everybody was authorized to say it and to keep on saying it."

IDEAS AS WEAPONS

The use of ideas to supplement or substitute for physical weapons
is as old as the tribal battle cry or the African tom-tom. In every
war the proponent tries by argument, suggestion, emotional appeal;
by the withholding of some information, the overemphasis of other
information; and by other tactics ranging down to organized deceit
and outright lying, to implant ideas which will be beneficial to his
cause and injurious to the enemy cause. He directs this effort (1)
at the enemy, to break down his resistance, (2) at the home front,
to strengthen support for the war effort, (3) at neutrals to win
their sympathy and if possible their alliance, (4) at the occupied
countries to sustain and direct their resistance, and (5) at his own
armed forces and allies to fortify and enlarge their morale. Whatever the methods used, whatever the fundamental policy adopted
and the various tactics employed to put it into operation, all such
activities are elements of the psychological technique known as
propaganda.

Whether Woodrow Wilson's words won the first world war may
be open to question, but there is no doubt that they and the other
words with which the Allied propaganda services bombarded the
Germans considerably shortened that war. German military prospects were favorable at the beginning of 1918, and well-informed
authorities on the Allied side then estimated that it would be
August, 1919, before the addition of American military might would
be sufficient to crush the Hindenburg armies.

The United States Army Intelligence Service had a Psychological
Subsection which kept a close watch on the morale of the German
troops and the German civilian population. By interviewing prisoners, intercepting and analyzing German military communications,
propaganda, newspapers and other publications, and through secret
agents behind the enemy line, these psychological warriors of
1917-'18 kept themselves informed of the temper of German opinion.

They even prepared a chart on which they plotted the ups and
downs of German civilian attitudes, taking the state of morale in
August, 1914, as 100 per cent. This chart showed that in February

and March of 1918 the enemy's morale stood above 90 per cent, following recent successes in the German military position. But toward the end of March, morale began to deteriorate, despite further gains of the army. By mid-June, although the German military situation stood at 90 per cent, the state of German civilian morale was below 80 per cent; and thereafter it crumbled at a rapid rate, accelerated by the mounting food shortage and the series of German military reverses which began in July. By October the morale curve stood at 39 per cent, the military curve at 20 per cent, and it was obvious that Germany was beaten. Shortly before the armistice the *London Times* estimated that "good propaganda saved a year of war, and this meant the saving of thousands of millions of money and probably at least a million lives."

What were the ideas which the Allies' propaganda sowed among the German troops and people? First, it told them facts of the Allied resources; manpower, industrial power, the coming of the Americans, the Allied war aims, the statistics of destroyed U-boats and other German losses. Daily newspapers in the form of one-page leaflets were prepared and dropped by airplane or balloon behind the German line. After a battle, tabulations telling the number of dead and wounded on each side were published, and their accuracy won eager and astounded readers among the Kaiser's soldiers. "The number lost in one of our regiments as given in the leaflets exactly tallied with the actual loss, and thereafter the entire contents of the leaflets were believed and one was stunned by the greatness of our losses," reported a German veteran after the war.

From flooding him with information which his government had withheld, the Allied propaganda moved on to destroy the German's hope of victory. There was a carefully wrought campaign of despair through leaflets picturing the frightfulness of war, the toll of death at the front, the toll of hunger and cold and other privations back home, with a query "Does it pay?" to headline the futility of the struggle. Another propaganda tactic was the appeal to hope, picturing the way of escape from the horrors of the war: personal escape for the soldier by desertion and surrender to a generous and humane foe, national escape for his people by accepting President Wilson's Fourteen Points, casting out the warmakers and setting up a democratic government with which other war-weary nations could join in a league of peace. This revolutionary appeal was also triggered to the prejudices of various elements of the German empire: *e.g.*, to detach Austria-Hungary and promote the disintegration of that polyglot state, to separate Alsace-Lorraine from the arrogant overlords who treated its inhabitants as "second-class citizens," to alienate Catholic Bavaria from Protestant Prussia, to inflame the proletariat and middle classes against the Junkers, and to incite everybody against the Hohenzollerns.

It is not unreasonable to believe that German military defeat would have resulted in a political revolution anyhow, even if there had been no skillful effort at organized propaganda. But the fact that the propaganda did get under the German skins, the fact that German military and naval officers found their men reading the Allied leaflets and later repeating the Allied arguments and phrases, the fact that a decay of civilian morale could be traced to the influence of the French, British and American propagandists—all made a profound impression on the German irreconcilables.

In particular, it impressed Corporal Adolf Hitler. When he sat down in the prison at Landsberg in 1924 to compose *Mein Kampf* he gave propaganda a primary place in the revolutionary program which he there outlined. Of Allied propaganda he said: "To what terrific consequences a rightly directed propaganda may lead could be observed for the first time during the war, though unfortunately it had to be studied on the other side. What we failed to do, the enemy did with unheard-of skill and a calculation that seems truly the work of genius. The war propaganda of the English and Americans was psychologically correct. In the beginning it sounded crazy and impudent; later it was no more than unpleasant; and finally it was believed. After four and one-half years a revolution broke out in Germany, whose slogans came from the enemy's war propaganda."

THE RAPE OF THE MASSES

Hitler's rise to power was forwarded by many different human forces, including thuggery and crime, the patronage of scared industrialists and other political reactionaries, the acquiescence of moral and religious groups that were later to feel the bite of his treachery, and the prestige of the aging and bewildered Hindenburg. But in the forefront of the revolutionary forces was the campaign of propaganda which played upon mob instinct in every conceivable way to accomplish what Serge Chakotin has called "the rape of the masses." Recognizing propaganda as the strongest weapon in his conquest of the state, the Nazi dictator saw it as equally indispensable in consolidating his control of the German people and retaining power. And so, on March 13, 1933, exactly two weeks after the audacious propaganda act of the Reichstag fire, Hitler as chancellor submitted a decree for the signature of Hindenburg as president. The old gentleman signed, and thereby created a new Cabinet office which was not provided in the constitution of the German republic. This creation was the Ministry of Public Enlightenment and Propaganda, and the decree named Paul Joseph Göbbels as minister.

Göbbels, who had been state propaganda leader for the National Socialist Party since 1929, and before that as editor of the Berlin party newspaper *Angriff* (Attack) its most ingenious, unscrupulous and successful publicist, had been a follower of Hitler since 1925. Nobody understood the dictator's mind more intimately than this gnomish, dark-haired, very non-"Aryan"-looking little man with the piercing black eyes and the big mouth and the talent for invective. "Hatred?" he once said, "that's my trade. It takes you a long way further than any other emotion." Like Hitler, he is a disappointed "artist." In youth he aspired to be a writer, but the Berlin theater managers rejected his two plays, the Berlin publishers found his novel unacceptable, and the *Tageblatt* declined to employ him as reporter. "When I think of the humiliation of my youth," reflected the Minister of Public Enlightenment and Propaganda, "I see no reason to shrink from applying any treatment to our adversaries."

The new ministry was housed in the former Leopold Palace in Berlin, and the conceited little "Doktor" (he had won a Ph.D. at Heidelberg in 1921, at the age of 24) was proud of the palatial premises. At his first meeting with the newspaper men, he assured them that the press would remain free, but "Do not imagine that we shall allow you to swindle the people out of our hands. We know only too well how this can be done." A few weeks later the new minister amplified this idea in a public address. "We are not satisfied with having 52 per cent of the nation, and terrorizing the other 48 per cent. We want the people as the people, not only passively but actively," he went on, "for if we have only a part, be it the majority of the nation, we shall be unable to realize the great tasks ahead of us in a larger frame."

In accordance with this totalitarian program, the new minister was given virtually unlimited authority over a wide range of agencies. This included supervisory powers over press and radio, the censorship of plays, books, motion pictures, paintings, sculpture, and other works of art; the administration of the state fairs and other industrial exhibitions, of agencies advertising the German railways and air lines, and the control of all German publicity in foreign lands. Some of these assignments encroached on functions already being exercised by the Ministry of Foreign Affairs, the Ministry of the Interior, the Ministry of Economics, and the Reich Post Office, and there were protests, clashes, struggles; but in the end propaganda usually won over the other ministries.

During the "peaceful" era 1933-'37, Dr. Göbbels was allotted $100,000,000 annually. "You wouldn't have to fight at all if I had my way," he said to Air Minister Göring, "I could win any number of wars for you with no losses but the suicides on the other side." Perhaps he proved this boast in the war against Austria, with victory without fighting; and in the war of nerves against Czechoslovakia, again with victory without fighting; but the story since then has been different and the appropriation for the Propaganda Ministry has had to be enlarged. No figures have been released by Germany, but estimates of Dr. Göbbels's annual wartime budget range all the way from $220,000,000 to $500,000,000. By contrast, the British Ministry of Information spent £8,600,000 in the fiscal year 1942, and the United States Office of War Information $37,-000,000.

THE MACHINERY OF PROPAGANDA

Woodrow Wilson's words were winged in the sense of their appeal to the hearts of a war-weary humanity, but they traveled on the leaden feet of print. This is not to slight the importance of the printed word, for in terms of volume even greater use is being made of leaflets in the present war than was the case in 1914-'18. There is rarely an Allied bombing expedition in Europe that is not accompanied by some planes which carry psychological bombshells, *i.e.*, leaflets, folders, pamphlets, news sheets, picture sheets, and other printed material. They are packaged in bundles. The cords that bind the bundle are of a material which under action of the air breaks when the bundle is fairly near the ground, and thus the package spills its contents over an area. There is plenty of evidence that these leaflets are read, and have had important effects, especially in occupied areas and satellite countries.

It is true also that there are various technological developments in the printing arts which have enhanced their mass appeal. Improved photography and improved methods of photo-engraving are reflected in the growth of tabloid newspapers and pictorial magazines. Such journals as the *New York Daily News* and *Life* have their counterparts in many countries, and they have built up circulations reaching into the millions without taking readers away from the older, more conventional publications. Impressed by the successful mass appeal of these new journalistic developments, some of the warring governments have issued picture papers as part of their propaganda.

But in the vastly quickened tempo of mechanized war, the war of ideas too has had to streamline its communications and speed up its pace. Its two most potent weapons are radio and moving pictures; to which the totalitarians have added a third—the organization in foreign countries of "Sudeten" minorities, Fifth Columns, and other groups of "racial brothers" to serve as human sounding boards, protagonists, and borers from within.

Radio is peculiarly powerful because it can cross frontiers and penetrate behind the enemy's lines. It provides the propagandist with a "psychological parachute." Moreover, radio communication is instantaneous; it can reach great multitudes; and above all, it carries the human voice. There are inflections in the spoken word; techniques of emphasis, of spontaneity, of pathos, of humor, of invective, of righteous indignation; tricks of emotional appeal which are beyond the artifices of the journalist or literateur. "Revolutionary movements are not the work of great writers, but of great orators," said Göbbels. And with Nazi logic his lieutenant, Hadamovsky, tells the Nazi reason: "The ordinary person, and the masses still more, will almost infallibly succumb to the power of the spoken word, no matter whether it is true or not."

Radio broadcasting was first used for war propaganda in 1931.

The Japanese military, during their invasion of Manchuria, kept the populace back home in a state of jubilant excitement with daily accounts of the successive victories. People in Tokio listened in open-mouthed amazement to the roar of battle as it was picked up by microphones at the front. After the conquest, the little men set to work to consolidate their gains with the help of radio. Cheap receiving sets were distributed among the Manchurians so that they could listen to the powerful station which the Japanese government immediately set up at Hsinking, and propaganda programs were broadcast in both the Japanese and native languages. But when it was found that many of those who had thus been favored were listening to the Nanking station, the "New Order" immediately began to jam the Chinese broadcasts, thereby mangling their own.

Jamming the wave lengths of rival stations and forbidding citizens and subjects to listen to "enemy lies" are fairly standard totalitarian policy. These practices are followed not only because the radio brings to the listener enemy lies, but above all because it brings the enemy voice. The hated foe also can talk the language of the people, and by talking as "folks" to "folks" can deflate the image of the "enemy beast" which propaganda has built up. Thus radio tends to break down attempts to organize simple stereotypes against the enemy. We depend on the voice more than on handwriting or print to evaluate character, and radio opens a door for this universal tendency to cross national frontiers. It is a continuing guarantee of the common humanity of the enemy. Of course, if the broadcaster is rabid of speech, vocally incoherent, intemperate and violent of utterance, if he behaves like a raving beast, that is his character, and that is the impression which the microphone transmits. But if he is human, something of the humanness of the enemy is what the listener gets; and this is why radio opens such dangerous pitfalls to dogmas of racial superiority.

The motion picture, as a propaganda weapon, is even more moving than radio, though its audience is more limited and its range more restricted. It cannot "parachute" behind the enemy's line as radio can, but it has been used with powerful effect in the homeland, among the armed forces, and among allies and neutrals. The movie, combining as it does both the appeal to the eye and the appeal to the ear, is almost a substitute for a visit. "Mrs. Miniver," for example, despite its Hollywood flavor, was an influence in upbuilding and strengthening American support of the British cause. The propaganda film "In Which We Serve" was far more poignant in its effect, and there are other documentary films which reflect the maturity of technique that has come from the early pioneering of the British Post Office in film production.

On the other side of the battlefront, Göbbels has made persistent use of movies to "enlighten" his fellow citizens, to terrorize and soften the governments and peoples of neutral lands, and to "educate" those of the occupied and satellite countries. In 1941, for example, soon after the stories of large-scale "mercy killings" in German institutions for the aged and feeble-minded began to leak out, a film "I Accuse" was produced and exhibited widely throughout Germany. It pictured the plight of a conscientious scientist whose young wife fell victim to an incurable disease, a somber fate for her which the husband finally relieved through merciful death by giving her an overdose of a beneficent drug. "There arises also the problem of the inmate of a hospital or asylum in whom illness seems to have destroyed the normal human faculties," said the *Frankfurter Zeitung*, drawing the plausible conclusion which all who saw it were intended to draw from this heart-tearing conflict between old ideas and new.

But it is in the newsreels that the Nazis have shown perhaps their greatest inventiveness in the use of cinematic devices for psychological warfare. This is particularly true of connected sequences portraying the triumph of German arms, such as "The Polish Campaign," "Victory in the West," and "The Struggle in the East." It is said that "Victory in the West," which "reports" the blitz through the Low Countries and the conquest of France, was made from 1,000,000 feet of film material. Out of that vast footage, taken by camera men at the front, behind the lines, and in various parts of the conquered area, a carefully selected 9,000 feet were cut and pasted together to produce the effects which Göbbels and his associates sought to produce in a one and one-half-hour film. Not only that, but additional cutting and piecing were done to suit the film to different audiences. Thus, as exhibited in theaters in Scandinavian countries, there were shots of French prisoners, showing a strange assortment of pinch-faced weaklings, mostly undersized brunettes, Negroes, and other alien types. Other scenes played up the "immorality" of the French by showing pictures of nude women found on the walls of forts in the Maginot Line. As prepared for distribution to South America, and doubtless for other Latin places, there were shots showing Hitler with his generals going into a Catholic church and standing in a spirit of great reverence; while other flashes portrayed the resistless sweep of the marching columns, rolling tanks, and roaring Stukas.

One episode, which was skillfully stage-managed to throw an aura of mysticism about the person of the Fuehrer, showed him at the Strasbourg Cathedral in reconquered Alsace. The camera was manipulated to produce shots which associated Hitler with parts of the ancient monument. In one, his head appears against the uprising spire of the cathedral; in another, taken in the shadowed nave, the jeweled rose-window provides the background for the Leader's face. The whole effect is to confer on the man something of the majesty and calm of the sacred building. And while this view of the "Deliverer of Alsace-Lorraine" appears on the screen, the sound track carries voices singing the old German folk song, "O Strasbourg, O Strasbourg, you wonderful town." Religion, patriotism, hero worship, antiquity, Gothic art—it would be difficult to concoct a more powerful combination of emotional appeals.

RACIAL BROTHERS

One thinks of the organization of propaganda service as lines of communication, by print, picture, radio, and other mechanisms, reaching out from a central originating body, such as that of Dr. Göbbels's outfit in Berlin or Mr. Brendon Bracken's in London or Mr. Elmer Davis's in Washington. Such bureaus naturally have their official branches and representatives in other lands, but in addition the totalitarians have exploited the idea of using groups of "racial brothers" which "spontaneously" develop in foreign countries to propagate the faith of the fatherland. Perhaps the most notorious example of this type of organization is the German American Bund, but the same device has been used in almost every country under other names.

The idea of promoting cultural cliques in other nations did not originate with the Nazis. German-American, Italian-American, and other hyphenated societies operated before the first world war. Although it could hardly be said that these organizations sped the Americanization of their members, their purposes were rarely totalitarian or seditious. But with the rise of Communism in Russia, Fascism in Italy, Naziism in Germany, and Falangism in Spain, cells or branches of the parent party organizations were formed in foreign regions. And when the war clouds began to gather in Europe in the 1930's, there was a network of these cells in almost every land. They provided foci of listeners for the short-wave broadcasts which were beamed to all countries, little foci which soon grew into large ones as the propaganda was spread by word of mouth and as additional listeners were won.

The tricks by which these groups operated to advertise their cause, terrorize opponents, intimidate newspaper and other criticism, and to bore into patriotic groups, relief societies, and other naive organizations, have been fully exploited and are well known. The groups were particularly serviceable in spreading rumors, and often they received their instructions as to which rumors to spread or were tipped off as to the timing by short-wave radio. It is doubtful, for example, if the German radio had any positive influence on public opinion in the United States in 1942, but its messages served to keep the unjailed Nazis and their sympathizers posted on the current propaganda line.

In 1914-'18 there were attempts to use German-American societies for propaganda for the German cause, but they were bungling and inexpert, as was much of the Kaiser's propaganda service. The German ambassador Bernstorff was in perpetual hot water, almost from the very beginning of the war. Perhaps the innate American leaning toward the Anglo-French cause was largely responsible, but certainly the inept German publicity added to the temperature. Later the ambassador wrote of the German wartime press service that it "never succeeded in adapting itself to American requirements," and "the same may be said of most of the German propaganda which reached America in fairly large quantities since the third month of the war, partly in German and partly in not always irreproachable English. This, like the press telegrams, showed a complete lack of understanding of American national psychology."

One may question if the Göbbels publicity pattern has not also shown a lack of understanding of American psychology. The Nazi broadcasts have never enjoyed respect in the United States, much less sympathy, beyond the few German partisans. Perhaps one reason for this failure has been the delusion of quick victory. After the easy takings in Austria and Czechoslovakia and the sudden crushing conquests of Poland, Norway, the Low Countries, and France, all of which were powerfully aided by propaganda, early termination of the war seemed assured. It didn't matter much what the United States thought or how it felt—and so, instead of carefully working out a distinctive line for America, the same symbolic appeals which had softened Europe were fed over the short waves. Possibly the only really effective Nazi propaganda in the United States has been its whispering campaign. There was an ingenious technique of spreading rumors designed to divide and divert and diminish American chances of getting into the war. Nazi rumor-mongers have been equally effective in promoting anti-Semitism, and their anti-Communist line has fanned the old suspicions of Russian integrity. Many Americans have repeated poisonous rumors which were planted by the "racial brothers" under instructions from the Wilhelmstrasse.

Göbbels has an advantage that was not possessed by his German predecessors in World War I. He is of the inner circle of the government, among the policy-making group, hand in glove with the chief of state; and that kind of relationship is highly important to the successful management of propaganda. Of course, it is inherent in the totalitarian form of government, but the same principle of intimacy between policy making and propaganda making applies to the successful management of public relations by a democratic government, a commercial corporation, or any other interest which seeks popular support.

Knowing the policy of the government, the military strategy and the changes made from day to day, it is a matter of simple common sense to shape the propaganda to the strategy. The war of ideas must be co-ordinated with the war of weapons. The ideas may be camouflaged, as the physical weapons often are. They too may be manipulated for surprise effects. There are psychological equivalents of booby-traps, time bombs, and other physical devices. The Nazi doctrine of "the new order," "the wave of the future," the necessity of having a strong Germany as the economic core of a prosperous Europe, all these ideas which were weapons of the psychological blitz of the 1930's, became of possible strategic value as political time bombs after the tide of war turned in 1942-'43. Although it was apparent by the latter year that the Axis could not win the war, by means of these ideas the totalitarians might be able to salvage something, perhaps a negotiated peace, perhaps a better place in the postwar world than unconditional surrender would seem to imply. And think of the potential high explosive planted in the plastic minds and hearts of the next generation by the Nazi youth movement. These tactics of education have been pushed in the occupied countries as well as in the homelands.

German propaganda has been variously described, and almost eulogized by some who seem to see in it, however devilish and nihilistic, a marvelous application of the subtleties of psychological science. But its strategy is only an expression of the tyrant's age-old technique. The totalitarians have simply streamlined and adapted to the radio, motion picture, and other modern vehicles of communication the concepts, rituals, and other schemes for seducing the mind which are universally characteristic of dictatorship. The whole bag of tricks may be described as "the strategy of despotism," borrowing the phrase of Dr. Harold D. Lasswell of the Library of Congress. For several years Dr. Lasswell has been making a study of the wartime propaganda of the various nations, and the discussion which follows is a reflection of his analysis and conclusions.

THE STRATEGY OF DESPOTISM

The psychological secret of Hitler's success in capturing Germany, with ambitions of "tomorrow the world," lies in the use of two primitive appeals: first, the appeal to self-interest; second, the appeal to mysticism. Each of these is an emotional lever of great power which has had centuries and even millenniums of testing, and nearly all the propaganda techniques of the dictators can be explained, says Dr. Lasswell, in terms of these two psychological forces.

The appeal to ruthless calculation of self-interest is demonstrated, for example, in the Quisling tactics. A trade is made: you give obedience to the leader, and he will give you dominion over an area. To a publisher or steel magnate the offer takes the form: you join us, and we will make you head of the country's publishing industry or of its steel industry. And this sort of trading goes all down the line, from gauleiter to deputy to party member. Even the janitor, as party member, may be charged with authority to keep watch and report on the tenants of his apartment house. The appeal is made on the national scale also: join the Nazi party, and we will wipe out the humiliation of the Versailles Treaty; we will make Germany great and win living space for Germans; we will annihilate her enemies, particularly the racial parasites whose greed betrayed us in 1918. Always there is the scapegoat, the underling, the inferior whom the lowliest Nazi can lord it over. There is thus a complete hierarchy in which the individual submits to those above him and dominates those below him.

The appeal to mysticism is exerted through Nazi symbolism, the great mass meetings, the marchings and heilings, the frenzied oratory with its slogans and catch-phrases, salutes, endless displays of the swastika, and other repetitions which merge the individual with the mass and give him the sense of spiritual identification with a great cause. Here you have the creation of a situation in which "little man, what now?" can participate in the emotional experience of belonging to something bigger than his frustrated existence. This mystical appeal combines with the appeal of self-interest to give the individual a sense of importance. He has at the same time the satisfaction of dominating those below him and of participating with his fellows in a ritual that is both consecration and release.

There is need for release, because in a dictatorship the people are continually humiliated by regimentation. The peremptory orders offend their dignity from childhood up, and their tendency is to defend the integrity of their personality. The natural target for their accumulating aggressions is the man at the top. The leader's natural tendency is to divert these aggressions downward and outward, away from himself. Ritual is one of the devices by which this is accomplished. When a man is riled, particularly if he is powerless to change the conditions which impose the frustration, have you noticed how he falls into a manner of repetition? He will repeat his complaint, often harping on some word or phrase as a slogan. He will go through the same motions, pace the floor, sit down and get up repeatedly, or perform some other act over and over again. This resort to stereotype is one way that the frustrated person deals with his own hostile intentions—and it is also a way the dictator deals with the hostile intentions of his followers. He provides marching, drilling, the repetitive ritual of the mass meeting, the outstretched arm, the recurring Heil Hitler. Through these stereotypes the frustrated one turns his aggressions inward and attains a measure of compensation within himself.

But his hostile intentions, which subconsciously are directed toward the leader, must also find some outside expression. The Nazi attains that outside expression by being ruthless with subordinates, lording it over inferiors, airing his racial animosities, burning books, and smashing synagogues. On the national scale, these suppressed aggressions find release in the various methods of intimidating neighboring countries, the tactics of threatening, terrorizing, asserting "our unshakable will," "our unalterable purpose," "our irrevocable hour of decision," and other saber-rattling words with which tyrant nations bulldoze, encroach upon, and possess their neighbors.

There are, of course, many different tactics from which the propagandist selects the psychological weapon to be used in any particular problem of public relations. But Dr. Lasswell's analysis of Axis propaganda material finds that all these techniques are grounded in the fundamental strategy of regimentation with its combination of the two appeals—to hard-boiled self-interest, and to stereotyped mysticism.

TECHNIQUES TO PARALYZE REASON

Dr. Ernst Kris has pointed out that the dictators rarely if ever broadcast from a studio. They do not usually talk into a microphone from the quiet of their homes or offices, as Churchill and Roosevelt do. Hitler and Mussolini invariably direct their remarks to a crowd, a mass of wildly cheering listeners, and the radio simply picks up and passes on what is spoken by the magnetic leader to his adoring and subservient followers. This observation fits in with the old theory of crowd behavior responding to the dominating personality of the orator as the subject responds to the dominating personality of the hypnotist.

Dr. Hans Herma, discussing this and other aspects of Nazi propaganda practices at a recent seminar in New York, suggested that the orator-crowd situation provides a means of paralyzing rational thinking. Of course, that is what hypnotism does; by its process of suggestion it causes its subject to accept anything that is told him by the hypnotist, no matter how ridiculous it may be. But Dr. Herma finds that this conspiracy against the reason, to paralyze rational thinking, applies to other Nazi propaganda situations in addition to that provided by leader-to-crowd oratory. For example, at a certain stage of the war the Nazis found it necessary to convince the German people that German morale was not impaired. This is the way they went about it:

"Reports were spread by the Nazis, in neutral countries, that Germany was on the verge of a revolt. One of the instances reported was the occupation of strategic spots of Berlin, such as the Wilhelmplatz, by Elite Guards, ready to meet any revolutionary uprising on the spot. These reports were quoted by press and radio of the democratic countries. The German people received the story as a report from Schenectady. The (German) radio star Hans Fritzsche (then) invited the people of Berlin to go and see whether there were Elite Guards on the Wilhelmplatz. He could confidently rely on the good judgment of the eyewitnesses and ridicule the democratic lies."

An ingenious transformation of ideas was thus accomplished. The original question, Is German morale impaired? had been shifted to a test of whether or not the enemy lies. Thereby attention was switched from the observation of German behavior to an observation of enemy behavior. Finally, the complex problem of the quality of home morale has been replaced by a "Go and see" which is so simple a proposition that it can be answered by "yes" or "no."

What would be the likely reaction of a German listening to this broadcast and following its injunction to go and see? "If he is a Nazi," said Dr. Herma, "he will feel relieved: 'Everything is going all right, nothing to worry about.' If he is an anti-Nazi he will be disappointed: 'Still no indication of growing unrest.' Each would react differently, but both would react *emotionally*. In both, the reaction corresponds to a conviction: 'Everything is quiet.' To create this conviction was the intention of the propagandist. The rational subject's capacity of analyzing the facts is outwitted, it plays no part in the situation, and a comprehension of the real situation is successfully forestalled by the propagandist. . . . Given the frame of reference created by the news manipulation, the man crossing the Wilhelmplatz is hardly aware that, in fact, he answers with 'no' the question, 'Is it true that morale in Germany is impaired?' when he vaguely takes notice of the absence of the Elite Guards."

This is but one of the innumerable trickeries by which propaganda is used to throw the reasoning faculty out of gear. Here it was applied in a "constructive" way to befuddle and thereby manage the thinking of the home front. In other procedures the principle of transfer is used to bewilder, confuse, unnerve, and so destroy the enemy front.

THE STRATEGY OF CLARIFICATION

The antithesis of this strategy of befuddlement is the strategy of clarification, which is or should be the working principle of democratic propaganda. In the democratic state, where the people have a voice in government, they must be informed to insure intelligent participation. The despot's technique is one of imposition, of regimentation, accomplished through the appeals to self-interest and to mysticism. The democracy's technique is one of participation, of collaboration, accomplished through the device of a system of balances. The people in office are balanced by the people out of office. Statements by the administration are subject to challenge by the loyal opposition, or by any individual, for that matter. Assertiveness is allowed to express itself in the democratic system, whereas in a despotism the chronic frustration imposed upon the citizenry by the perpetual regimentation turns normal assertiveness into aggression, with results as already outlined. A propaganda of clarification would wreck a totalitarian state, whereas it is the only kind of propaganda that can truly serve a democracy.

It is no accident that in 1917, when President Wilson appointed

an agency to look after the wartime propaganda of the United
States, he called it the Committee on Public Information. In 1942
President Roosevelt set up, as the corresponding agency of his government, the Office of War Information. The British call theirs
the Ministry of Information. The use of this word "information"
to designate these propaganda services is not posturing, or other
pretense, but is a reflection of their primary purpose. Those of
us who remember how George Creel, as chairman of the Committee on Public Information, was flailed in Congress and in the
press for alleged manipulation of truth in 1917-'18 are not surprised
to find Elmer Davis the target of partisan attacks in 1943. The
record of Mr. Creel's performance is now far enough in the past
to permit an unemotional appraisal, and one finds that the performance was professionally honest and operationally successful.

The democracies would be shortsighted indeed if they did not
go out for factual information, since the dictators have made truth
a scarce and precious commodity in their homelands, occupied
areas, and satellite countries. "Many millions of people are completely dependent for any truthful account of what is going on
on what we and our Allies tell them," said Davis in discussing the
job of OWI. "Thanks to this very repression, to the endeavor of
totalitarian governments to suppress all news and all opinion except
what they choose to give out, the truth itself has become a more
powerful weapon than ever before."

AMERICAN AND BRITISH PROPAGANDA

From the start of their services, news has been the primary
material for distribution by the Ministry of Information in London
and the Office of War Information in Washington. There has been
a close collaboration between the two agencies. Beginning soon
after the Pearl Harbor raid the British Broadcasting Corporation
began to relay to the Continent a daily feature picked up from
the United States, "America Calling Europe." On their part, the
United States services have transmitted to Japan material prepared
by the British. All the various mediums of communication have
been utilized; all the various audiences, at home, in neutral countries,
in the Allied countries, and in the enemy and enemy-held lands, have
been addressed; and the military agencies of both the British and

United States governments have recognized the value of the propaganda services by giving them confidence and co-operation. There is reason to believe that the propaganda which bombarded the Axis forces in Tunisia aided their decision to capitulate before their munitions were spent, though of course the most powerful propaganda was provided by attacking bombers, tanks, and the never silent artillery of the Allied offensive. "Without military success, propaganda is a weak sister."

British propaganda output, particularly that sent over the radio waves, has leaned heavily on big personalities; whereas an American program may quote some well-known radio personality, but it rarely uses him as a featured speaker. The tendency of OWI has been to focus attention on the Voice of America.

Very often a news broadcast will carry no comment, and will depend entirely on the juxtaposition of the various news items to provide emphasis. A BBC program addressed to German working men, for example, contained brief one-paragraph items telling of an increase in the wage of British mine workers, the number of Belgian workers now employed in Great Britain, the number of women received in British engineering societies, a current trade-union demand in Britain. The overworked German may be reminded in this way of his lost labor unions, for which the Nazi Labor Front is hardly a substitute, and informed that outside the Axis the union movement is still alive, active, and kicking. Similarly, the BBC has programs addressed especially to German seamen, the German army, the Luftwaffe, and other groups.

Behind the enemy line, the overseas broadcasters have three main groups of listeners. First are the official listeners, the government agency. They record everything that comes over the air, take it down, analyze it, try to find out what are the intentions and implications of the broadcaster.

Then there are the leaders of the underground movements. They may be only fifty or sixty people in an entire country, but they are vital to the whole hope of revolt and internal revolution. They also take down all that they hear over the radio, both in order to keep posted on developments and to provide information for distribution through the underground press and by word of mouth.

The third group is the mass audience, a rather floating and

uncertain element. They listen not because they are sympathetic, but because they are curious, or are suspicious of the home broadcasts and wish to check up or at least prospect the outside news sources. Some of them may listen in a spirit of dare, just because the thing is verboten. It has been found that these mass listeners often tune in on a program in some language other than their own. Italians prefer to listen in French, Germans in English. The theory seems to be that if the enemy is sending a broadcast in German, for example, it is likely to be doctored, whereas in English it is more likely to be the truth.

Also, Dr. Göbbels has a policy of jamming the incoming German-language broadcasts, whereas the English broadcasts are on the air almost continuously and jamming becomes too much of a job.

There is evidence of a great deal of this cross-listening by curious or suspicious persons in the enemy countries. Some time ago the British Broadcasting Corporation organized a program called "What Do You Want to Know?" It followed somewhat the plan of "Information Please." There was a panel of experts to answer questions, and some questions asked by prisoners and refugees were submitted. Pretty soon inquiries began to filter in from the Axis-dominated lands. There were occasional letters from Germany, usually smuggled into Switzerland where they were mailed to the British ambassador at Berne.

Further evidence of the degree to which the Allied propaganda has reached behind the enemy lines is the effort that Göbbels makes to discredit its news. An example, and it is quite typical, may be cited from a British experience in 1941. An American correspondent leaving Berlin stopped in London on his way home, and said to a BBC man, "Be careful, in reporting on your air raids, not to claim specific hits. The time you reported that the Anhalter Station in Berlin had been struck left a bad effect, for people in Berlin went to see, found there was no hit, and it made them doubt your veracity." A little later another traveler out of Berlin brought the same warning. "That claim of a hit on the Anhalter Station gave you a black eye." Others mentioned it, and finally the BBC management decided to check through their transmissions—for every broadcast is recorded—and see what exactly had been said. They were unable to find any such statement. The whole thing was a fake. Dr. Göbbels had fabricated the claim, then published it as a quotation from a British broadcast, thus repeating the Nazi technique of planting a lie where it will do the most harm—in this case, in the minds of those who were surreptitiously listening to the British news.

It is part of Nazi logic that the rule of consistency, which is repeatedly invoked to discredit the adversary, may be openly violated by Dr. Göbbels without scruple. In December, 1939, when the captain of the scuttled *Graf Spee* committed suicide in Buenos Aires, the Berlin broadcast reporting the funeral said: "At the end of the ceremony some British seamen threw a dead cat into the grave." In the next few days, as the story was rebroadcast to different countries, the species of the animal was changed to represent the beast most detested by the local populace. To India it was a dead dog, to the Moslems a pig, to others a rat—and all these variations were beamed from one German station!

Actually, the British seamen sent a wreath of flowers to Captain Langsdorff's funeral.

THE COVENANT OF THE GANGSTERS

There is one consistency which Göbbels and his aids have cultivated with rare fidelity. Dr. Ernst Kris recently published a penetrating analysis of German home-front propaganda in which he shows that the method in the Nazi madness has been to treat the German people as accomplices, following the psycho-dynamics of the criminal gang.

In the familiar picture of the gang, as portrayed in thrillers, the leader, threatened with arrest by society, wards off desertion and strengthens his hold on followers by three kinds of appeal. First, he emphasizes the advantages of the criminal association, pointing out the loot to be gained by a new and final enterprise of great daring. Second, he threatens traitors with relentless revenge, at the same time pointing to the safety of those who remain under his protection. Finally, with the wavering follower who unwittingly became an accomplice, he uses the argument that nobody will believe his innocence, no alibi will save him, and he, the leader, will prevent his securing one. This complicity, which thereby becomes the center of their pact for common loot and common safety, sealed by the unifying force of association in crime, is what Dr. Kris calls the covenant of the gangster.

He proceeds to show that it is precisely this sort of relationship that Hitler and his group have cultivated in their psychological manipulation of the German people. The United Nations occupy the role of outraged society. Hitler and his Germans represent the gang. "Indicted by the United Nations, they attempt to retain the loyalty of the people by presenting them with a set of arguments similar to those used by the gang leader of our model."

First, there is the argument of loot. "The war, as Dr. Göbbels says, is an investment. And the word quickly goes the rounds and gains acceptance. Even the military experts use the term. The battles of the summer of 1942, which led to the conquest of the Donets Basin, are termed investments by Lieut. General Dietmar, a military expert who broadcasts his comments on the German home radio. Victory is made concrete. The German occupation army in Norway was told in October, 1942, what it will mean: no more wars to wage after conquest, a house for each on his own soil, and a car for each home."

Second, there is the argument of revenge. "The memory of the years following the first world war is dramatized, and unrepresentative or spurious voices from Allied countries are quoted to add color to old patterns. There is Lord Vansittart's pamphlet (*The Black Record: Germans Past and Present*), there is the unfortunate venture of a Mr. Kaufman of New York who advocates the sterilization of all Germans (*Germany Must Perish*), there is a harmless letter of a Dutch correspondent to one of the emigré papers in London (*The Vry Netherlands*), who recommends that German children be educated for some years in the democratic countries to let them see what free society can achieve. And this becomes, in Dr. Göbbels's version, 'Mr. Churchill's plan for the disruption of the German family.' "

Third, there is the threat of retaliation, of punishment for betrayal. This argument has its roots far back, in that version of 1918 which depicts Versailles as a consequence of the defection of the German people from the German military. "Germany's army," it said, "was never conquered. Unvanquished, it surrendered to an enemy who proved superior only in the arts of deceit." But, continues the propagandist, "this time Germany will not surrender.

They have, Dr. Göbbels says, a prophet who warns them; the prophet, of course, is the skillful doctor himself." Responsibility for the atrocities, persecutions, and announced plan to extirpate a whole racial group from Europe, is turned with terrifying weight upon the whole German people, to implicate them in Nazi guilt and press upon them the inescapable necessity for victory.

Thus, as outraged society, in the might of the United Nations, presses harder and closer upon the gangsters, the temper of the leader's argument becomes ever more hard-boiled, aggressive, implicating. "We did this for you" becomes "we did this together" and, to paraphrase a sentence of Dr. Göbbels, "if only because of the terrible retribution that would follow defeat, we *must* win this war."

Dr. Kris's paper was published in, appropriately, *The Journal of Criminal Psychopathology*.

PSYCHOLOGY IN WAR AND PEACE

But psychological warfare is more than a system of terrorism, whether applied against the home front as in the covenant of the gangster, or against the enemy front as in the war of nerves. Indeed, these may be regarded as pathological aberrations. They are techniques of psychotherapy in reverse—*i.e.*, schemes to produce mental disorder instead of to cure it. Psychological warfare also has its constructive responsibilities and techniques, and includes the mental preparation of the soldier for battle.

One may say that all warfare, except that waged by purely automatic weapons, is fundamentally psychological. For brains and muscles must be trained if they are to perform efficient military service, and the spirit must be fortified by a high morale to sustain brains and muscles in the hour of battle. High morale derives from a sense of competency quite as much as from a sense of rectitude. Therefore, in providing tests which weed out those who are constitutionally unfitted for military service, in providing systems of selecting men according to their aptitudes and then training them to a high level of performance, psychology upbuilds morale along with efficiency.

Psychologists have been called into consultation by designers of aircraft and other weapons, in which problems involving the relation of seeing, hearing, and other sensory functions are involved.

Certain groups have developed tests for the acuity of night vision. Others have worked on problems of audition. The placing and lighting of dials and other gadgets on the instrument board, questions as to the number of instruments that an aircraft pilot can reasonably give attention to, and the relation of these problems to fatigue and mental alertness in flight—all are subjects for psychology, and have received attention in the psychological laboratories. The successful solution of these problems also contributes to military morale.

Psychology is not an exact science. If it were, history would be different. A chemist can predict precisely what will happen as a result of bringing two compounds together, but no psychologist can predict precisely anything about human relations. We do know something about crowd reactions, about the power of prejudice, the influence of example, the tenacity of youthful indoctrination, the tendency of the emotions to take the reins from the reason. We have accumulated a large miscellany of observations about human behavior, and some of them have been found to fit into orderly systems; but psychology is not yet an exact science. The "yet" is an admission of our hope in its continuing progress.

For this science needs to progress if mankind is to be freed from war. We have the spectacle of Wilson, whose words contributed so powerfully to the victory of 1918, and yet were impotent to win the peace. You may say that in peacetime his followers deserted him—but if that is the explanation of the failure at Versailles and after, the event is still a psychological tragedy that needs to be understood if its recurrence is to be avoided. Fortunately, the necessity for some system of international co-operation for world order has been so generally emphasized in discussions of the last three years, and is so widely echoed by citizens of all sorts and conditions, that the psychological effect of repetition has operated to build up a considerable mass sentiment for a practical world system. The durability of this sentiment remains to be demonstrated. Its ultimate test will come when our peace architects sit down to plan the framework of the new world association and our statesmen begin to administer it. The test will be *integrity*, the degree to which utter honesty is present, both in the planning and in the administering.

EPILOGUE

Science and the New World

The end of our foundation is the knowledge of causes
and secret motions of things; and the enlarging of the
bounds of human empire, to the effecting of all things
possible.

—Francis Bacon, THE NEW ATLANTIS

THE future comes. Never in human history has it come with pace
so swift and bringing promises so world-sweeping as now. For these
violent times are no ordinary struggle between national sovereignties. They are the hammer strokes forging a new world. It must be
new, for forces have been set loose which can not be crowded back
into the old familiar patterns, forces of human aspiration as well
as forces of physical power. It is idle to think of these forces as
evil. The future *can* be better than our past—if we have the courage
and the intelligence to accept change and adapt ourselves to the
new conditions.

As science conditioned the conduct of the war, so science ines-
capably will affect the structure of the postwar. Many contingencies
could mar or poison the peace settlement, but nothing more dis-
astrously than a failure to understand the central place which science
occupies in modern civilization. Indeed, the whole hope and probability of a permanent peace will depend to a large extent on the
attitude that politics takes toward the opportunities opened and
the limitations imposed by technology.

Science will emerge from the war with greatly enhanced resources of manpower, knowledge, techniques, and reputation. Certainly Britain can never forget the men of the laboratories who designed the Spitfire. And through numerous other developments, known better to the men of the armed services than to civilians, "the covering wings of science" protected our ships, our coasts, our homes, and our men at the front. Soldiers and sailors will return to civilian life with skills and an acquaintance with electrical, mechanical, optical, aeronautical, and other scientific devices far beyond that contributed by World War I; and the leaven of their practical knowledge and personal interest will be felt among the general population.

The wartime training programs in schools and colleges, with emphasis on the physical sciences, can hardly fail to affect postwar attitudes, interests and loyalties. Education in the future is likely to find an increasing demand for courses in mathematics, physics, chemistry, biology, and other fundamentals. History courses focused on the personalities and contributions of science may conceivably give youth a sounder orientation to the human scene than is afforded by the traditional round of kings, conquerors, and politicians. I for one should not wish to lose the human values contributed by the arts, literature, and other "humanities." It would be a drab world without the wingéd words, the music, humor, aspiration, entertainment, and color of the liberal arts; and there is small likelihood that mankind will deliberately debase and stultify these precious resources, or abolish them from education, as some doleful prophets seem to fear. What is to be desired is a balanced education in which science becomes co-ordinate with the humanities as a subject of popular educational interest. Too long has it been regarded as a thing apart from public comprehension, as something too technical for the citizen, a specialty to be left to the expert. As if the very basis of our civilization, the lever that has raised democracy from the slough of feudalism, were of concern to only a select few! Tradition has its lore, picturesque and appealing, but there is no true scale of human values in which lore is superior to knowledge.

Professor John Dewey has gone so far as to say that "only the gradual replacing of a literary by a scientific education can assure to man the progressive amelioration of his lot." And Professor

George A. Lundberg, who agrees with Dewey, finds that "the unifying discipline of modern education lies in modern science, which is simply the distilled essence of the classics of all time." Attitudes have changed since those Nineteenth-century days when students at the Lawrence Scientific School of Harvard were a breed apart—stepchildren perhaps, but hardly of the legitimate line—and not admitted to residence in the Yard.

SCIENCE AS HUMANISM

The idea that science is something outside of humanity, or is of a lower order of human interest than poetry, painting, architecture, or the other arts, is one of the oddest quirks of casuistry. The whole fabric of science is man's work and achievement, and if it still be fragmentary and incomplete that also is a reflection of its human origins. Art is not the sole invoker of beauty. The pure delight which the discoverer derives from his explorations of nature is comparable to the delight of the creative artist. Clerk Maxwell's theory of the nature and interrelationship of electricity and magnetism was the work of a creative artist as well as an exploring scientist. It took imagination in addition to mathematics to conceive that majestic generalization. It is true that the number of persons who respond to the beauty of Maxwell's creation is limited to the few who understand the language in which it is written—and not all of these are moved by it aesthetically—but the appeal of literature and the other fine arts also meets its irresponsive clods, stone walls of indifference, and yawns of boredom. More people can understand Shakespeare than can understand Maxwell, but not all who understand the Shakespearian words find enjoyment in the Shakespearian poetry.

The panorama of science at war is more than the pageant of weapons. These ingenious machines of the air, land, and sea, with their audacious applications of "the knowledge of causes and secret motions of things"; the bold new ventures in physics, chemistry, and other sciences, with their fringes of mystery and whispers of wonders yet to be spoken aloud, are creatures of the brain of man. They are as authentic products of the human spirit as a novel, a painting, or a work of architecture. A scientific achievement like radar is a cumulative creation. It is the total expression of the observation, curiosity, imagination, thought, experiment, and physical labor of many minds and many hands, like a cathedral whose final splendor is the joint contribution of successive generations of architects and builders.

"It would be a crime to exhibit the fine side of war, even if there were one!" wrote Henri Barbusse from the battlefield wreckage, squalor, and putrefaction of the first world war. And we who are now familiars of the Great God Mars will be wise if we continue to class it where it belongs—an anachronism that belongs far back in human history, in the Bronze Age or earlier; a hangover from savagery that is civilization's disgrace. It is our shame that the future has to come this way. The fact that it does is a perpetual denial of our religion, our morality, our intelligence; a ghastly reproach and betrayal of our science. For science has opened doors to unbelievable riches; it has provided the possibility of wiping out disease, want, and war; but its resources have been only partly recognized and nowhere fully accepted and put to work.

The scientific mind is essentially constructive. The creative spirit does not take a healthy delight in destruction. The discoverers have been men of peace. Distinctions of race and boundaries of nationality have offered no bar to the exchange of their findings and ideas. Sulfanilamide was a German development, penicillin an English discovery, the method of drying blood plasma in the frozen state an American contribution; and knowledge of all three has repeatedly crossed national lines. But war imposes unaccustomed and stifling restrictions on the natural impulses, desires, and habits of these citizens of the world republic of science—as it does, of course, on all people in a democracy. They accept it only as a means, what Leonardo da Vinci called "a means of offense and defense in order to preserve the chief gift of nature, which is liberty."

THE UNITY OF MANKIND

But human liberty requires more than war to insure its protection and prosperity. It requires more than the successful completion of this war. "Peace is not mere absence of war," said Spinoza, "but a virtue which arises from strength of soul." That is why "peace in our time" could not last. It had no strength of soul.

When Neville Chamberlain returned from Munich in 1938, to

report on the betrayal of Czechoslovakia, he dismissed the problem, you remember, as "a quarrel in a far-away country between people of whom we know nothing." The stupidity, the blindness, and the lack of integrity which made war inevitable are all compacted in that statement. For the Earth is round, and the trade ways, air ways and radio waves encircle it. There are no far-away countries. There is no people of whom we can afford to know nothing. The central fact of our civilization is the essential unity of mankind. We ignored and denied, or at least made no intelligent effort to recognize, this unity in our political systems; we wasted or misused the engines of democracy which science had provided and which could have insured the prosperity and peace of all; and we stumbled into the dark abyss of war.

Although it is not listed among the war aims, this is what the war is about—the unity of mankind. And this is what any lasting peace will have to recognize and embody in a world order.

A PLANETARY ECONOMY

Several years before Mr. Wendell Willkie embarked on his tour of discovery of the One World, a professor of government sat down in his quiet study to write a book. His writing—*World Economy in Transition*, by Eugene Staley—finally reached publication in the early summer of 1939, a few months before the war which it foreshadowed. Professor Staley was by no means the first to discuss the impact of science on civilization; indeed, his book is replete with acknowledgments to earlier writers on the subject; but the antithesis of technology versus politics has never been better set forth than in this able analysis. Here you find in interesting detail (1) the rate at which science has shrunk the world in terms of travel-time and communication-time; the factors which have made for increased production, lowered costs, and other effects of advancing technology; with contrasting details of (2) the obstructions that nations have erected which hamper travel, defeat the full use of the advantages of instantaneous communication, reduce production, and limit the extent of intercourse between peoples.

"One set of men build tunnels through mountains, span oceans with steamships and planes, develop better engines for transport, erect industrial enterprises designed to use the products of far places and to distribute goods in far places. Another set of men erect barriers to increase the cost of transporting goods from one place to another, devise new means of keeping capital within national boundaries, restrict the movement of persons, and slow down the interchange of ideas. A conflict rages between technology and politics. Economics, so closely linked to both, has become the major battlefield. Stability and peace will reign in world economy only when, somehow, the forces on the side of technology and the forces on the side of politics have once more been accommodated to each other."

The trend of modern science has been in the direction of multiplying the exchanges between nations—toward a planetary economy. Whereas, and with increasing velocity since World War I, the tendency of governments has been to restrict these activities, to intensify efforts to bolster up the self-sufficiency of states and combinations of states. In this struggle it is not difficult to see on which side lie the wider interests of mankind.

The future that presses for a decision will not be put off with quibbles about national sovereignties, vested rights, monopoly devices hallowed by precedent, and other relics. The dangerous imbalance of the world can be resolved only by a frank recognition of the unity of mankind. The international fellowship of science is itself a mirror of that essential unity. The uneven distribution of mineral wealth and other resources is part of the evidence. The ability of a scientific development in one country (such as Fritz Haber's process of nitrogen fixation in Germany) to upset a vital element in the economy of another country (such as the nitrate industry of Chile) also enters into our picture.

If you can abolish synthetic chemistry, radio, and air transport; restrict motion-picture themes to the homeland; put quotas on the dynamo; drastically limit the number and horsepower of gasoline, Diesel, and steam engines per million of the population, and in addition padlock all research laboratories, you may be able to push the next generation back into the Nineteenth century of nostalgic memory, or at least to pre-1914. But there were wars in the Nineteenth century, and there came a war in 1914.

No, the past is gone. We have eaten of the tree of knowledge and there is no turning back. Our home is a planet, one world; we are one human race, and the future must be ours together. "He hath made of one blood all nations of men for to dwell on all the face of the Earth."

POSSIBLE WORLDS

Each man envisions a world nearer to his heart's desire, but few of us know enough about the results already bubbling in the laboratories to give solid foundation to our dreams. President Karl T. Compton, the physicist who directs the Massachusetts Institute of Technology, was asked on a radio program to outline his anticipation of America's future. Certainly no one is closer to the activities of current research than President Compton; therefore he speaks from knowledge of what is scientifically probable:

"I look to see a race of Americans made healthier by medical progress and better living conditions. I look to see them gainfully employed in industries now undreamed of or only in the embryo stage. I look to see more wealth distributed, not by taking it away from someone else who has a good share, but by creating it—for that is the proved way of science. I look to see people living in homes of new designs, greater convenience and attractiveness, based on new structural materials and methods, and located in groups planned for effective community life. I look to see great cyclotrons operating as chemical factories instead of as laboratory instruments. I may see great power plants in which the fuel under the boilers need not be replenished in a thousand years. I shall certainly expect to see rain and fog eliminated from the list of hazards to travel by sea or air. These are only a few samples of what America's future looks like to me."

America's future is keyed to our endowment of natural resources, industrial plant, and trained man power. The vast expansion of industry forced by the war, plus many entirely new technological developments stimulated by the emergency, can be supported only by a globe-encircling structure of world trade. The bomb-blasted, shell-torn, starved and naked nations of the European and Asiatic war areas will have colossal needs to be satisfied. There are demolished cities to be cleared and rebuilt, ruined factories and other production plants to be reconstructed. Of work and markets there will be no lack in the postwar world; the problem will be one of financing and integrating. Successful management may call for bold and unprecedented policies—social inventions as unlike our old ways of economy as the cyclotron of today is unlike the chemical plant of the 1920's.

Such wartime developments as rocket propulsion, the mining of the sea for metals and other chemicals, and advances in the problem of unlocking the nuclear energy of the atom will inevitably affect peacetime industry. The transoceanic air-ferry services have provided a demonstration which would have taken decades of peacetime development to attain. These swift, direct, convenient freight carriers will affect the accustomed traffic by sea and by rails. In the course of the years, the extension of air transport may render obsolete the Panama Canal and other waterways. New York as an airport may become more important than New York as a seaport, and may be overshadowed by even more important inland airports nearer to the industries and populations. The use of helicopters to transport mails, with landing stations on the roofs of postoffices, is already indicated in an application filed with the Civil Aeronautics Authority for the establishment of a mail-passenger service in New England and upstate New York. A subsidiary of the Chicago, Burlington & Quincy Railroad applied in 1943 for permission to operate 6,380 miles of helicopter service in the western states. Other corporations, both transportation and industrial, have "committees on the future" studying possible postwar developments and adjustments.

The war has set precedents in public service which cannot be forgotten or ignored. For example, the rate of malaria infection in the armed forces was drastically reduced by a campaign of mosquito eradication in areas occupied by military encampments. Why cannot the same system be applied to states and regions? And if a region can be rid of mosquitoes, why not of other nuisances—the parasites which prey on crops and mar the beauty of the countryside, and disease-producing plants such as ragweed and poison ivy? The price of one battleship would probably suffice to control the Japanese beetle, which is rapidly spreading to new areas of the United States. The price of a few battleships might so reduce the mosquito population of North America as to render malaria as little known there as yellow fever.

THE EFFECTING OF ALL THINGS POSSIBLE

Francis Bacon, in his vision of the future in *The New Atlantis*, looked to science for "the enlarging of the bounds of human empire, to the effecting of all things possible." Can those "all things" include the conquest of war, the establishment of permanent world peace?

Why not? It is only defeatism to view war as inevitable, to call it irresistible destiny. The whole course of science is proof that destiny is irresistible only when it is not resisted. Famine was the periodic fate of the majority of Europeans two centuries ago. Until fairly modern times floods were accepted as one accepted the lightning bolt and the smallpox: fate had decreed the destructive waters, the electric fire, the deadly disease, and one could only submit. But today we have turned the raging rivers into irrigation canals, power systems, and other harnessing of their forces; we have tamed the lightning, and made smallpox a rarity.

The causes of war are as specific as those of smallpox, though more numerous and subtle. There are tensions in international relations analogous to those atmospheric tensions that give rise to the sudden ionic breakdown which is lightning. There are floods in human affairs as there are floods in hydraulic affairs, and each has natural causes which are ascertainable. The scientific method— the method which gave us smallpox vaccination, lightning-arrester devices, and flood-control systems—can also investigate the causes of war and the means of neutralizing or controlling them. Our social scientists are competent to make such objective studies. They can tell us what are the alternative courses of action, and what are the approximate costs and risks of each. For peace has its costs, and we cannot expect to get it without paying for it.

The costs of peace involve certain renunciations of sovereignty. They require a certain sharing of responsibility. Inevitably they will impose some money expense. But against these costs, set down the costs of the war: the billions of dollars poured into the military and naval establishments; the uncounted billions yet to be paid in the restoration of wrecked cities and devastated areas; the millions of human lives destroyed; the other millions of human bodies maimed; the additional millions stunted by starvation, pestilence, cold, and other privations. Four years of war have cost more blood and nerves and treasure than a century of peace could possibly cost. And it is not implacable fate that imposes these tolls on the human species. It is only our ignorance, our blindness, our deep-rooted prejudice, our fear of change.

Against the cost of peace we can set down also the gifts which peace can bring: the harmonious development of the rich resources of the planet; the distribution of these goods and services on a global scale; the lifting of the race to new standards of health, wealth, and happiness; above all, banishment of the fear of war.

It will take the collaboration of all our spiritual, intellectual and physical forces to accomplish the peace that can banish war. The scientist and the humanist must work together heart and soul; the politician and the technologist, with a full appreciation of the capacities and integrity of each other; and there must be mass support, a wide popular affirmation of the program that is adopted. For the present, perhaps, our strongest scaffolding of popular support will be remembrance of what the war has done. It has cut too deeply into our lives for even the most reactionary traditionalist to view an unorganized future with complacency. This thing must not happen again! It will not happen again if we have courage to blaze new trails in international relations. Also necessary is a measure of magnanimity: we must trust one another's good faith in the new experiment of a planetary order. The final requisite is intelligence to make full use of the mighty forces which science has released "to the effecting of all things possible."

NOTE OF ACKNOWLEDGMENT

A number of men in various positions of science, industry, and military affairs were consulted during the preparation of this book. Of some, I sought advice on the current developments that would be available for publication. Others provided information in their special fields. Many read, checked, and criticized drafts of the chapters. The book in its final form owes a great deal to the generous co-operation of these whom I can only regard as collaborators, though in calling them such I do not mean to imply that they have endorsed the book or are responsible for any of its shortcomings. I am wholly responsible for the conception and execution, but the job could not have been done without access to trustworthy sources of counsel, information, and criticism. Those to whom I am indebted for one or more of these services are:

Edwin H. Armstrong, Columbia University, New York
W. L. Barrow, Massachusetts Institute of Technology, Cambridge
Henry A. Barton, American Institute of Physics, New York
Rear Admiral H. G. Bowen, U. S. Navy Department, Washington
Detlev W. Bronk, University of Pennsylvania Medical School, Philadelphia
Charles F. Brooks, Blue Hill Meteorological Observatory, Milton, Mass.
Dean Burk, National Institute of Health, Bethesda, Maryland
George H. Burnham, American Institute of Physics, New York
Vannevar Bush, Office of Scientific Research and Development, Washington
O. H. Caldwell, *Electronic Industries*, New York

Walter B. Cannon, Harvard Medical School, Boston
Ernest E. Charlton, General Electric Company, Schenectady
Edwin J. Cohn, Harvard Medical School, Boston
E. U. Condon, Westinghouse Electric & Manufacturing Company, East Pittsburgh
F. G. Cottrell, Washington
Eugene DuBois, Cornell University Medical College, New York
Gano Dunn, J. G. White Engineering Corporation, New York
F. G. Fassett, Jr., *The Technology Review*, Cambridge
George Freyermuth, Standard Oil Company of New Jersey, New York
Thornton C. Fry, Bell Telephone Laboratories, New York
John F. Fulton, Yale Medical School, New Haven
Brigadier General D. N. W. Grant, air surgeon, U. S. Army Medical Corps, Washington
John S. Gray, U. S. Army School of Aviation Medicine, San Antonio
Alan Gregg, Rockefeller Foundation, New York
Colonel L. E. Griffis, U. S. Army Medical Corps, Air Forces, Washington
Hermann R. Haber, Great Neck, N. Y.
Major James H. Hammond, U. S. Army Medical Corps, Air Forces, Washington
Frank Blair Hanson, Rockefeller Foundation, New York
James G. Harbord, Radio Corporation of America, New York
Roger W. Hickman, Harvard University, Cambridge
Jerome C. Hunsaker, National Advisory Committee for Aeronautics, Washington
James K. Hunt, E. I. du Pont de Nemours & Company, Wilmington
H. R. Isenburger, St. John X-Ray Service, Long Island City
Frank B. Jewett, National Academy of Sciences, Washington
Chester S. Keefer, Boston University School of Medicine, Boston
F. P. Kerschbaum, Washington
Robert W. King, American Telephone & Telegraph Company, New York
Sidney D. Kirkpatrick, *Chemical and Metallurgical Engineering*, New York
Ernst Kris, New School for Social Research, New York
Harold D. Lasswell, Library of Congress, Washington

Paul F. Lazarsfeld, Columbia University, New York

John S. Lockwood, University of Pennsylvania Medical School, Philadelphia

W. W. MacDonald, *Electronics*, New York

John Marshall, Rockefeller Foundation, New York

John J. Moorhead, Postgraduate Medical School, New York

A. N. Richards, Office of Scientific Research and Development, Washington

William J. Robbins, Botanical Gardens, New York

Arthur L. Schade, Overly Biochemical Research Foundation, New York

George T. Seabury, American Society of Civil Engineers, New York

Kurt G. Stern, Overly Biochemical Research Foundation, New York

James Stockley, General Electric Company, Schenectady

E. K. Thayer, E. I. du Pont de Nemours & Company, Wilmington

Richard C. Tolman, Office of Scientific Research and Development, Washington

S. A. Tucker, *Power*, New York

Arthur Van Dyck, Radio Corporation of America, New York

John H. Van Vleck, Harvard University, Cambridge

Warren Weaver, Rockefeller Foundation, New York

S. R. Williams, Amherst College, Amherst, Massachusetts

Joseph H. Willits, Rockefeller Foundation, New York

Carroll L. Wilson, Office of Scientific Research and Development, Washington

Reviewing the history of science and war and the files of technological journals and other publications, I made much use of the resources of the New York Public Library, the Engineering Societies Library, and the Rockefeller Foundation Library. I should like to express thanks to the librarians of these institutions for their help on many occasions.

The quotations from Leonardo da Vinci which appear on the title page and in Chapter II are from Edward MacCurdy's translation of *The Notebooks of Leonardo da Vinci*, published by Reynal & Hitchcock, to whom I am indebted for my use of them. The story of Archimedes' defense of Syracuse is based on the account in the chapter on Marcellus in *Plutarch's Lives*, and the quotations are from the translation by John Dryden. For many historical details I am indebted to *Engineers and Engineering in the Renaissance* by William Barclay Parsons (The Williams & Wilkins Company), *The Social Function of Science* by J. D. Bernal (The Macmillan Company), *Technics and Civilization* by Lewis Mumford (Harcourt, Brace and Company), and *A History of the World War* by B. H. Liddell Hart (Little, Brown & Company). Professor A. M. Low's *Mine and Countermine* (Sheridan House) was of help in reviewing the history of explosive devices, particularly the magnetic mine. *The Chemistry of Powder and Explosives* by Tenney L. Davis (John Wiley & Sons) was my reference book on the history of explosives; and *Chemicals in War* by A. M. Prentiss (McGraw-Hill Book Company), on the history of gas warfare. Many stories of the early services of electricity in war are in *Old Wires and New Waves* by Alvin F. Harlow (D. Appleton-Century Company, Inc.). The extended quotation from *Flying Dutchman* by A. H. G. Fokker and B. Gould in Chapter IV is used with the permission of the publishers, Henry Holt and Company, Inc.; this book has interesting anecdotes of the adaptation of the airplane to warfare. In the Epilogue I have cited Eugene Staley's *World Economy in Transition* (published by the Council on Foreign Relations); and a booklet which also bears on the economic consequences of technology is William F. Ogburn's *Machines and Tomorrow's World* (published by the Public Affairs Committee, Inc.). All of these publications are commended to readers who wish to go further into the historical, technological, sociological, and economic subjects which they present.

Among the periodicals which were of assistance as sources of news of war and its repercussions in science, in addition to those whose editors have already been mentioned in this note, acknowledgment is made to *Army Ordance*, *The Infantry Journal*, *The Military Engineer*, *Nature* (London), *The Journal of Applied Physics*, *Electrical Communications*, *The Sperryscope*, *Aeronautics* (London), *Aviation*, *Flying*, *The Journal of Aviation Medicine*, and *War Medicine*.

G. W. G.

INDEX

Set in Linotype Janson
Format by A. W. Rushmore
Manufactured by the Haddon Craftsmen
Published by HARPER & BROTHERS
New York and London